COOK ONCE
DINNER FIX

quick & exciting ways to transform tonight's dinner into tomorrow's feast

COOK ONCE
DINNER FIX

Cassy Joy Garcia

Photography by Kristen Kilpatrick

SIMON & SCHUSTER

NEW YORK   LONDON   TORONTO   SYDNEY   NEW DELHI

Simon & Schuster
1230 Avenue of the Americas
New York, NY 10020

First Simon & Schuster hardcover edition September 2021

SIMON & SCHUSTER and colophon are registered trademarks
of Simon & Schuster, Inc.

For information about special discounts for bulk purchases,
please contact Simon & Schuster Special Sales
at 1-866-506-1949 or business@simonandschuster.com.

The Simon & Schuster Speakers Bureau can bring authors to
your live event. For more information or to book an event,
contact the Simon & Schuster Speakers Bureau at 1-866-248-3049
or visit our website at www.simonspeakers.com.

Interior design by Jennifer K. Beal Davis

Manufactured in China

1   3   5   7   9   10   8   6   4   2

Library of Congress Cataloging-in-Publication Data

Names: Garcia, Cassy Joy, author. | Kilpatrick, Kristen,
photographer. Title: The cook once dinner fix / Cassy Joy Garcia ;
photography by Kristen Kilpatrick.
Identifiers: LCCN 2021013328 | ISBN 9781982167264 |
ISBN 9781982167271 (ebook)
Subjects: LCSH: Make-ahead cooking. | Cooking (Leftovers)
Classification: LCC TX652 .G3612 2021 | DDC 641.5/55—dc23
LC record available at https://lccn.loc.gov/2021013328

ISBN 978-1-9821-6726-4
ISBN 978-1-9821-6727-1 (ebook)

For my dear Fed + Fit readers. Whether
you're new to my work or have been
around from the beginning, this book
is for you. I'm honored by your trust
and hope this book serves you well.

Contents

intro

I have to be honest with you. Unlike any resource I've created before, *this* book feels like the most *me*. You see, this is how I really cook (well, 90 percent of the time). I've spent nearly ten years publishing recipes in digital and print formats, and while I still stand by those recipes, the meals that appear on our family's table night after night aren't a patchwork of stand-alone dishes. Instead, they're meals that nod to one another by way of strategic time- and money-saving ingredient hacks. While I will meal prep when needed (such as before a week when our schedule is especially packed), and while I do sometimes throw myself into the production of more-involved one-off dishes (like slow-roasted lamb for a special occasion), those meals are the exception to my household rule.

What's the rule? Get a healthy, delicious dinner on the table as painlessly as possible. Spend just enough time in the kitchen to enjoy the cooking process, make sure the food is flavorful, and be proud that you pulled off *yet another* crowd-pleasing meal without breaking the bank—or your back.

As both a personal and a professional pursuit, my job is to "fix dinner." I personally fix dinner for my family almost daily, and as a professional pursuit, I also work to fix the dinner approach. For many people, the current model for getting dinner on the table is broken.

It feels hard! Why is that?

My theory is that we're all overcomplicating and overcommitting, and I want to guide you through how to make dinner an easier process. I want to show you that dinner doesn't have to be difficult to be delicious, and it doesn't have to be expensive or consume all of our precious time. We can have our cake and eat it, too: we can enjoy dinner without feeling exhausted or depleted from the effort. *That* is the purpose of this book: to give you confidence, ease, and prowess in the kitchen, all in a way that fits your budget.

Meet Cassy Joy and Fed + Fit

I started fedandfit.com way back in the summer of 2011, when you still had to explain what a "blog" was if you mentioned you had one at a cocktail party. Before launching my healthy-recipe website, I went on a long personal journey toward a healthier, happier me. In my early twenties, I struggled with chronic pain, headaches, what felt like a constantly growing waistline, and an addiction to restrictive, dogmatic diets. In order to really break the yo-yo diet cycle, I committed myself to learn about *real* nutrition and how to just *be well* (versus losing the same twenty pounds over and over again). I discovered the power of real food, of still enjoying indulgences, of moving my body, and of giving myself grace and freedom from my physical expectations.

My world changed, but it changed slowly—the way I now understand is best. Over several years, I healed my body, my gut, and my mind. On a mission to help others find true wellness, I launched fedandfit.com as a destination for "no-rules wellness."

For the past ten years, the content on Fed + Fit has maintained its orientation toward our true north: to empower health. With a growing team of staff writers and editors, in addition to our expanding list of guest contributors, we are working hard to bring you a well-rounded approach to wellness. At Fed + Fit, you won't find us "shoulding" on you about endless wellness trends. Instead, you'll find a distilled collection of our very best healthy lifestyle tips and tricks.

From casual blogger to editor in chief of an online wellness destination, I have been honored to continue to serve our larger community with a grace-filled approach to healthy living. May we enjoy the occasional indulgent sweet, may we find joy in fitness, may we feel confident with our nutrition choices, may we be kind to our bodies, and may we not sacrifice our stability in the name of dinner. May we have it all—just maybe not in the way we expected to.

What's Different about This Book?

What makes this book different from other recipe books out there? That's a great question, and I'd be asking it, too. Let me break it down for you.

THE DINNER SERIES CONCEPT

To put it as briefly as possible, the dinner series concept involves transforming one (or more) cooked component from one meal into a second, completely different meal. Picture cooking a fabulous classic pot roast for one dinner and planning ahead to have purposeful "leftovers," then strategically transforming those leftovers into the best shredded beef (I call it barbacoa) tacos you've ever tried.

It's efficient meal planning that acknowledges a desire to still do *some* cooking each night. You'll find that getting dinner on the table is easier, more enjoyable, and maybe even more delicious. You may find that your grocery bill is lightened, as is your stress around that daily (possibly haunting) question: "What's for dinner?"

Cook Once Dinner Fix answers that question by way of sixty dinner series, with the bold assertion that a delicious meal doesn't have to be difficult. That we don't have to spend a fortune or hours in the kitchen each day to nourish ourselves and our families. That dinner is finally fixed.

RECIPES BUILT BY NUTRITIONISTS

As a holistic nutritionist leading a team of health-minded recipe developers, I designed these recipes with balanced health in mind. Though some are wonderfully indulgent, they were mindfully designed that way. In other words, extreme care was taken to ensure that every bite of each dish is as flavorful and healthful as possible.

Additionally, because of my background in nutrition, I can't help but give you ingredient modifications so you can accommodate your personal or your family's dietary needs. I spent a good portion of my career helping people with dietary restrictions figure out what to eat, by creating specific meal plans that met their needs, or authoring recipes with several "choose your own adventure"–style ingredient list options. You'll find that same spirit throughout this book. The dietary modifications taken into account include:

- Vegetarian
- Dairy-Free
- Grain-Free
- Gluten-Free
- Low-Carb

Note: wherever a recipe is listed as "gluten-free," for example, that means that the dish is already gluten-free by nature. When you see "gluten-free option," it means that the recipe can be made gluten-free with our modification instructions.

YOU'RE UNIQUE

I know you—and anyone you nourish—are unique. You have unique tastes, schedules, food allergens, food preferences, budget, and mealtime goals. Maybe you're tracking macros. Maybe you're grain-free or dairy-free. Maybe you're working to keep your weekly groceries under a certain dollar amount. Or maybe you only have thirty minutes

each day to dedicate to dinnertime. *I see you.* I see you so clearly, and I worked incredibly hard with the team here at Fed + Fit to come up with the tips, techniques, and mealtime hacks on the following pages. My hope is that these act as a compass to help you navigate this book and use it to its fullest potential. My goal is to make dinner as easy on you as possible, and helping you find the right meals for your unique self is a huge part of that.

YOU WANT MORE

Though you may enjoy the content of this book, you want more. To satisfy that craving, we've made the following tools available at cookonce.com:

- **TEN WEEKLY MEAL PLANS:** These meal plans mix and match the dinner series contained here into delicious weekly menus that will keep your taste buds on their toes.
- **SHOPPING LISTS:** You'll also find consolidated shopping lists that pair with the weekly meal plans to help make your grocery runs as easy and efficient as possible.
- **SUBSTITUTION TIPS:** Though we've included several dietary modification substitutions in this book, our unabridged guide can be found online.
- **METHOD DEMONSTRATIONS:** Looking for a demonstration or two of the concepts used in this book? It's likely we have them waiting for you on the website.

Substitution Guide

I pride myself on my ability to pivot in the kitchen, and I want you to feel comfortable with the occasional pivot, too. In this section, I'll walk you through some of the most common questions about ingredient substitutions. Let's say you've got your heart set on an Asian-inspired chicken-and-rice dish. What if you open the fridge and there's no chicken? I say, no problem! No rice? Not an issue. As long as you have the basic flavors for a sauce on hand, a protein with a similar texture, and a base that makes you happy, you can make something very similar. I hope this serves you as a useful guide as you customize these dinners to fit your dietary needs and ingredient availability.

PROTEINS

- **Shredded poultry, pork, and beef** are *all* interchangeable with each other.
- **Ground poultry, pork, and beef** are *all* interchangeable with each other. While the fat content of the ground meat will make a small difference in the end product, it's not a large enough difference that it should prevent you from making the dish you want to make. I say, use what you want!
- **Sliced poultry, pork, and beef** are *all* interchangeable with each other.
- **Vegetarian swaps:** Wherever shredded or ground animal proteins are used, you can swap in an equivalent volume of cooked or canned beans, lentils, or another legume of your choosing.
- **Many types of fish** are interchangeable with each other, as long as they have similar thickness and/or fat content. If a recipe calls for salmon but you can only find snapper, use the snapper. Cooking times will vary slightly depending on the fat content of the fish and the thickness of the cut you're cooking, so just make sure you're paying attention to the color and texture of the fish as it cooks.

VEGETABLES

- **Bell peppers:** Use carrots or, if you're up for a creative adventure, a cruciferous veggie like purple cabbage or Brussels sprouts.
- **Cruciferous veggies:** All cruciferous vegetables (think cabbage, cauliflower, broccoli, Brussels sprouts, and more) are interchangeable with one another because their water content is relatively consistent across the board. Though it may seem strange to make a slaw with cauliflower instead of purple cabbage, it will still work.
- **Herbs:** Just about all mild fresh herbs (cilantro, parsley, chives, dill, etc.) are interchangeable. Parsley can be used instead of cilantro, and vice versa. Swap bolder-flavored herbs (sage, thyme, rosemary, etc.) with others within that category.
- **Leafy greens:** Almost all leafy greens are interchangeable with one another. Some are more obvious swaps (kale, collards, and Swiss chard are all easy substitutions), while others require a little creative thinking (like using mustard greens instead of spinach). Just about all salads can be made with whatever greens you have on hand.
- **Onions and garlic:** Omit or use leeks or shallots, either raw or cooked.
- **Summer squash:** All summer squash (yellow squash, zucchini, etc.) are interchangeable with one another. You can also omit them, or use

tomatoes in their place, as they have a similar water content.

- **Tomatoes:** Either omit them (if you can), or use summer squash as a replacement.

STARCHES

- **Carrots:** Use beets, parsnips, or potatoes.
- **Beets:** Use potatoes, carrots, or parsnips.
- **Potatoes:** Just about all potatoes are interchangeable with one another. If you want to make sure your finished dishes are as close to the intended recipe as possible, try to swap sweet potatoes with other sweet potatoes (yams, purple-skinned sweet potatoes, white sweet potatoes, etc.) and all other potatoes with one another (Yukon Gold, russet, fingerling, etc.).
- **Winter squash:** All winter squashes (butternut, acorn, pumpkin, etc.) are interchangeable with one another. Just make sure the weight of the squash and the cut size or shape are the same as called for in the recipe so the cooking time will be the same.
- **Rice:** All varieties of rice are interchangeable with one another, as long as you use an equal volume of uncooked rice. Cooking times will vary based on the type of rice, so make sure you take that into account when using longer-cooking rice (like brown rice) in place of white rice. You can also use cauliflower rice in its place—substitute 4 cups cooked cauliflower rice for each 1 cup uncooked rice called for in the recipe.
- **Beans:** Just about all beans are interchangeable with one another, as long as you use an equal quantity by weight. You can also substitute canned beans for dried beans instead of cooking them from scratch, and vice versa.

PANTRY INGREDIENTS

- **Wine:** If you'd prefer not to use wine, you can swap in vinegar for about one-third of the amount of wine called for in the recipe. Use apple cider vinegar to replace white wine and balsamic vinegar for red wine.
- **Fats:** For savory cooking, nearly all fats (butter, ghee, olive oil, coconut oil, bacon fat, duck fat, etc.) are all interchangeable at an equal volume.
- **Vinegar:** Though there will be a slight variation in flavor, vinegars are generally interchangeable at an equal volume. Red wine vinegar, white wine vinegar, apple cider vinegar, and rice wine vinegar can be substituted for one another. If a recipe calls for balsamic vinegar, though, I recommend not swapping it for another vinegar. Balsamic is sweeter and has an ability to caramelize that the others do not.
- **Citrus:** I tend to cook with a good amount of fresh lemon and lime juice. As a nutritionist, I'm a fan of the vitamin C available in these superfoods and of their ability to satisfy our taste buds' need for acid. If you have one but not the other, the good news is that they're interchangeable with each other at an equal volume.
- **Flour:** Any recipe that calls for all-purpose flour can use an equal amount of a cup-for-cup gluten-free flour.

Adjusting Yield: Making More or Less Food

If you're looking to use this book to fit your family's needs but you don't fit the typical mold, let's go over how you can apply the strategy to still enjoy a dinner-fix win.

NEED FEWER SERVINGS

The easiest thing to do is to make the recipes as written and store the leftovers to enjoy another day. Leftovers can be enjoyed from the refrigerator within three to five days, or you can follow the freezing guide on page 14 to build up a stash of "in case of emergency" freezer meals. If you're single, I recommend storing leftovers in single-serving portions. In my years of cooking for one, I found that single servings were much more likely to be enjoyed than large batches.

Your second option is to halve the recipes, but this requires some math.

The last option is to give the food you won't be able to enjoy to a friend, coworker, or neighbor. You never know how a prepared meal can truly bless someone.

NEED MORE SERVINGS

The easiest thing to do is to double the recipes until you have the yield you need. Don't be afraid to lean on prepared proteins (think rotisserie chicken) and larger cuts of meat (like a beef brisket or a turkey) when you want a break in the kitchen. These large proteins stretch a dollar and make the best use of your time.

If your family doesn't enjoy eating leftovers, then you'll be cooking more often, but you can still take advantage of the cook-once method by preparing proteins and starches in bulk and repurposing them later in new and fresh dishes.

SAMPLE MEAL PLAN: FAMILY OF TWO

SUNDAY: Sun-Dried Tomato Bacon Chicken Pasta (page 36)

MONDAY: Leftover Sun-Dried Tomato Bacon Chicken Pasta

TUESDAY: Jamaican-Inspired Bowls with Mango Salsa and White Rice (page 37)

WEDNESDAY: Leftover Jamaican-Inspired Bowls

THURSDAY: Perfect Carnitas with Roasted Mexican Street Corn (page 172)

FRIDAY: Sticky Honey-Garlic Pork with White Rice (page 173)

SATURDAY: Leftover Perfect Carnitas and Sticky Honey-Garlic Pork

SAMPLE MEAL PLAN: FAMILY OF FOUR

SUNDAY: Sun-Dried Tomato Bacon Chicken Pasta (page 36)

MONDAY: Jamaican-Inspired Bowls with Mango Salsa and White Rice (page 37)

TUESDAY: Enchilada-Stuffed Zucchini Boats (page 234)

WEDNESDAY: Vegetarian Chili with Vegan Corn Bread (page 235)

THURSDAY: Perfect Carnitas with Roasted Mexican Street Corn (page 172)

FRIDAY: Sticky Honey-Garlic Pork with White Rice (page 173)

SATURDAY: Free night (grab pizza or takeout, visit a restaurant, or make that random dish you printed off Pinterest and have been meaning to try)

Twelve Time-Saving Kitchen Tips

By now you've caught on that efficiency is the name of the game. Your time is precious, so I want to make sure that any time you spend making my recipes is as easy and efficient as possible. I've collected time-saving tips for over a decade and am thrilled to share them with you here. Some require nonessential kitchen equipment, while others are ideas on how to best manage your time while preparing a meal. I hope you find them helpful.

1. Use a stand mixer to shred large proteins. If you own a stand mixer, this is a major game changer. Place the still-hot protein in the bowl of a stand mixer fitted with the paddle attachment. If the bowl is especially full, drape a kitchen towel over the top to help keep any pieces from flying out. Mix on medium-low speed for 1 to 2 minutes, then peek to see if the meat has been shredded—if so, you're done! Gone are the days of hand cramps from shredding massive amounts of protein with two dinner forks.

2. Need to mash something? Use a hand mixer to mash anything, including cooked squash, cauliflower, and especially potatoes—all "mash" incredibly well with a hand mixer, and your arm and shoulder are saved the work of using a potato masher. Just put the ingredient in a large bowl and mix on low speed until you get your desired consistency.

3. Instead of baking a potato, shave off significant time by microwaving it instead. Just wrap the potato (any type) in a damp paper towel (wrap them individually if you're cooking more than one) and microwave until the flesh is tender—1 pound of potatoes will cook in 5 to 6 minutes, 2 pounds in 8 to 9 minutes, and 3 pounds in 10 to 15 minutes. Stop and give them a pinch halfway through to see how much more time is needed. (If you like, you can transfer the cooked potato to the oven and bake it at 425°F for 10 minutes to crisp the skin and get that perfect texture.)

4. Prep often-used ingredients—such as garlic, onions, bell peppers, kale, fresh herbs, cabbage, etc.—as soon as you get them home from the grocery and then store them in airtight containers or zip-top bags. Finely chop garlic, dice onions and bell peppers, stem and

chop kale leaves, and so on, so they're ready to add to recipes later on, saving you prep time on busy nights.

5. If your hand grater brings back memories of injured knuckles, use a food processor to quickly slice or grate veggies like carrots, Brussels sprouts, and cabbage. There's no shame in saving time *and* your knuckles by shredding veggies with your food processor. Bonus: if you're prepping raw veggies, the cleanup is incredibly easy.

6. If you have some downtime while cooking Meal 1—say, you're waiting for the chicken to finish roasting—use that time to get some prep done for the next night's meal. Make sauces or cook grains like rice or quinoa and store them to use the next day.

7. If you need to save time, buy prechopped veggies and prepared sauces or dressings. Prepped vegetables are sold in the produce section of your grocery store; you can also save money and time by buying frozen prepped veggies. And feel free to substitute store-bought versions for any of the home-made sauces and dressings in this book.

8. Another time-saver? Opt for canned beans over dried—there's no shame in it! Canned beans take only a few minutes to prep and cook, while cooking dried beans from scratch means an overnight soak and at least an hour of simmering.

9. Need to get dinner on the table especially fast one night? Chop your veggies smaller. For example, if a recipe calls for sliced bell peppers, diced will take less time to cook.

10. Before you start cooking, read through the recipe in its entirety, then take out all the ingredients you'll need and prep them as directed in the ingredient list. This is a practice known as mise en place, from the French "put in place," and it will allow you to move faster as you're cooking and eliminate mistakes. It also ensures you don't get halfway through a recipe only to discover you're missing an important ingredient!

11. Lean on tools like a pressure cooker or Instant Pot to help speed up your protein cooking time. I personally love my Instant Pot and have included method adaptations for several of the meals in this book.

12. Spend just a little time, maybe at the beginning of the week, to plan your meals out. Bookmark the dishes you want, write down your plan, and tape it so it's visible. This way, you won't need to spend any time trying to sort out what you'll make for dinner each night; the decision is already made!

Fresh Cooked vs. Made Ahead

If I've accidently become an expert on anything, it's the subject of which foods are best made ahead and which are best made fresh. You might be surprised by what lands on the make-ahead list. The trick to ensuring your make-ahead foods turn out great—not just okay—is in *how* you reheat them (more on that on page 14).

WHAT TO MAKE FRESH

Some foods are best cooked fresh because their texture changes too much when they're reheated. These include:

- Dressed salads made with delicate greens (think butter lettuce, romaine, fresh herbs, fresh spinach, etc.). If you want to prepare this type of salad in advance, simply store the assembled, undressed salad and the dressing separately, then dress the salad just before serving.
- Steak meant to be enjoyed as a steak. We do re-purpose steak for a second meal in a few recipes in this book, but if you want a classic steak dinner, it's best to cook the steak and enjoy it immediately.
- Soft-boiled and fried eggs. While soft-boiled eggs can be reheated in a warm water bath and fried eggs in a pan over low heat, reheating them is almost as much work as cooking them from scratch.
- Sautéed greens. While you absolutely *can* eat left-over sautéed spinach, kale, etc., the bright color of the freshly cooked greens will dull and brown over time. If that bothers you, cook your greens fresh.

WHAT TO MAKE AHEAD

- Hearty salads and slaws. Hearty salads and slaws made with sturdy greens like kale or cabbage will hold up wonderfully for a day or two (though if they contain fresh herbs, these may look a little wilted after storage).
- Cooked shredded or ground proteins. If there were ever an obvious choice for make-ahead proteins, it's these two. This is because these broken-down proteins maintain their textures exceptionally well when reheated.
- Rice. Just about every variety of rice is perfectly fine to make ahead. While the texture may get slightly stickier when you reheat it, it'll still be really close to freshly cooked.
- Beans and lentils. You'd be hard-pressed to find a bean or lentil that isn't just as great the day after it was cooked.
- Sauces. All the sauces! Just about every sauce under the sun is totally fine to make ahead. Mayo, aioli, salad dressings, marinades, hoisin sauce, teriyaki sauce, Peruvian green sauce—you name it. They're all great for days after they're prepared.
- Baked potatoes. Baked potatoes, especially those cooked whole, are a no-brainer for making ahead. If you want to reheat them to serve as a baked potato, that's doable. If you want to turn them into mashed potatoes, doable. If you want to slice them into rounds and sear them until crispy, or even make a crispy hash, *doable*!
- Winter squash. Winter squash, especially if roasted in large pieces, is great to cook ahead. Unless you're serving the squash straight-up, you'll need to let it cool enough to handle anyway. Roasting and cooling the squash ahead of time takes away the pressure of the dinnertime countdown.

The Trick to Reheating Foods

Reused ingredients are essentially completely different on day two. The texture won't be exactly the same, so don't treat them as you did on day one. Extra sauce, fat, seasoning, and cooking method are key to delicious leftovers.

- Apply concentrated heat via a skillet or in the oven. This will recrisp the food.
- Apply extra sauce to cooked proteins. If you're sensitive to proteins that seem even just a bit dry (think shredded chicken), don't be afraid to apply more sauce. Toss the cooked protein with the sauce and then reheat as you like.
- Apply dry seasonings to bring cooked foods back to life.
- Squeeze some fresh lemon or lime juice over the cooked food.
- Garnish with fresh herbs.

Freezing Foods 101

One question that easily falls into the most-asked category is "Can I freeze that?" If the answer is yes, this question is then followed by "But . . . how do I freeze it? And for up to how long? And then how do I defrost it?"

All great questions.

In this section, instead of providing an extremely exacting encyclopedia of foods with their freezing specifications, I want to teach you how to figure this out for yourself. In essence, this guide is more of a "teach you to fish" vs. "hand you the fish" kind of activity.

CAN YOU FREEZE THAT?

There are certain kinds of foods that don't hold up well in the freezer. Let's talk about the science of freezing to help tease this out.

First, most food is made up mostly of water. What happens to water when it freezes? It solidifies, and as it solidifies, it expands. If you've ever frozen a too-full container and come back to find that it's popped its lid or split the container, you know what I mean. This expansion is the biggest factor to consider when freezing foods. As an example, let's envision a raw sweet potato. The sweet potato is made up of cellular walls, the water contained within them, and a variety of other components (some protein, vitamins, minerals, etc.). If you freeze that raw sweet potato (either chopped or whole), it may not look, to the naked eye, very different from its original form, but on a cellular level, things have definitely changed. The water inside the cells of that sweet potato has expanded, destroying the cellular walls and therefore changing the texture of the potato.

Does this mean you can't freeze raw sweet potatoes? Absolutely not. You can still freeze them and cook them, but do so knowing that the texture may be different than if you'd cooked raw potatoes. This information raises a great question, too: Is there a way to freeze sweet potatoes that will reduce the likelihood of an altered texture?

Now we're getting somewhere.

Though there's nothing wrong with freezing raw fresh sweet potatoes, I prefer freezing them in a form that will have little to no impact on their texture once they're thawed. What form is that?

Cooked! If you were to compare the cells of that raw sweet potato from our original example with the cells of cooked sweet potato, you'd see things are already different. The cellular walls have been broken down by the cooking process, giving the potato that wonderful cooked texture we love. The water has already been allowed to escape, making the flesh more malleable and able to stand up to freezing much better. Though a freezer won't maintain a sweet potato fry's outside crisp, it will maintain its almost-exactly-the-same interior texture.

So, when you want to know the answer to "Can I freeze that?" you need to first visualize the water content of the food. If it's cooked, the cell walls have been broken down, and you can very likely get away with an easy freeze/thaw with little or no change to the food's texture. If the food is uncooked, know that its texture may change after freezing/thawing.

HOW DO YOU FREEZE IT?

There are three main options for freezing food:

1. **Raw, mostly whole.** This is a great way to freeze animal proteins (including eggs—just make sure they're out of the shell), grains, nuts and seeds, some dairy products, and butter. Raw vegetables and fruits can also be frozen, but this option could result in the greatest change in texture after thawing.

   Great foods to freeze raw and whole: animal proteins, beaten raw eggs, low-water-content whole fruits and vegetables (think avocado), leafy greens (as long as you cook them after thawing vs. serving them raw), fresh berries

2. **Raw, manually broken down.** Some fresh foods do really well in the freezer, but they need just a touch of work to be freezer-ready for the best application later. That means chopping, shredding, or otherwise prepping the foods before freezing.

   Great foods to break down raw and freeze: herbs (chopped or minced), potatoes (shredded; you won't really notice a texture difference after thawing due to the small pieces), stone fruit (pitted and chopped or sliced), peppers (seeded and chopped), winter squash (peeled and chopped; the texture will be altered, but unappealing), onions (chopped), garlic (chopped or minced), and fresh ginger (peeled and grated or just peeled).

3. **Cooked.** Some foods really excel at freezer life as fully cooked components. This is mostly because the change from prefrozen to postfrozen is minimal in my experience. Foods that we freeze most often include soups, stews, casseroles, and chili. I've found that these food formats help protect the ingredients from freezer burn and yield a perfectly enjoyable meal once they're thawed and reheated.

   Great foods to cook and freeze: stews, soups, fully assembled casseroles, chili, lasagna, rice and other grains or grain dishes (think cheesy polenta), beans, roasted vegetables, fruit reductions, etc.

HOW DO YOU REHEAT FROZEN COOKED FOODS?

The million-dollar question! My answer is very simple: the best way to reheat a food is by the same method you cooked it originally. So if you baked a casserole before freezing it, reheat it in the oven; if you cooked chili on the stovetop, reheat it in a saucepan.

If you can plan ahead, transfer the food to the refrigerator and let it thaw overnight before reheating. If planning ahead isn't in the cards, don't fret. Just thaw it enough that you can transfer it from the freezer container into a vessel for reheating (a saucepan, baking dish, etc.).

- **Soups/stews/chili:** My favorite way to reheat soup, stew, or chili is from frozen, right in a pan on the stove. Let the food thaw just enough that you can slip it out of the freezer container, plop it into a large pot, cover, and heat over low heat for a good 30 minutes to 1 hour, until it's completely thawed and evenly heated through.
- **Casseroles:** The best place to reheat a casserole is in the oven. If it's thawed (good for you for thinking ahead), use the baking temperature and time from the original recipe. If it's still frozen, know you're in for a bit of a wait, but that's okay. For a 4-quart or larger frozen-solid casserole, cover with aluminum foil and bake in a preheated 325°F oven for 2 hours, then check to see if the center has thawed. If not, bake for 30 minutes more, still covered, then check again; continue until the center has thawed. Once the center has thawed, uncover the casserole, raise the oven temperature to 375°F and bake for 30 to 45 minutes more, until the casserole is heated through (if you can, take a small bite or slice from the center to check for doneness—that's where the casserole takes longest to reheat). Once the casserole comes out of the oven, feel free to garnish it with fresh herbs to liven it back up.
- **Rice/other grains/beans:** Reheat these either on the stovetop or in the microwave, which does a great job with grains and legumes.
- **Roasted vegetables:** If they're thawed, spread them out on a baking sheet, pop them into a preheated 350°F oven, and roast again for 15 to 20 minutes. If they're frozen solid, let them cook for 30 minutes, or until they start to sizzle and look like new again. Just keep an eye on them so they don't burn.

HOW LONG CAN I STORE FROZEN FOODS?

Great question! On average, I operate within the following rough parameters:

- **Frozen raw proteins:** Use within 5 months.
- **Frozen dairy:** Use within 5 months.
- **Frozen raw produce:** Use within 3 months.
- **Frozen uncooked grains/legumes:** Use within 9 months.
- **Frozen cooked foods:** Use within 6 months.

After thawing, it's best to reheat and serve formerly frozen foods within 24 hours and use leftovers within 3 to 5 days.

If your foods partially thaw and then refreeze, there's a good chance you can leave them be without any worry. According to the USDA, "Once food is thawed in the refrigerator, it is safe to refreeze it without cooking, although there may be a loss of quality due to the moisture lost through thawing. After cooking raw foods which were previously frozen, it is safe to freeze the cooked foods. If previously cooked foods are thawed in the refrigerator, you may refreeze the unused portion. Freeze leftovers within 3–4 days. Do not refreeze any foods left outside the refrigerator longer than 2 hours." (Source: fsis.usda.gov/wps/portal/fsis/topics/food-safety-education/get-answers/food-safety-fact-sheets/safe-food-handling/freezing-and-food-safety/CT_Index)

WILL COOKED FOODS TASTE DIFFERENT AFTER FREEZING AND REHEATING?

In my experience, you can expect the following taste and texture differences:

- **Little to no change in texture or flavor:** soups, stews, chili, grains, beans, shredded proteins, ground proteins
- **Some change in texture or flavor:** roasted vegetables, whole baked potatoes, fresh fruit, fresh vegetables, fresh herbs
- **Different texture, but okay to eat:** mashed potatoes, dairy-heavy foods (like cream-based pasta sauce), any food that was originally intended to be "crispy" (think fries, hash browns, breaded chicken)

Kitchen Equipment: Ten Must-Have Pieces

To get dinner on the table with ease, you need a plan, a good attitude, a little time, the right foods to prep, and efficient equipment. Let's zero in on that last item.

This conversation merits a disclaimer: I'm not one for single-use gadgets and kitchen gizmos. I'm decidedly against kitchen tools that get used once a month (at most) but clutter my counters or cabinets, finances, and mind. Just as how I approach getting dinner on the table in the dinner fix (with incredibly efficient ingredients and steps), I recommend you approach your kitchen tools and equipment in the same manner.

If I had to start all over and stock my kitchen with a brand-new set of equipment, these are the ten items I'd buy, the tools I think should show up on every wedding registry or on the wish list of every young professional responsibly stocking their cabinets. They're multiuse (with one exception), high quality, and feel like part of the solution, rather than part of the dinner problem.

1. **A SHARP CHEF'S KNIFE** (or several sharp knives). If you don't currently have a knife you actually look forward to using while you work in the kitchen, consider this your sign to take the plunge and get one. Whether you have a birthday coming up or you can forgo your next shopping spree and grab a quality kitchen knife instead, this item is number one for a reason. While you lovingly pour your time and energy into preparing dinner, a knife that works with you (rather than against you) can speed up your prep time, make for a better product, and (maybe most important) make cooking a more enjoyable experience. A 6- to 10-inch chef's knife is a great place to start. If possible, go to a store in person so you can pick up the knife and see how it feels in your hand. The grip shouldn't feel uncomfortable and the knife shouldn't feel unwieldy; if it does, try a shorter one.

    Keeping your knife (or knives) sharp is important—a dull knife is actually more dangerous than a sharp one, because you have to apply more pressure to cut through foods, making a slip more likely. A dull knife also makes chopping and slicing feel like more work. If you already have a great knife but it has dulled, consider this your reminder to get it professionally sharpened. Your nearest kitchen store can likely assist. Sharpening is relatively inexpensive and will feel like some of the best money you've spent in a while.

2. **A GOOD SKILLET**. I'm not saying you need to invest in a $300 copper skillet that you'll mark as an heirloom one day. I just want you to have a large skillet (about 12 inches in diameter) that will stand up to daily use and can go from the stovetop to the oven. Stainless steel is ideal, though pricey, and ceramic-coated is acceptable. If you opt for nonstick, make sure the skillet doesn't have a coating that will flake (like old Teflon); if you're using a nonstick pan right now with a damaged surface or flaky nonstick coating, replace it if you can. If you want to go bargain hunting, you may be able to find a great deal on cookware at outlets and off-season/off-price retailers (think T.J. Maxx).

3. **A STURDY CUTTING BOARD**. If you have those flimsy plastic cutting boards that were popular in 2002, I need you to take this one seriously. You may be frustrated with your dinner experience because the dang cutting board scoots all over the place, making chopping, slicing, and dicing an unenjoyable (and potentially unsafe) experience. A sturdy cutting board will provide stability and safety as you prepare your ingredients. Pro tip: place your cutting board on a lightly dampened kitchen towel to keep it from moving while you chop.

4. **MEASURING CUPS AND SPOONS**. Have you been eyeballing ingredient quantities and finding yourself frustrated with inconsistent recipe results? Grabbing a basic set of metal measuring cups for dry ingredients (the kind with a flat top and a handle, in increments of ¼, ⅓, ½, and 1 cup) and a set of metal measuring spoons could make a huge difference in your cooking experience. I also recommend having at least one basic glass measuring cup for liquids (the type with a spout) that holds at least 2 cups.

5. **DUTCH OVEN** (enameled cast iron). This will become a well-used and well-loved kitchen tool. You'll notice that pots didn't make my top-ten list—that's because a Dutch oven can double as a pot for boiling water for pasta, making soup, whipping up chili, etc. These can range in price, but don't feel like you have to buy the most expensive one—I recommend finding one that holds at least 3¾ quarts (or up to 6 quarts) and that fits your budget. You can also use it as a casserole dish and skip item seven. Talk about efficiency!

6. **QUALITY SPATULAS, SPOONS, AND WHISKS**. You really only *need* one of each of these, but I'd probably grab a couple of sizes of spatulas, stirring spoons, and whisks to make my life as easy as possible. If the spatula/spoon crock sitting next to your stove looks more like a Chia Pet *bursting* with every spoon you've ever been given, consider this permission to thin the herd. (I recommend tossing anything that isn't heatproof to start.) You just need a few, and it'll feel so much easier to find what you need when you need it.

7. **CASSEROLE/BAKING DISH**. If you want to get fancy, an 8-inch square and a 9 x 13-inch baking dish are the two to have. If you have to choose just one, grab the larger one. These can be metal, ceramic, or glass. All will work.

Baking foods like lasagna, enchiladas, etc., in a casserole dish (as opposed to in your Dutch oven) gives them more surface area and will help give them the perfect finish.

8. **MEAT THERMOMETER**. Though you can technically get by without one, an instant-read meat thermometer can offer a lot of peace of mind as you learn how to navigate the kitchen and cook various cuts of meat. It's incredibly validating to see exactly what the temperature is inside that lovely roast so you can pull it from the oven when it's done to your liking. These are inexpensive and don't take up much room in a drawer.

9. **RIMMED BAKING SHEETS (TWO)**. The two basic stainless-steel rimmed baking sheets I have in my kitchen are possibly my most-used equipment, next to my citrus squeezer (see item ten) and my knives and cutting boards. Also called sheet pans or jelly-roll pans, these are ideal for baking or roasting just about anything: broccoli, chicken thighs, french fries, cookies, you name it! Don't stress over their changing looks as they age with use. I actually have some of my grandmother's baking sheets, and their patina and history make them a real treasure.

10. **CITRUS SQUEEZER**. Okay, this may seem like an odd addition to a "multiuse kitchen equipment" list, but hear me out. In my home, the citrus juicer is used daily. You might keep reaching for the salt jar to add flavor to a dish, but your taste buds are actually craving an acidic note. I take this into account with all the recipes I develop, which is why you'll notice that they're relatively lemon- and lime-heavy. My advice when choosing a citrus squeezer: don't get a metal one with a painted finish (it will flake). Opt instead for a good-quality heavy-duty plastic squeezer that will stand the test of time. The energy saved by this one gadget, keeping you from squeezing by hand and having to fish out seeds, is not insignificant.

Enjoying Your Time in the Kitchen Even More

Are you catching on to a massive theme here? With this book, my job is to make sure the get-dinner-on-the-table process is as easy and enjoyable as possible, and to do that, I'm giving you every tool I have in my tool chest. Now that we've got endless guides for food storage, recipe customizing, equipment advice, and time-saving tips under our belt, I want to zero in on an often-forgotten subject, the other equally valuable things you can do to make dinner prep even more enjoyable.

- **HAVE A PLAN.** Your plan can come together a week ahead, a day ahead, hours ahead, or minutes ahead, but spend at least five minutes making a plan. This will make a *big* difference in how you feel as you go about prepping dinner. Planning could be as simple as flipping this book open to your favorite dinner series, taking a moment to quickly envision your process, and deciding what time you'd like dinner to hit the table. It could also be as simple as sitting at the kitchen table for ten minutes, jotting down a week of planned meals that fit your family's packed schedule, and brainstorming your grocery list. Any way you do it, having some kind of a plan will bring you peace and confidence, and help you avoid that directionless "I have no idea what I'm making" feeling while you stare into the open door of your refrigerator with a ticking clock counting down thirty minutes to dinner.

My recommendation on when to plan dinner? Ideally, by 2 p.m. day-of. This should give you enough time to pull out any frozen proteins, assess what produce you've got on hand, choose side dishes, and decide what time you'll start the cooking process.

- **FIND A GOOD PLAYLIST.** This may sound a little silly, but it can make a world of difference. Even if you just ask Alexa to "play the latest Justin Bieber," tunes twirling in the background while you get to work chopping and searing can build the ambience and enjoyability of the experience. Because the process of making dinner is such a chapter in my day (a chapter that tells me work is over and we're moving on to family time), background music signifies to myself and my family that it's time to unwind, dance, dirty a few dishes, and gather to discuss our day.

- **POUR YOURSELF A SPECIAL DRINK.** This could be sparkling water with lemon or a glass of wine, but make it special. Cooking dinner is work, and I believe you should feel pampered as you do it! Sometimes a special drink in a special glass can be just enough to put a little spring in your step as you bounce toward the kitchen to start cooking.

- **INVITE HELP.** Though getting your helpers going on their own tasks takes a bit of extra work to start, it can be such a joy. Delegating easier tasks to family members (asking your teenager to assemble the salad and/or your partner to chop the potatoes, for example) also helps make dinner feel easier. Even giving my two-year-old some nontask "tasks," like handing her a bowl of ingredients to play with, brings me joy, as I get to watch her learn about food and see how her dinner comes together.

- **GATHER QUALITY KITCHEN TOOLS.** We've talked about this extensively, but it's worth another mention. Swapping out a few of your most-used and worn-down kitchen tools for good-quality pieces can make a big difference in how much you enjoy dinner prep.
- **ORGANIZE YOUR KITCHEN TOOLS.** Though the act of pulling everything out of your cabinets and drawers may feel a little like intense spring cleaning, the end result is therapeutic in and of itself. My recommendation: declutter your cabinets, shelves, and drawers by pulling everything out. Give all the drawers and shelves a good wipe-down and then put back only those items you know you'll use. There's no award for hanging on to that frog-shaped cake pan, broken hand mixer, or plastic storage containers without matching tops. Donate what you can, recycle what you can't donate, and bask in the glory of a kitchen stocked with tools you'll actually use. Best of all? Because you just touched each item, you'll know where everything is.
- **DEEP CLEAN YOUR FRIDGE AND PANTRY.** Similar to the previous task, going through an intense sorting and clean-out of your food inventory can feel like a real chore, but goodness, does it help relieve stress when meal planning and prepping. Just as you did with your kitchen equipment, I recommend pulling everything out of your cabinets and fridge. Give each surface a wipe-down and then only put back what you'll use. Discard expired foods and recycle their packaging, and donate unexpired pantry items you know you won't get around to using or that your family doesn't enjoy.
- **WASH AS YOU GO.** I know there are two kinds of cooks out there: the wash-as-you-go folks and the let-the-dishes-pile-up folks. Even though my husband will gladly wash dishes after dinner is done, watching the sink fill up as I cook just adds to my stress. I'm a big fan of washing dishes as I work, because it keeps my sink empty and my countertops visually uncluttered. Then, when we sit down for dinner, the only dishes I have to contend with are our dinner plates and servingware. This makes for a "kitchen shutdown" process that's so simple: put away leftovers, wash/rinse what's left, turn off the lights, and go read books in our daughters' room.

poultry

Barbeque Chicken Casserole

WITH SWEET POTATO

/ RECIPE PAGE 30 /

ABOUT

This dinner series is smack-dab in the middle of my recipe creation wheelhouse. Shredded chicken is given two totally different treatments, both of which are fun and family friendly. The first dinner is a healthy casserole: shredded chicken is tossed in barbecue sauce and then piled high on tender kale and mashed sweet potatoes. It's a complete meal in a scoop! The second dinner—Baked Chicken Chimichangas with Beans and Slaw—is one of my favorites in the whole book. The chicken is seasoned with vibrant Tex-Mex flavors and loosely rolled up with beans and cheese in a tortilla of your choosing. The chimichangas then get brushed with butter, baked, and served with sauce and slaw.

▧ $$

▧ DAIRY-FREE OPTION

▧ EGG-FREE

▧ GLUTEN-FREE OPTION

▧ GRAIN-FREE OPTION

▧ NUT-FREE

▧ FREEZER-FRIENDLY

Baked Chicken Chimichangas

WITH BEANS AND SLAW

/ RECIPE PAGE 31 /

SUBSTITUTIONS

Make It Dairy-Free:

- **MEAL 1:** Use olive oil in place of the butter in the barbecue chicken casserole.

- **MEAL 2:** Omit the cheese blend from the chimichangas. Use ⅓ cup coconut cream (scooped from the top of a chilled can of full-fat coconut milk) in place of the sour cream in the chimichanga sauce, and omit the sour cream used for garnish. Brush tortillas with olive oil before baking.

Make It Gluten-Free:

- **MEAL 2:** Use gluten-free wraps or tortillas for the chimichangas. If you can't find 12-inch tortillas, you'll need about 14 smaller (7-inch) tortillas.

Make It Grain-Free:

- **MEAL 2:** Use grain-free tortillas for the chimichangas. These will be smaller, about 7 inches in diameter, so you'll need about 14 tortillas total.

MEAL 1

BARBECUE CHICKEN CASSEROLE WITH SWEET POTATO

Serves 6

Active time: 30 MINUTES

Total time: 1 HOUR 30 MINUTES

3 pounds sweet potatoes

4 pounds boneless, skinless chicken breasts or chicken breast tenders

¾ cup barbecue sauce

3 tablespoons salted butter

½ teaspoon fine sea salt

¼ teaspoon ground black pepper

1 tablespoon extra-virgin olive oil

1 bunch collard greens, leaves stemmed and coarsely chopped

Juice of 1 lemon

¼ cup finely chopped red onion, for garnish

1. Preheat the oven to 400°F.

2. Spread the sweet potatoes evenly over a rimmed baking sheet. Bake for 45 to 55 minutes, until the potatoes are soft when pinched (wear an oven mitt!).

3. Meanwhile, place the chicken in a large pot and add water to cover (3 to 4 cups). Bring to a simmer over medium heat. Cover and simmer for 15 to 20 minutes, until the chicken pulls apart easily with a fork. Remove the chicken from the pot and transfer to a large bowl; discard the cooking water.

4. To shred the chicken by hand, use two forks to pull the meat apart into roughly ½-inch pieces. To shred the chicken using a stand mixer, transfer it to the bowl of a stand mixer fitted with the paddle attachment. Beat on low speed for 15 to 25 seconds, until the chicken is evenly shredded. Transfer about 2⅔ cups shredded chicken to an airtight container

and refrigerate to use for Meal 2 (it will keep for up to 5 days).

5. Pour about ½ cup of the barbecue sauce over the shredded chicken remaining in the bowl. Toss to combine evenly; set aside.

6. Remove the sweet potatoes from the oven and set aside to cool slightly. Reduce the oven temperature to 350°F.

7. When the sweet potatoes are cool enough to handle, peel them and put the flesh in a large bowl. Add the butter, salt, and pepper and mash well. Spread the sweet potatoes evenly over the bottom of a 9-inch square baking dish.

8. In a 10-inch skillet, heat the olive oil over medium heat. Add the collards and toss to coat with the oil. Cover and cook for 4 to 5 minutes, until the collards have wilted and reduced in volume. Add the lemon juice and toss. Remove from the heat and spoon the collards over the mashed sweet potatoes in the baking dish.

9. Spread the barbecue shredded chicken over the collards. Bake the casserole for 30 minutes, until the top is browned. Remove from the oven and let cool for 10 minutes.

10. Drizzle the remaining barbecue sauce over the casserole, garnish with the onion, and serve.

TIPS

- The chicken breasts in this recipe yield approximately 8 cups shredded cooked chicken (enough for both Meals 1 and 2). If you have leftover cooked chicken from another meal, you can substitute it here—just shred enough to make 4 cups and mix it with the barbecue sauce as directed.

- If you have cooked sweet potatoes on hand, you can use those instead—just melt the butter before adding it to the bowl with the sweet potatoes.

CALORIES: 571   FAT: 14.8G   CARBS: 62.9G   PROTEIN: 45.6G

MEAL 2

BAKED CHICKEN CHIMICHANGAS WITH BEANS AND SLAW

Serves 4

Active time: 35 MINUTES   **Total time:** 50 MINUTES

For the Chimichangas

4 cups shredded cooked chicken (reserved from Meal 1; see page 30)

1 tablespoon ground cumin

1 tablespoon mild chili powder

½ teaspoon garlic powder

½ teaspoon onion powder

½ teaspoon dried oregano

½ teaspoon fine sea salt

¼ teaspoon ground black pepper

1 cup refried beans

8 large (12-inch) flour tortillas

2 cups shredded Mexican-style cheese blend

2 tablespoons salted butter, melted

For the Slaw

¼ cup fresh lime juice (from about 2 limes)

¼ cup extra-virgin olive oil

½ teaspoon ground cumin

¼ teaspoon fine sea salt

¼ teaspoon ground black pepper

½ head purple cabbage, shredded (about 4 cups)

½ cup shredded carrots

½ cup packed fresh cilantro, coarsely chopped

1 jalapeño, seeded and thinly sliced

To Serve

1 cup red salsa

½ cup sour cream

2 tablespoons finely chopped fresh cilantro

1. Make the chimichangas: Preheat the oven to 375°F. Line a rimmed baking sheet with parchment paper.

2. In a large bowl, stir together the chicken, cumin, chili powder, garlic powder, onion powder, oregano, salt, and pepper until evenly combined.

3. Spread 2 tablespoons of the refried beans down the middle of a tortilla, then spoon about ⅓ cup of the seasoned chicken on top. Top with about ¼ cup of the cheese. Roll up the tortilla to enclose the filling. Secure the stuffed tortilla with a toothpick and place it seam side down on the prepared baking sheet. Repeat to fill and roll the remaining tortillas.

4. Brush the stuffed tortillas with the melted butter. Bake for 30 minutes, or until the tops are golden brown. Remove from the oven and let cool for 5 minutes.

5. Meanwhile, make the slaw: In a small bowl, whisk together the lime juice, olive oil, cumin, salt, and pepper until the dressing is fully combined.

6. In a large bowl, combine the cabbage, carrots, cilantro, and jalapeño, then pour the dressing over. Toss to combine and set aside.

7. In a small bowl, stir together the salsa and ⅓ cup of the sour cream.

8. Divide the chimichangas among four plates and top evenly with the creamy salsa and the remaining sour cream. Garnish with the cilantro and serve with the slaw alongside.

TIPS

- Warmed tortillas will roll more easily than room temperature or chilled ones from the refrigerator. If you find that your tortillas break, add a few sprinkles of water or microwave wrapped in a moistened paper towel.

- If you don't want to shred your own cabbage and carrots for the slaw, substitute 4½ cups coleslaw mix instead.

CALORIES: 999   FAT: 47.5G   CARBS: 77.6G   PROTEIN: 66.4G

Chicken Sloppy Joes

WITH GINGER CARROT SLAW

/ RECIPE PAGE 34 /

ABOUT

I cannot wait for you to make these two dinners! They're both *big* hits in my house, adored by two-year-olds and sixty-two-year-olds alike. A heaping helping of shredded chicken is divided between two festive dinners. First up is a perfectly tangy and sweet sloppy joe paired with my favorite ginger carrot slaw. You can enjoy this meal as a piled-high sandwich or serve it bunless in a bowl. The second dinner is a white chicken enchilada casserole that you are going to want to make again and again. It's incredibly easy to whip up. I like to serve it with a bright tomato and avocado salad for a touch of color and freshness.

- $$
- EGG-FREE
- GLUTEN-FREE OPTION
- GRAIN-FREE OPTION
- NUT-FREE
- FREEZER-FRIENDLY

MEAL 2

White Enchilada Casserole

WITH TOMATO AVOCADO SALAD

/ RECIPE PAGE 35 /

SUBSTITUTIONS

Make It Gluten-Free:

- **MEAL 1:** Use gluten-free buns for the sloppy joes.

Make It Grain-Free:

- **MEAL 1:** Skip the buns and serve the sloppy joes in individual bowls instead.

- **MEAL 2:** Use grain-free tortillas for the enchilada casserole.

Freezer-Friendly Tip:

- Both the chicken filling for the sloppy joes and the enchilada casserole freeze beautifully. (I don't recommend freezing the ginger carrot slaw or the tomato avocado salad, so make those fresh the day you plan to serve them.)

CHICKEN SLOPPY JOES WITH GINGER CARROT SLAW

Serves 4

Active time: 35 MINUTES   **Total time:** 35 MINUTES

For the Chicken Sloppy Joes

4 pounds boneless, skinless chicken breasts or chicken tenders

½ cup ketchup

¼ cup prepared yellow mustard

2 tablespoons honey

½ teaspoon garlic powder

½ teaspoon onion powder

½ teaspoon fine sea salt

For the Ginger Carrot Slaw

6 to 8 medium carrots, shredded

1 bunch radishes, shredded

1 (1-inch) piece fresh ginger, peeled and grated

1 bunch fresh cilantro, coarsely chopped

Juice of 3 limes

1 teaspoon fine sea salt

½ teaspoon ground black pepper

6 hamburger buns, toasted, for serving

1. Make the chicken sloppy joes: Place the chicken in a large pot and add water to cover (3 to 4 cups). Bring to a simmer over medium heat. Cover and simmer for 15 to 20 minutes, until the chicken pulls apart easily with a fork. Remove the chicken from the pot and place it in a large bowl; discard the cooking water.

2. To shred the chicken by hand, use two forks to pull the meat apart into roughly ½-inch pieces. To shred the chicken using a stand mixer, transfer it to the bowl of a stand mixer fitted with the paddle attachment. Beat on low speed for 15 to 25 seconds, until the chicken is evenly shredded. Transfer half the shredded chicken (about 4 cups) to an airtight container, let cool, and refrigerate to use for Meal 2 (it will keep for up to 5 days).

3. Transfer the remaining shredded chicken to a large pot. Add the ketchup, mustard, honey, garlic powder, onion powder, and salt and stir to combine. Bring to a simmer over medium heat, cover, and simmer for 5 to 10 minutes, until the chicken is warmed through.

4. Meanwhile, make the slaw: In a large bowl, stir together the carrots, radishes, ginger, cilantro, lime juice, salt, and pepper to combine.

5. To assemble the sloppy joes, spoon about ½ cup of the chicken onto the bottom half of each toasted bun and top with about ¼ cup of the slaw. Add the toasted bun tops and serve.

TIPS

- The chicken breasts in this recipe yield approximately 8 cups shredded cooked chicken (enough for both Meals 1 and 2). If you have leftover cooked chicken from another meal, you can substitute it here—just shred enough to make 4 cups and mix it with the sauce as directed.

- Use your food processor's shredding blade to shred the carrots and radishes for the slaw, or buy about 3 cups pre-shredded carrots and 1 cup preshredded radishes.

- The sloppy joes can be served as an assembled sandwich as shown on page 32, or served in a bowl over the slaw, without the bun.

CALORIES: 547   FAT: 8.7G   CARBS: 57.8G   PROTEIN: 53G

WHITE ENCHILADA CASSEROLE WITH TOMATO AVOCADO SALAD

Serves 6

Active time: 30 MINUTES   **Total time:** 45 MINUTES

For the White Enchilada Casserole

2 tablespoons salted butter

1 cup sour cream

1 cup milk or chicken broth

3 cups shredded Monterey Jack cheese

1 teaspoon fine sea salt

¼ teaspoon ground black pepper

4 cups shredded cooked chicken (reserved from Meal 1; see page 34)

1 (4.5-ounce) can green chiles, with their liquid

1 teaspoon ground cumin

1 teaspoon garlic powder

2 tablespoons fresh lime juice (from 1 lime)

12 corn tortillas

For the Tomato Avocado Salad

1 avocado, cut into 1-inch chunks

1 pint cherry tomatoes, halved

¼ red onion, thinly sliced

¼ cup chopped fresh cilantro

2 tablespoons extra-virgin olive oil

½ teaspoon coarse sea salt

¼ cup fresh cilantro leaves, for garnish (optional)

1. Make the casserole: Preheat the oven to 350°F.

2. In a large sauté pan or skillet, combine the butter, sour cream, milk, 1 cup of the cheese, ½ teaspoon of the salt, and the pepper. Heat over medium heat, whisking continuously, until the ingredients are evenly combined and the cheese has melted. Remove from the heat.

3. In a large bowl, stir together the chicken, green chiles and their liquid, cumin, garlic powder, lime juice, and remaining ½ teaspoon salt until evenly combined.

4. Arrange 3 tortillas over the bottom of a 9-inch-square baking dish (breaking the tortillas as needed to fit). Spoon 1 cup of the seasoned chicken mixture evenly over the tortilla layer, then sprinkle ½ cup of the cheese evenly over the top. Repeat these layers three more times, using the remaining tortillas, chicken, and cheese. Pour the white sauce over the top of the casserole.

5. Bake for 30 minutes, or until the top starts to look golden brown.

6. Meanwhile, make the salad: In a large bowl, combine the avocado, tomatoes, onion, cilantro, olive oil, and salt and toss to combine.

7. Serve the casserole with the salad alongside, garnished with the cilantro, if desired.

CALORIES: 676   FAT: 39.8G   CARBS: 26.1G   PROTEIN: 54G

Sun-Dried Tomato Bacon Chicken Pasta

/ RECIPE PAGE 38 /

ABOUT

In this dinner series, we get to lean on one of my favorite proteins to meal prep: chicken thighs. These chicken thighs are simply seasoned and then baked (or grilled, if you're up for it). The cooked chicken is then put to great use in two incredible dinners. The first is a pasta dish made fabulous by way of a sun-dried tomato sauce, plenty of crunchy bacon, and a generous sprinkling of Parmesan cheese. The second dinner is a bowl bursting with enormous Jamaican-inspired flavors. The cooked chicken thighs are brought back to life with a spice blend that draws influence from traditional jerk seasoning. They're recrisped in a hot pan and then served over rice, with a generous scoop of mango salsa.

- $$
- DAIRY-FREE OPTION
- EGG-FREE
- GLUTEN-FREE OPTION
- GRAIN-FREE OPTION
- LOW-CARB OPTION
- NUT-FREE

MEAL 2

Jamaican-Inspired Bowls

WITH MANGO SALSA AND WHITE RICE

/ RECIPE PAGE 39 /

SUBSTITUTIONS

Make It Dairy-Free:

- **MEAL 1:** Use olive oil in place of the butter for the pasta, substitute full-fat coconut milk for the heavy cream, and omit the Parmesan.

Make It Gluten-Free:

- **MEAL 1:** Use gluten-free pasta for the sun-dried tomato bacon chicken pasta.

Make It Grain-Free:

- **MEAL 1:** Substitute zucchini noodles or cooked spaghetti squash for the pasta.

- **MEAL 2:** Serve the chicken over cooked cauliflower rice instead of the white rice.

Make It Low-Carb:

- **MEAL 1:** Substitute zucchini noodles or cooked spaghetti squash for the pasta.

- **MEAL 2:** Omit the beans and the mango salsa from the chicken bowls, and serve the chicken over 4 cups cooked cauliflower rice instead of the white rice.

SUN-DRIED TOMATO BACON CHICKEN PASTA

Serves 4

Active time: 30 MINUTES   **Total time:** 50 MINUTES

DINNER SERIES 3

For the Chicken Thighs and Bacon

3 pounds boneless, skinless chicken thighs, patted dry

1 teaspoon fine sea salt

½ teaspoon ground black pepper

1 pound sliced bacon

For the Sun-Dried Tomato Pasta Sauce

½ cup sun-dried tomatoes (drained, if packed in oil)

⅓ cup extra-virgin olive oil

½ cup chicken broth

¼ cup heavy cream

3 tablespoons fresh lemon juice (from about 1½ lemons)

½ teaspoon fine sea salt

¼ teaspoon ground black pepper

For the Pasta

12 ounces dried penne

½ teaspoon fine sea salt

Fresh parsley, for garnish

2 tablespoons grated Parmesan cheese, for garnish

1. Preheat the oven to 400°F. Bring a large pot of water to a boil for the pasta.

2. Cook the chicken and bacon: Spread the chicken thighs out on a rimmed baking sheet and season with the salt and pepper, then place in the oven on the lower rack and cook for 10 minutes. On a separate rimmed baking sheet, arrange the bacon slices in an even layer. Once the timer for the chicken goes off, place the bacon on the top rack of the oven and cook the chicken and bacon for 20 minutes, until the bacon is crispy and an instant-read thermometer inserted into the chicken registers 165°F.

3. Meanwhile, make the pasta sauce: In a blender, combine the sun-dried tomatoes, olive oil, broth, heavy cream, lemon juice, salt, and pepper and blend until smooth. Set aside.

4. Make the pasta: Add the pasta to the boiling water and cook according to the package instructions. Drain the pasta and return it to the pot. Immediately add the salt and sun-dried tomato sauce and toss to coat the pasta.

5. When the chicken and bacon are done, remove from the oven. Chop the chicken into ½-inch cubes, then transfer half the chicken thighs (about 3 cups) to an airtight container and refrigerate for up to 5 days to use for Meal 2. Chop the bacon.

6. Divide the pasta among four bowls and top with the chicken and bacon. Garnish with the parsley and Parmesan and serve.

TIPS

- If the weather is nice, grill the seasoned chicken thighs for both meals at about 400°F for 3 to 5 minutes on each side, until grill marks appear and the chicken is cooked through.

- Once the chicken has 15 minutes left to cook, add the pasta to the boiling water.

CALORIES: 839   FAT: 55.7G   CARBS: 53.8G   PROTEIN: 30.1G

MEAL 2

JAMAICAN-INSPIRED BOWLS WITH MANGO SALSA AND WHITE RICE

Serves 4

Active time: 30 MINUTES   **Total time:** 30 MINUTES

1 cup uncooked white rice, rinsed

1 (15-ounce) can black beans, drained and rinsed

For the Chicken

¼ cup fresh lime juice (from about 2 limes)

¼ cup soy sauce or tamari

1 teaspoon garlic powder

1 teaspoon onion powder

2 teaspoons ground allspice

2 teaspoons dried thyme

½ teaspoon ground black pepper

¼ teaspoon ground cinnamon

¼ teaspoon ground nutmeg

3 cups cooked cubed chicken thighs (reserved from Meal 1; see page 38)

1 tablespoon extra-virgin olive oil

For the Mango Salsa

1 large ripe mango, cut into ¼-inch cubes

1 red bell pepper, cut into ¼-inch pieces

2 tablespoons fresh lime juice (from 1 lime)

½ teaspoon fine sea salt

¼ cup chopped fresh cilantro, for garnish

1. Cook the rice according to the package instructions.

2. Pour the beans into a small saucepan and add 1 cup water. Cover and bring to a simmer over medium heat. Cook for about 5 minutes, until heated through. Remove from the heat and keep warm until ready to serve.

3. Make the chicken: In a food processor or blender, combine the lime juice, soy sauce, garlic powder, onion powder, allspice, thyme, pepper, cinnamon, and nutmeg and process into a paste.

4. Transfer the seasoning paste to a large bowl, add the cubed chicken, and toss, coating each piece of chicken as evenly as possible.

5. In a large skillet, heat the olive oil over medium-high heat until the oil shimmers and runs easily when you tilt the pan. Add the chicken and cook for 3 to 4 minutes on each side, until darkened in color.

6. Meanwhile, make the slaw: In a medium bowl, combine the mango, bell pepper, lime juice, and salt and toss until well combined. Set aside until ready to serve.

7. Divide the rice among four bowls and top with the chicken, slaw, and black beans. Garnish with the cilantro and serve.

TIP

- If you didn't make the chicken ahead of time, make the mango salsa and start the rice right after the chicken goes into the oven, then finish by heating the black beans.

CALORIES: 455   FAT: 7.1G   CARBS: 76.1G   PROTEIN: 23.4G

Teriyaki Chicken

WITH BROWN RICE

/ RECIPE PAGE 42 /

/ RECIPE PAGE 42 /

ABOUT

Chicken breasts are back in the spotlight for this dinner series. Boneless, skinless breasts are seasoned with salt and pepper, then baked (or grilled, if you prefer) and used to make two dinners you're sure to love. The first is a simple chicken teriyaki bowl, served over brown rice. The chicken is sliced and then tossed in my go-to teriyaki sauce, though you absolutely could use your favorite teriyaki from the store. The rest of the chicken is then enjoyed in some bacon ranch loaded potatoes. This is one of those dinners that will leave you feeling full and so satisfied.

▨ $$
▨ DAIRY-FREE OPTION
▨ EGG-FREE OPTION
▨ GLUTEN-FREE
▨ GRAIN-FREE OPTION
▨ NUT-FREE

DINNER SERIES 4

MEAL 2

Bacon Ranch Loaded Potato

/ RECIPE PAGE 43 /

SUBSTITUTIONS

Make It Dairy- and Egg-Free:

- **MEAL 2:** Use vegan ranch for the loaded baked potatoes.

Make It Grain-Free:

- **MEAL 1:** Substitute cooked cauliflower rice for the brown rice in the teriyaki chicken.

Tip

- To save time on the loaded baked potatoes, bake the potatoes while the chicken for Meal 1 is in the oven, let cool, then store them in an airtight container in the refrigerator. Reheat the potatoes in a preheated 350°F oven for 15 minutes before stuffing and topping them.

TERIYAKI CHICKEN WITH BROWN RICE

Serves 4

Active time: 10 MINUTES   **Total time:** 45 MINUTES

For the Baked Chicken

3 pounds boneless, skinless chicken breasts

1 tablespoon extra-virgin olive oil

1 teaspoon fine sea salt

½ teaspoon ground black pepper

1 cup uncooked brown rice, rinsed

For the Teriyaki Sauce

1½ cups coconut aminos

1½ tablespoons rice vinegar

2 teaspoons toasted sesame oil

½ teaspoon garlic powder

½ teaspoon ground ginger

¼ teaspoon fish sauce

For the Bowls

6 cups broccoli florets (from about 2 medium heads)

2 tablespoons chopped fresh cilantro, for garnish

1 teaspoon black sesame seeds, for garnish

1. Bake the chicken: Preheat the oven to 400°F.

2. Place the chicken breasts on a rimmed baking sheet. Rub the olive oil over the chicken to coat, then season with the salt and pepper. Bake for 30 minutes, or until an instant-read thermometer inserted into the thickest part of each breast registers 165°F.

3. While the chicken is in the oven, cook the brown rice according to the package instructions.

4. Make the teriyaki sauce: In a large skillet, bring the coconut aminos to a simmer over medium heat, then simmer for 10 to 15 minutes, until it thickens enough to coat the back of a spoon. Stir in the vinegar, sesame oil, garlic powder, ginger, and fish sauce and remove from the heat.

5. Place the broccoli in a large glass bowl and add about ¼ cup water. Cover with a microwave-safe lid or plastic wrap and microwave on high for 5 minutes, or until the broccoli is tender. (Alternatively, place the broccoli in a medium pot and add ¼ cup water. Bring the water to a simmer over medium heat, then cover and cook the broccoli for 10 minutes, or until tender.) Drain the broccoli and set aside.

6. When the chicken is done, remove it from the oven and let cool slightly, then chop it into 1-inch cubes. Set aside 3 cups of the cubed chicken to use in the teriyaki bowls, then transfer the remainder to an airtight container and refrigerate for up to 5 days to use for Meal 2 (this will keep for up to 5 days).

7. Assemble the bowls: Reheat the teriyaki sauce over medium heat until it begins to bubble, then add the chicken and toss to coat in the sauce. Cook for 2 minutes, or until the chicken is warmed through. Divide the brown rice among four bowls, then top with the chicken and broccoli. Garnish with the cilantro and sesame seeds and serve.

TIPS

- Get the rice started as soon as the chicken goes into the oven.
- Substitute ½ cup of your favorite store-bought teriyaki sauce instead of making your own.

CALORIES: 569   FAT: 11.7G   CARBS: 76.1G   PROTEIN: 39.9G

MEAL 2

BACON RANCH
LOADED POTATO

Serves 4

Active time: 25 MINUTES   **Total time:** 55 MINUTES

1 tablespoon extra-virgin olive oil

1 pound Yukon Gold potatoes

1 teaspoon fine sea salt

8 ounces sliced bacon

3 cups cubed cooked chicken breast (reserved from Meal 1; see page 42)

¼ cup ranch dressing, for serving

¼ cup chopped green onions, for garnish

1. Preheat the oven to 375°F.

2. Rub the olive oil over the potatoes. Place them on a rimmed baking sheet and sprinkle with ½ teaspoon of the salt. Bake for 45 minutes, or until easily pierced with a fork.

3. Meanwhile, place the bacon in a large skillet and cook over medium-high heat for 5 to 10 minutes, flipping the slices about every 3 minutes, until crispy. Transfer the bacon to a paper towel to drain and let cool slightly, then coarsely chop.

4. Remove the potatoes from the oven and place one in each of four bowls. Split the potatoes open lengthwise and stuff them with the chicken, dividing it evenly among them. Top with the bacon and ranch dressing, garnish with the green onions, and serve.

CALORIES: 590   FAT: 36.3G   CARBS: 21.7G   PROTEIN: 41.9G

Green Curry Meatball Bowls

WITH WHITE RICE

/ RECIPE PAGE 46 /

ABOUT

I hope you're ready to have your socks blown off by the flavors and versatility of these chicken meatballs! Ground chicken is simply seasoned, formed into balls, and baked, then the meatballs are split between two exciting dinners. The first is a fabulous Thai-inspired green curry bowl, which I recommend enjoying with white rice (though I've included grain-free and low-carb substitutions for you on the opposite page). Then, come hungry to the second dinner, because we're using the rest of the meatballs in a riff on cheesy chicken, complete with butter-garlic pasta.

- $$
- DAIRY-FREE OPTION
- EGG-FREE
- GLUTEN-FREE OPTION
- GRAIN-FREE OPTION
- LOW-CARB OPTION
- NUT-FREE
- FREEZER-FRIENDLY

Chicken Parm Meatball Skillet

WITH BUTTER-GARLIC PASTA

/ RECIPE PAGE 47 /

RECIPE PAGE 47

SUBSTITUTIONS

Make It Dairy-Free:

- **MEAL 2:** Omit the mozzarella and Parmesan cheese on the chicken Parmesan meatballs, and use ghee in place of butter on the noodles.

Make It Gluten-Free, Grain-Free, and Low-Carb:

- **MEAL 1:** Substitute cooked cauliflower rice for the white rice in the green curry bowls.

- **MEAL 2:** Substitute zucchini noodles or cooked spaghetti squash for the pasta that accompanies the chicken Parmesan meatballs.

Tip

- Lightly seasoning the meatballs makes them versatile enough to top with sauces with very different flavors.

GREEN CURRY MEATBALL BOWLS WITH WHITE RICE

Serves 4

Active time: 20 MINUTES **Total time:** 40 MINUTES

1 cup uncooked white rice, rinsed

For the Meatballs

3 pounds ground chicken

1 teaspoon garlic powder

1 teaspoon onion powder

1½ teaspoons fine sea salt

½ teaspoon ground black pepper

For the Green Curry Sauce

1 (13.5-ounce) can full-fat coconut milk

3 tablespoons green curry paste

¼ teaspoon fish sauce

¼ cup fresh lime juice (from about 2 limes)

¼ cup chopped fresh cilantro, for garnish

1 lime, cut into wedges, for serving

1. Preheat the oven to 400°F. Line a rimmed baking sheet with parchment paper.

2. Cook the rice according to the package instructions.

3. Make the meatballs: In a large bowl, combine the ground chicken, garlic powder, onion powder, salt, and pepper. Mix until just combined (do not overwork the mixture or the meatballs will be tough). Form the chicken mixture into approximately 1-inch balls, setting them on the prepared baking sheet as you go. You'll have approximately 32 meatballs total.

4. Bake the meatballs until fully cooked through, about 18 minutes.

5. Meanwhile, make the green curry sauce: In a large sauté pan or pot, whisk together the coconut milk, curry paste, and fish sauce. Bring to a simmer over medium heat, then cook, stirring occasionally, for about 5 minutes to reduce the sauce.

6. When the meatballs have finished baking, remove them from the oven. Transfer half to an airtight container and refrigerate to use for Meal 2 (this will keep for up to 5 days).

7. Add the remaining meatballs and the lime juice to the pan with the curry sauce and toss to coat them evenly. Bring the sauce back to a simmer and cook, stirring occasionally, for 5 minutes, then remove from the heat.

8. Serve the meatballs and curry sauce over the rice, garnished with the cilantro, with lime wedges alongside.

TIP

- Opt for a store-bought green curry sauce instead of making your own to make this meal even easier.

CALORIES: 626   FAT: 34.3G   CARBS: 46.3G   PROTEIN: 35.7G

CHICKEN PARM MEATBALL SKILLET WITH BUTTER-GARLIC PASTA

Serves 4

Active time: 15 MINUTES   **Total time:** 35 MINUTES

For the Chicken Parm Meatball Skillet

- ½ batch cooked chicken meatballs (approximately 16, reserved from Meal 1; see page 46)
- 1 (24-ounce) jar prepared pasta sauce
- ½ cup grated mozzarella cheese
- ½ cup grated Parmesan cheese

For the Butter-Garlic Pasta

- 12 ounces dried spaghetti
- 2 tablespoons salted butter
- 1 tablespoon extra-virgin olive oil
- ½ teaspoon garlic powder
- ½ teaspoon fine sea salt

- 2 tablespoons chopped fresh parsley, for garnish

1. Preheat the oven to 375°F. Bring a large pot of water to a boil.

2. Make the chicken Parm meatball skillet: In a large oven-safe skillet, toss the meatballs with the pasta sauce. Sprinkle the mozzarella and Parmesan cheese evenly over the top. Bake for 25 minutes, or until the cheese is bubbling and starting to turn golden brown.

3. Meanwhile, make the butter-garlic pasta: Add the spaghetti to the boiling water and cook according to the package instructions. Drain the pasta and return it to the pot.

4. Immediately add the butter, olive oil, garlic powder, and salt. Briefly toss to combine, then cover the pot so the heat of the pasta melts the butter. After about 3 minutes, uncover the pot and toss again.

5. Divide the pasta among four bowls. Serve the meatballs from the skillet, family style, garnished with the parsley.

TIP

- Start boiling the water for the pasta as soon as the skillet goes into the oven. Once the meatballs have 15 minutes left to cook, add the pasta to the boiling water.

CALORIES: 767   FAT: 26.8G   CARBS: 78.6G   PROTEIN: 52.1G

Buffalo Zucchini Boats

WITH RANCH ROASTED POTATOES

/ RECIPE PAGE 50 /

ABOUT

In this meal series, we get to show off the flexibility of ground chicken. After seasoning and browning, ground chicken is elevated in some flavorful Buffalo zucchini boats. Though they're a great low-carb meal when enjoyed on their own, I like to serve them with ranch-flavored roasted potatoes. The rest of the ground chicken is used to make the most wonderful chicken Alfredo lasagna. It's the easiest lasagna you'll ever make, and I round out the meal with the addition of a simple Italian side salad.

- [ ] $$
- [ ] EGG-FREE OPTION
- [ ] GLUTEN-FREE OPTION
- [ ] NUT-FREE
- [ ] FREEZER-FRIENDLY

Alfredo Chicken Lasagna

WITH SIMPLE ITALIAN SALAD

/ RECIPE PAGE 51 /

SUBSTITUTIONS

Make It Egg-Free:

- **MEAL 1:** Use vegan ranch for the ranch roasted potatoes and zucchini boats.

Make It Gluten-Free:

- **MEAL 2:** Use gluten-free lasagna noodles.

Tips

- Ground chicken is easy to cook, store, and reheat, so preparing enough for both meals in one go is a great time-saver. But if you plan on preparing just one of these meals, make just a half batch of chicken.

- To make a half batch of ground chicken (enough for one meal in this series), use 1½ pounds ground chicken, ¾ teaspoon fine sea salt, and ¼ teaspoon ground black pepper.

BUFFALO ZUCCHINI BOATS WITH RANCH ROASTED POTATOES

Serves 4

Active time: 25 MINUTES   **Total time:** 1 HOUR

For the Ranch Roasted Potatoes

1 pound red potatoes, cut into ½-inch pieces

¼ cup ranch dressing

½ teaspoon fine sea salt

¼ teaspoon ground black pepper

For the Buffalo Zucchini Boats

3 pounds ground chicken

1½ teaspoons fine sea salt

½ teaspoon ground black pepper

½ cup Frank's RedHot or other hot sauce

4 tablespoons (½ stick) salted butter, melted

6 zucchini, halved lengthwise and soft seedy cores scraped out with a spoon

¼ cup ranch dressing

2 tablespoons chopped fresh cilantro, for garnish

1. Preheat the oven to 350°F.

2. Roast the potatoes: In a large bowl, toss the potatoes in the ranch dressing to coat. Spread them out evenly over a rimmed baking sheet and sprinkle with the salt and pepper. Roast for 45 minutes, or until the potatoes are crispy but not burned.

3. Meanwhile, make the zucchini boats: Put the chicken in a large skillet and season with the salt and pepper. Cook over medium heat, breaking up the meat with a wooden spoon as it cooks, for 6 to 7 minutes, until the chicken is crumbled and fully cooked through. Transfer half the cooked chicken (3½ cups) to an airtight container and refrigerate to use for Meal 2 (this will keep for up to 5 days). Transfer the remaining chicken to a medium bowl.

4. Add the hot sauce and melted butter to the bowl with the chicken. Toss to combine.

5. Place the zucchini boats cut side up in a large baking dish, arranging them in a single layer. (If you don't have a baking dish large enough to fit them all, use two.) Stuff each zucchini boat with an equal amount of the chicken mixture.

6. Bake for 25 minutes, or until the zucchini has released its juices and the chicken is slightly crispy.

7. Divide the zucchini boats among four plates. Drizzle with the ranch dressing and garnish with the cilantro. Serve with the roasted potatoes alongside.

TIP

- To make sure all meal components are hot and ready at the same time, when the potatoes have 25 minutes left to bake, put the zucchini boats in the oven.

CALORIES: 560   FAT: 38.9G   CARBS: 20.9G   PROTEIN: 33G

MEAL 2

ALFREDO CHICKEN LASAGNA WITH SIMPLE ITALIAN SALAD

Serves 6

Active time: 30 MINUTES   **Total time:** 1 HOUR 5 MINUTES

For the Alfredo Chicken Lasagna

2 cups heavy cream

1½ cups grated Parmesan cheese

1 cup milk

4 tablespoons (½ stick) salted butter

1½ teaspoons garlic powder

1½ teaspoons fine sea salt

½ teaspoon ground black pepper

1 (15-ounce) container ricotta cheese

12 ounces frozen spinach, thawed and drained

9 ounces no-boil lasagna noodles

3½ cups cooked ground chicken (reserved from Meal 1; see page 50)

1½ cups grated mozzarella cheese

For the Simple Italian Salad

¼ cup extra-virgin olive oil

¼ cup red wine vinegar

2 teaspoons honey

½ teaspoon fine sea salt

¼ teaspoon ground black pepper

4 cups chopped romaine lettuce

1 tomato, cut into ½-inch-thick wedges

¼ red onion, finely sliced

¼ cup kalamata olives, pitted and halved

2 tablespoons chopped fresh parsley, for garnish

1. Make the lasagna: Preheat the oven to 350°F.

2. In a 3-quart pot, whisk together the cream, Parmesan, milk, butter, garlic powder, 1 teaspoon of the salt, and ¼ teaspoon of the pepper. Bring to a simmer over medium heat and cook, whisking, until the Parmesan has completely melted and the sauce is well combined. Remove from the heat and set aside.

3. In a large bowl, stir together the ricotta, spinach, remaining ½ teaspoon salt, and remaining ¼ teaspoon pepper.

4. Spread about ½ cup of the sauce evenly over the bottom of a 9 x 13-inch baking dish. Place a layer of the lasagna noodles over the sauce, then spread half the ricotta mixture over the noodles. Top evenly with half the chicken, then pour 1 cup of the sauce over the chicken. Add a second layer of noodles, the remaining ricotta mixture, the remaining chicken, and the remaining sauce, and finally sprinkle the top evenly with the mozzarella.

5. Cover the baking dish with aluminum foil and bake for 30 minutes, then remove the foil and bake for 10 to 15 minutes more, until the noodles are soft and the sauce is bubbling. Remove the lasagna from the oven and let cool slightly before serving, if desired.

6. Meanwhile, make the salad: In a small bowl, whisk together the olive oil, vinegar, honey, salt, and pepper.

7. Put the romaine, tomato, onion, and olives in a large bowl. Pour the dressing over the salad and toss to combine.

8. Garnish the lasagna with the parsley and serve with the salad alongside.

TIP

- If you'd like to get the top of the lasagna browned and bubbling, switch your oven to broil and broil for about 1 minute, watching closely, until the desired finish is achieved

CALORIES: 845   FAT: 50.4G   CARBS: 45.5G   PROTEIN: 52.6G

Herb-Crusted Roasted Chicken

WITH LEMON-GARLIC ORZO

/ RECIPE PAGE 54 /

DINNER SERIES 7

ABOUT

This dinner series illustrates how a whole chicken can be creatively put to good use. First, a chicken is liberally seasoned with fresh herbs and lemon, then roasted to perfection and the breasts served fresh out of the oven over a fabulous lemon-garlic orzo. The wings, legs, and thighs get a makeover for the second dinner, an easy sheet pan curried chicken. The chicken pieces are tossed with curry powder–spiced coconut milk, roasted with veggies, and served over white rice.

- $
- DAIRY-FREE OPTION
- EGG-FREE
- GLUTEN-FREE OPTION
- GRAIN-FREE OPTION
- LOW-CARB OPTION
- NUT-FREE OPTION

MEAL 2

Curried Chicken Sheet Pan Dinner

/ RECIPE PAGE 55 /

SUBSTITUTIONS

Make It Dairy-Free:

- **MEAL 1:** Use olive oil in place of the butter for the roasted chicken.

Make It Gluten-Free:

- **MEAL 1:** Use gluten-free orzo.

Make It Grain-Free and Low-Carb:

- **MEAL 1:** Substitute the roasted veggies on page 58 for the lemon-garlic orzo.

- **MEAL 2:** Substitute cooked cauliflower rice for the white rice served with the curried chicken.

Make It Nut-Free:

- **MEAL 2:** Omit the peanut garnish for the curried chicken.

Tip

- Both meals can be doubled to serve 4.

MEAL 1

HERB-CRUSTED ROASTED CHICKEN WITH LEMON-GARLIC ORZO

Serves 2 OR 3

Active Time: 25 MINUTES   **Total Time:** 90 MINUTES

For the Herb-Crusted Roasted Chicken

1 (3½- to 4-pound) whole chicken

4 tablespoons (½ stick) salted butter, at room temperature

1 teaspoon dried oregano

1 teaspoon dried rosemary

1 teaspoon dried thyme

1 teaspoon fine sea salt

½ teaspoon ground black pepper

For the Lemon-Garlic Orzo

12 ounces dried orzo

1 cup cherry tomatoes, halved

½ small red onion, finely chopped

2 tablespoons fresh lemon juice (from 1 lemon)

2 tablespoons extra-virgin olive oil

½ teaspoon fine sea salt

¼ teaspoon ground black pepper

2 tablespoons chopped fresh parsley, for garnish

1. Roast the chicken: Preheat the oven to 400°F.

2. Remove the giblets from the cavity of the chicken and pat the chicken dry with a paper towel.

3. In a small bowl, mix the butter, oregano, rosemary, and thyme until well combined.

4. Rub about half the herb butter over the outside of the chicken. Using your fingers, gently lift the skin from the breast and smear the rest of the herb butter under the skin.

5. Place the chicken in a roasting pan or on a rimmed baking sheet. Tuck the wing tips under the joint where the wing meets the chicken's body. Using about 6 inches of kitchen twine, tie the ends of the drumsticks together.

6. Season the chicken with the salt and pepper. Roast for 1 hour 10 minutes, or until the juices run clear and/or an instant-read thermometer inserted into the thickest part of the thigh registers 165°F. If the skin starts to brown too deeply, simply tent the chicken with a piece of aluminum foil.

7. Meanwhile, make the lemon-garlic orzo: Cook the orzo according to the package instructions. Drain and transfer to a large bowl.

8. Add the tomatoes, onion, lemon juice, olive oil, salt, and pepper to the orzo and stir to combine.

9. Remove the chicken from the oven, tent it with foil (if it's not already tented), and let rest for 10 minutes. Carve the legs, thighs, and wings from the chicken, transfer to an airtight container, and refrigerate to use for Meal 2 (it will keep for up to 5 days). Carve the breasts from the chicken and slice them.

10. Divide the chicken breasts and orzo between two plates. Garnish with the parsley and serve.

TIPS

- If you have extra time while the chicken is roasting, go ahead and chop the veggies for the curried chicken and store them in the fridge, so all you have to do tomorrow night is toss everything together.

- Once the chicken has about 15 minutes left to cook, get started on the orzo. It will be ready as soon as the chicken is done resting.

CALORIES: 697   FAT: 23.2G   CARBS: 92G   PROTEIN: 30.9G

MEAL 2

CURRIED CHICKEN SHEET PAN DINNER

Serves 2 OR 3

Active time: 15 MINUTES   **Total time:** 50 MINUTES

1 cup full-fat coconut milk

¼ cup fresh lime juice (from about 2 limes)

2 tablespoons curry powder

1 teaspoon fine sea salt

Cooked chicken thighs, legs, and wings (reserved from Meal 1; see page 54)

1 red bell pepper, cut into ½-inch-thick strips

6 large carrots, cut into 1-inch-thick rounds

1 cup uncooked white rice, rinsed (optional)

¼ cup chopped peanuts, for garnish

2 tablespoons chopped fresh cilantro, for garnish

1. Preheat the oven to 400°F.

2. In a small bowl, whisk together the coconut milk, lime juice, curry powder, and salt.

3. Add the chicken pieces, bell pepper, and carrots to the curry sauce and toss to combine. Spread the chicken and vegetables over a rimmed baking sheet. Discard the remaining curry mixture. Bake for 40 minutes, or until the chicken starts to look crispy but not overbrowned and the vegetables are tender.

4. Meanwhile, cook the rice (if using) according to the package instructions.

5. Garnish the chicken and vegetables with the peanuts and cilantro and serve over the rice, if desired.

TIP

- Start the rice when the chicken has 20 minutes left in the oven.

CALORIES: 779   FAT: 40.8G   CARBS: 73.4G   PROTEIN: 32.3G

Lemon-Garlic Roasted Chicken and Veggies

/ RECIPE PAGE 58 /

DINNER SERIES 8

ABOUT

I love this dinner series because it does such a great job of showing the flexibility and versatility of a roasted whole chicken. First, the chicken is flavored with my go-to lemon-garlic mix, then roasted alongside some fresh vegetables that remind me of summer. The first dinner is already done! Enjoy some of the chicken alongside the veggies for a healthy, complete meal. For the second dinner, the remaining chicken is shredded and then transformed into the most delicious no-fry sesame chicken dish. The sauce on this chicken is sticky, sweet, and sure to become your new favorite.

$

DAIRY-FREE OPTION

EGG-FREE

GLUTEN-FREE OPTION

GRAIN-FREE OPTION

NUT-FREE

FREEZER-FRIENDLY

Sesame Chicken

WITH WHITE RICE

/ RECIPE PAGE 59 /

Make It Dairy-Free:

- **MEAL 1:** Use olive oil in place of the butter for the roasted chicken.

Make It Gluten-Free:

- **MEAL 2:** Use gluten-free soy sauce or tamari.

Make It Grain-Free:

- **MEAL 2:** Use arrowroot powder or tapioca starch in place of the cornstarch for the sesame chicken, and serve it with cooked cauliflower rice in place of the white rice.

MEAL 1

LEMON-GARLIC ROASTED CHICKEN AND VEGGIES

Serves 2

Active time: 30 MINUTES   **Total time:** 1 HOUR 30 MINUTES

For the Roasted Chicken

- 1 (3½- to 4-pound) whole chicken
- 4 tablespoons (½ stick) salted butter, at room temperature
- 4 garlic cloves, grated
- 1 lemon, zested and cut in half
- 1 teaspoon fine sea salt
- ½ teaspoon ground black pepper

For the Roasted Veggies

- 4 carrots, cut into ½-inch pieces
- 2 large tomatoes, cut into ½-inch-thick wedges
- 1 yellow bell pepper, cut into ½-inch-thick strips
- ½ red onion, cut into ¼-inch-thick wedges
- 2 tablespoons extra-virgin olive oil
- 1 teaspoon fine sea salt
- ½ teaspoon ground black pepper

- 2 tablespoons chopped fresh parsley, for garnish
- 1 lemon, cut into wedges, for serving

1. Roast the chicken: Preheat the oven to 400°F.

2. Remove the giblets from the cavity of the chicken and pat the chicken dry with a paper towel.

3. In a small bowl, mix the butter, garlic, and lemon zest until well combined.

4. Rub about half the garlic butter over the outside of the chicken. Using your fingers, gently lift the skin from the breast and smear the rest of the garlic butter under the skin.

5. Place the chicken in a roasting pan or on a rimmed baking sheet. Stuff the cavity of the chicken with the lemon halves. Tuck the wing tips under the joint where the wing meets the chicken's body. Using about 6 inches of kitchen twine, tie the ends of the drumsticks together.

6. Season the chicken with the salt and black pepper. Roast for 1 hour 10 minutes, or until the juices run clear and/or an instant-read thermometer inserted into the thickest portion of the thigh registers 165°F. If the skin starts to brown too deeply, tent the chicken with a piece of aluminum foil.

7. Meanwhile, roast the vegetables: Place the carrots, tomatoes, bell pepper, and onion on a rimmed baking sheet. Drizzle with the olive oil and toss to coat, then spread the vegetables into an even layer and season with the salt and black pepper.

8. When the chicken has been roasting for 25 minutes, put the vegetables in the oven and roast for 45 minutes, or until they start to look wilted and lightly golden brown but not burned.

9. Remove the chicken and vegetables from the oven. Tent the chicken with foil (if it's not already tented) and let rest for 10 minutes. Carve the breasts from the chicken, transfer to an airtight container, and refrigerate to use for Meal 2 (it will keep for up to 5 days). Carve the legs, thighs, and wings from the chicken and divide them between two plates.

10. Serve the chicken and vegetables garnished with the parsley, with the lemon wedges alongside.

CALORIES: 445   FAT: 31.3G   CARBS: 18.9G   PROTEIN: 24G

MEAL 2

SESAME CHICKEN WITH WHITE RICE

Serves 2 OR 3

Active time: 25 MINUTES   **Total time:** 25 MINUTES

1 cup uncooked white rice, rinsed

2 tablespoons salted butter

Cooked chicken breasts (reserved from Meal 1; see page 58), skin removed, cut into 1-inch chunks

¼ cup soy sauce

¼ cup rice vinegar

¼ cup honey

2 teaspoons toasted sesame oil

½ teaspoon garlic powder

1 tablespoon cornstarch

2 tablespoons white sesame seeds, for garnish

1. Cook the rice according to the package instructions.

2. Meanwhile, in a large sauté pan or skillet, melt the butter over medium-high heat. Add the chicken and sear, undisturbed, for about 3 minutes, until it crisps slightly, then stir and sear for 3 minutes more. Remove from the pan and set aside on a plate.

3. In the same skillet, whisk together the soy sauce, vinegar, honey, sesame oil, and garlic powder to combine. Bring the mixture to a simmer over medium-high heat.

4. In a small bowl, stir together the cornstarch and 2 tablespoons water until the cornstarch has completely dissolved, then pour the mixture into the pan and whisk to combine. Simmer, stirring, until the sauce thickens, 3 to 4 minutes.

5. Return the chicken to the pan and toss to coat with the sauce.

6. Serve the chicken and sauce with the rice, garnished with the sesame seeds.

CALORIES: 650   FAT: 18.1G   CARBS: 79.6G   PROTEIN: 41.3G

MEAL 1

Paprika Spatchcocked Chicken
WITH GREEN SAUCE AND PLANTAINS

/ RECIPE PAGE 62 /

ABOUT

Never have I ever been more excited about a dinner series than I was about this one. Ask anyone—I couldn't stop talking about it! It combines two of my favorite dinners and makes them possible because this method is so easy. First is a Peruvian-inspired spatchcocked chicken. Spatchcocking is an easy way to prep a whole chicken so it lays flat while baking, which, in my experience, allows the skin to get crispy all around. The flavorful crispy-skinned chicken is served with the most delicious green sauce and sweet plantains (similar to a banana, but they need to be cooked and are a great option when you're tired of potatoes) for the first meal. Then the rest of the chicken is put to delicious use in a dish modeled after my favorite Thai noodle dish: pad see ew.

- $
- DAIRY-FREE
- EGG-FREE OPTION
- GLUTEN-FREE OPTION
- NUT-FREE

MEAL 2

Stir-Fried Noodles

WITH CHICKEN

/ RECIPE PAGE 63 /

SUBSTITUTIONS

Make It Egg-Free:

- **MEAL 1:** Use vegan mayo in the green sauce for the paprika chicken. You can also substitute olive oil for the mayo, but the sauce won't be as creamy.

- **MEAL 2:** Omit the egg from the stir-fried noodles and substitute an egg-free linguine.

Make It Gluten-Free:

- **MEAL 2:** Use gluten-free noodles.

PAPRIKA SPATCHCOCKED CHICKEN WITH GREEN SAUCE AND PLANTAINS

Serves 2

Active time: 40 MINUTES   **Total time:** 1 HOUR 15 MINUTES

For the Spatchcocked Chicken

1 tablespoon garlic powder

1 tablespoon ground cumin

1 tablespoon paprika

1 teaspoon dried oregano

1 teaspoon fine sea salt

½ teaspoon ground black pepper

¼ cup fresh lemon juice (from about 2 lemons)

2 tablespoons extra-virgin olive oil

1 (3½- to 4-pound) whole chicken

For the Green Sauce

1 cup packed fresh cilantro

1 medium jalapeño, seeded

1 garlic clove, peeled

⅓ cup mayonnaise

2 tablespoons fresh lime juice (from 1 lime)

1 tablespoon extra-virgin olive oil

¼ teaspoon fine sea salt

For the Pan-Fried Plantains

2 large ripe plantains

¼ cup extra-virgin olive oil, or 4 tablespoons (½ stick) salted butter

½ teaspoon fine sea salt

1. Roast the chicken: Preheat the oven to 400°F.

2. In a small bowl, whisk together the garlic powder, cumin, paprika, oregano, salt, pepper, lemon juice, and olive oil.

3. Remove the giblets from the cavity of the chicken and pat the chicken dry with a paper towel. To spatchcock the chicken, use a sharp knife or kitchen shears to cut along each side of the backbone and remove it, then open the chicken, place it skin side up on your cutting board, and press down on the breastbone to crack it so the chicken lays flat.

4. Using your fingers, gently lift the skin from the breast and thighs and rub about 1 teaspoon of the herb mixture in each of these cavities, using 4 teaspoons total of the seasoning. Rub the remainder of the herb mixture over the outside of the chicken.

5. Place the chicken skin side up on a large rimmed baking sheet or in a large roasting pan. Roast for 50 minutes to 1 hour, until the skin is a deep red, the juices run clear, and/or an instant-read thermometer inserted into the thickest portion of a thigh registers 165°F. If the skin begins to crisp too quickly, simply tent a piece of foil over the top of the chicken.

6. Meanwhile, make the sauce: In a blender, combine the cilantro, jalapeño, garlic, mayonnaise, lime juice, olive oil, and salt. Blend until smooth. Refrigerate the sauce until ready to serve.

7. Make the plantains: Peel the plantains and cut them on an angle into 1-inch-thick pieces.

8. In a large skillet, heat the olive oil over medium heat. Once the oil runs when swirled, it's hot enough to start frying the plantains.

9. Working in batches, add the plantains to the pan in an even layer and fry for 3 to 4 minutes, until they start to look golden brown on the bottom. Flip the plantains and cook for 3 to 4 minutes on the second side, until golden brown. Transfer the plantains to a paper towel to drain and sprinkle with the salt.

10. Remove the chicken from the oven, tent it with a piece of aluminum foil, and let rest for 10 minutes. Carve the breasts from the chicken, transfer to an airtight container, and refrigerate to use for Meal 2 (it will keep for up to 5 days). Carve the legs, thighs, and wings from the chicken and divide them between two plates.

11. Serve the chicken with the plantains alongside and the green sauce spooned over the chicken.

CALORIES: 601   FAT: 40.3G   CARBS: 40G   PROTEIN: 23.2G

MEAL 2

STIR-FRIED NOODLES WITH CHICKEN

Serves 2 OR 3

Active time: 35 MINUTES   **Total time:** 35 MINUTES

9 ounces uncooked egg noodles

1 (8-ounce) bottle coconut aminos

1 teaspoon fish sauce

1 teaspoon toasted sesame oil

2 tablespoons coconut sugar

3 tablespoons extra-virgin olive oil, plus more if needed

2 garlic cloves, minced

1 large egg

1 bunch broccoli rabe, cut into 1-inch pieces

Cooked chicken breasts (reserved from Meal 1; see page 62), skin removed, thinly sliced

1 lime, cut into wedges, for serving

1. Cook the egg noodles according to the package instructions. Drain and set aside.

2. Meanwhile, in a medium skillet, bring the coconut aminos to a simmer over medium heat. Simmer for 6 to 8 minutes, until the coconut aminos have reduced enough to coat the back of a spoon. Add the fish sauce, sesame oil, and coconut sugar and whisk until the sugar has dissolved. Remove from the heat and set aside.

3. In a large skillet, heat the olive oil over high heat. Add the garlic and sauté for about 2 minutes, until lightly browned.

4. Add the egg to the skillet and cook, stirring to scramble the egg, for 2 to 3 minutes.

5. Add the broccoli rabe, reduce the heat to medium-high, and cover the pan. Cook until the broccoli rabe has wilted, 2 to 3 minutes, then add the chicken and the cooked egg noodles. If there isn't any oil visible in the pan at this point, add at least 1 tablespoon more. Let the chicken and noodles sit in the pan, undisturbed, for 2 to 3 minutes, until they brown and become slightly crispy on the bottom, then flip them and cook, undisturbed, for 3 minutes more.

6. Add the sauce to the skillet and toss to combine. Cook, stirring occasionally, for 3 to 4 minutes more, then remove from the heat.

7. Serve with the lime wedges alongside for squeezing over the top.

CALORIES: 772   FAT: 20.2G   CARBS: 100.2G   PROTEIN: 45.5G

Roasted Chicken & Potatoes

WITH FRESH ARUGULA SALAD

/ RECIPE PAGE 66 /

ABOUT

In this series, we're showing off a classic roasted chicken in the most delicious way. The whole chicken is simply seasoned, then roasted along with some wedge-cut oven fries. The breasts and fries are served with a generous helping of a fresh arugula salad for the first meal in the series. The wings, legs, and thighs are then transformed into my interpretation of butter chicken. The creamy red sauce is served over fluffy white rice and topped with plenty of cilantro (which you can omit if you don't have a taste for it).

▨ $

▨ DAIRY-FREE OPTION

▨ EGG-FREE

▨ GLUTEN-FREE

▨ GRAIN-FREE OPTION

▨ LOW-CARB OPTION

▨ NUT-FREE

▨ FREEZER-FRIENDLY

Butter Chicken Bowls

WITH WHITE RICE

/ RECIPE PAGE 67 /

SUBSTITUTIONS

Make It Dairy-Free:

- **MEAL 1:** Use olive oil in place of the butter for the roasted chicken.

- **MEAL 2:** Use olive oil in place of the butter in the butter chicken and replace the yogurt and heavy cream with 1½ cups full-fat coconut milk.

Make It Grain-Free:

- **MEAL 2:** Use cooked cauliflower rice in place of the white rice served with the butter chicken bowls.

Make It Low-Carb:

- **MEAL 1:** Omit the roasted potatoes served with the roasted chicken, or make a simple roasted cauliflower side: Instead of the potatoes, toss 1 pound cauliflower florets with the salt and olive oil and roast alongside the chicken at 400°F for 30 minutes, until tender and golden brown.

- **MEAL 2:** Use 4 cups cooked cauliflower rice in place of the white rice served with the butter chicken bowls.

ROASTED CHICKEN AND POTATOES WITH FRESH ARUGULA SALAD

Serves 2

Active time: 30 MINUTES

Total time: 1 HOUR 30 MINUTES

For the Roasted Chicken

1 (4- to 4½-pound) whole chicken

4 tablespoons (½ stick) salted butter, at room temperature

4 garlic cloves, minced

1 teaspoon fine sea salt

¼ teaspoon ground black pepper

For the Roasted Potatoes

1 pound red potatoes, cut into ½-inch-wide wedges

2 teaspoons extra-virgin olive oil

½ teaspoon fine sea salt

For the Fresh Arugula Salad

4 cups arugula

2 tablespoons fresh lemon juice (from 1 lemon)

1 tablespoon extra-virgin olive oil

½ teaspoon fine sea salt

¼ teaspoon ground black pepper

1. Preheat the oven to 400°F.

2. Roast the chicken: Remove the giblets from the cavity of the chicken and pat the chicken dry with a paper towel.

3. In a small bowl, stir together the butter and garlic until well combined.

4. Rub about half the garlic butter over the outside of the chicken. Using your fingers, gently lift the skin from the breast and smear the rest of the garlic butter under the skin.

5. Place the chicken in a roasting pan or on a rimmed baking sheet. Tuck the wing tips under the joint where the wing meets the chicken's body. Using about 6 inches of kitchen twine, tie the ends of the drumsticks together.

6. Season the chicken with the salt and pepper. Roast for 1 hour 10 minutes, or until the juices run clear and/or an instant-read thermometer inserted into the thickest portion of a thigh registers 165°F. If the skin starts to brown too deeply, tent the chicken with a piece of aluminum foil.

7. Meanwhile, roast the potatoes: In a large bowl, toss the potatoes with the olive oil. Spread them out over a rimmed baking sheet and season with the salt.

8. When the chicken has been in the oven for 35 minutes, put the potatoes in the oven and roast for 45 minutes, or until they start to look golden brown.

9. When the chicken is done, remove it from the oven, tent it with foil (if it's not already tented), and let rest for 10 minutes.

10. Meanwhile, make the arugula salad: Place the arugula in a large bowl. Add the lemon juice, olive oil, salt, and pepper and massage the dressing into the leaves.

11. Remove the potatoes from the oven. Carve the legs, thighs, and wings from the chicken, transfer to an airtight container, and refrigerate to use for Meal 2 (it will keep for up to 5 days). Carve the chicken breasts from the chicken and divide them between two plates.

12. Serve the chicken with the potatoes and arugula salad alongside.

TIP

- Start working on the arugula salad once you've pulled the chicken out of the oven.

CALORIES: 400   FAT: 12.9G   CARBS: 25.8G   PROTEIN: 44.4G

BUTTER CHICKEN BOWLS WITH WHITE RICE

Serves 2

Active time: 35 MINUTES   **Total time:** 40 MINUTES

1 tablespoon paprika

1 tablespoon garam masala

1 teaspoon ground coriander

1 teaspoon ground cumin

1 teaspoon ground turmeric

1 teaspoon fine sea salt

Cooked chicken legs, thighs, and wings (reserved from Meal 1; see page 66), skin removed, cut into 1-inch pieces

4 tablespoons (½ stick) salted butter or ghee (see Tip)

1 tablespoon grated garlic (about 3 cloves)

1 tablespoon grated fresh ginger (from about ½ inch)

2½ cups crushed tomatoes (from one 18-ounce can)

1 cup plain Greek yogurt

½ cup heavy cream

2 tablespoons fresh lemon juice (from 1 lemon)

1 cup uncooked white rice, rinsed

2 tablespoons chopped fresh cilantro leaves, for garnish

1. In a small bowl, whisk together the paprika, garam masala, coriander, cumin, turmeric, and salt. Add the chicken and toss to coat in the spice mixture.

2. In a large sauté pan, melt the butter over medium heat. Add the garlic and ginger and sauté for 3 to 4 minutes, until fragrant but not browned.

3. Add the seasoned chicken to the pan, reserving any spice mixture left in the bowl, and sear, undisturbed, for 3 minutes, or until lightly browned on the bottom, then stir and sear for 3 minutes more. Remove the chicken from the pan and set aside on a plate.

4. In the same pan, whisk together the tomatoes, yogurt, cream, lemon juice, and any remaining spice mixture until combined. Bring to a simmer over medium-low heat and cook, stirring occasionally, for 15 to 20 minutes, until fragrant and slightly reduced in volume.

5. Meanwhile, cook the rice according to the package instructions.

6. Return the chicken to the sauce and simmer for 5 minutes more, then remove from the heat.

7. Serve the chicken over the rice, garnished with the cilantro.

TIPS

- Once you set the butter chicken to simmer in step 4, start the rice.

- Ghee (a clarified butter popular in Indian cooking) is sold in many large grocery stores—since it's shelf-stable, look for it in the baking aisle or the international foods aisle. It's also available at Indian markets and health food stores, as well as online.

CALORIES: 756   FAT: 31.5G   CARBS: 71.5G   PROTEIN: 45.2G

Crispy Roasted Duck

WITH WARM BEET SALAD

/ RECIPE PAGE 70 /

DINNER SERIES 11

ABOUT

I am so excited for you to make this dinner series! Though you can adapt these dinners to use roasted chicken, try to get your hands on a duck so you'll be able to experience the full flavors intended. The first meal centers around a perfectly crispy roasted whole duck. To highlight this special protein, I'm serving it alongside a warm beet salad. Then, for the second meal, the remaining roasted duck is shredded and used to the make the most delicious duck fried rice. You are going to love these dinners and how easy they are to prepare.

- $$
- DAIRY-FREE OPTION
- EGG-FREE OPTION
- GLUTEN-FREE OPTION
- GRAIN-FREE OPTION
- LOW-CARB OPTION
- NUT-FREE
- FREEZER-FRIENDLY

Duck Fried Rice

/ RECIPE PAGE 71 /

SUBSTITUTIONS

Make It Dairy-Free:

- **MEAL 1:** Omit the goat cheese in the warm beet salad.

Make It Egg-Free:

- **MEAL 2:** Omit the eggs in the duck fried rice.

Make It Gluten-Free:

- **MEAL 2:** Use gluten-free soy sauce or tamari in place of the soy sauce in the duck fried rice.

Make It Grain-Free:

- **MEAL 2:** Substitute 4 cups cooked cauliflower rice for the white rice in the duck fried rice.

Make It Low-Carb:

- **MEAL 1:** Serve the roasted veggies on page 58 in place of the warm beet salad.

- **MEAL 2:** Substitute 4 cups cooked cauliflower rice for the white rice in the duck fried rice.

CRISPY ROASTED DUCK WITH WARM BEET SALAD

Serves 2

Active time: 40 MINUTES

Total time: 2 HOURS 50 MINUTES, PLUS 24 TO 48 HOURS TO CURE

For the Crispy Roasted Duck

1 (4- to 5-pound) whole duck, thawed if frozen

¼ cup plus 1 teaspoon fine sea salt

½ teaspoon ground black pepper

For the Warm Beet Salad

1½ pounds red beets, peeled and cut into roughly ½-inch-thick wedges

3 tablespoons extra-virgin olive oil

¼ cup fresh lemon juice (from about 2 lemons)

1 tablespoon chopped fresh dill, plus more for garnish

½ teaspoon fine sea salt

¼ teaspoon ground black pepper

¼ cup thinly sliced red onion

¼ cup crumbled goat cheese

1. Roast the duck: Rub the outside of the duck and inside its cavity with ¼ cup of the salt. Place the duck in a large bowl or roasting pan, cover, and refrigerate for 24 to 48 hours.

2. When ready to cook the duck, preheat the oven to 300°F.

3. Rinse the duck completely and pat it dry with paper towels as well as you can. Using a small knife, prick the skin of the duck all over, piercing the skin about every inch.

4. Season the duck with the remaining 1 teaspoon salt and the pepper. Place the duck in a roasting pan. Cover the pan with aluminum foil and bake for 2 hours.

5. Meanwhile, make the beet salad: In a large bowl, toss the beets with 1 tablespoon of the olive oil. Spread them out over a rimmed baking sheet.

6. When the duck has been in the oven for 2 hours, place the beets in the oven, uncover the duck, and raise the oven temperature to 400°F. Roast the duck for 30 minutes more, or until an instant-read thermometer inserted into the thickest portion of the breast registers 165°F and the skin starts to look golden and crispy. Remove the duck from the oven and let rest for about 10 minutes; if necessary, roast the beets for up to 15 minutes more, until they're easily pierced with a fork, then remove from the oven.

7. Carve the duck, transfer the thigh and leg meat to an airtight container, and refrigerate to use for Meal 2 (it will keep for up to 5 days). Divide the remaining duck between two plates.

8. In a large bowl, whisk together the remaining 2 tablespoons olive oil, the lemon juice, dill, salt, and pepper. While the beets are still warm, add them to the bowl and toss until each piece is coated in the dressing. Lightly stir in the onion and goat cheese and garnish with additional dill.

9. Serve the duck with the beet salad alongside.

TIPS

- Before roasting, the duck needs to cure in salt for 24 to 48 hours, so be sure to plan ahead.

- Place the beets in the oven when the duck has 30 minutes left to roast.

- The light meat and dark meat of the duck work equally well with the beet salad and in the fried rice, so carve the duck and divide the pieces however you like.

- The roasted duck will release quite a bit of fat and I recommend saving it. Pour skimmed fat into a jar and refrigerate until using, best within 1 month of rendering.

CALORIES: 514   FAT: 39.4G   CARBS: 18.9G   PROTEIN: 22.5V

DUCK FRIED RICE

Serves 4

Active time: 25 MINUTES   **Total time:** 45 MINUTES

1 cup uncooked white rice, rinsed

3 tablespoons extra-virgin olive oil

2 large eggs

Cooked duck (reserved from Meal 1; see page 70), skin removed, meat shredded or finely chopped (about 1½ cups)

1 tablespoon grated fresh ginger

4 teaspoons minced garlic

2 cups frozen peas and carrots

¼ cup plus 2 tablespoons thinly sliced green onions

2 tablespoons soy sauce

2 tablespoons fresh lime juice (from 1 lime)

2 teaspoons toasted sesame oil

¼ teaspoon red pepper flakes

1 tablespoon white sesame seeds, for garnish

1. Cook the rice according to the package instructions.

2. Meanwhile, in a large skillet or wok, heat 1 tablespoon of the olive oil over medium heat. Whisk the eggs together in a small bowl, then pour them into the pan. Cook, without stirring, for about 2 minutes, then flip the egg as best you can and cook for 1 minute more, or until no liquid egg remains. Break up the cooked eggs with a spoon or spatula and transfer to a clean bowl.

3. In the same pan, heat the remaining 2 tablespoons olive oil over medium-high heat. Add the duck and cook, stirring occasionally, for 3 to 4 minutes, until it starts to crisp and brown.

4. Add the ginger, garlic, and peas and carrots and stir to combine. Cook, stirring occasionally, for 3 to 4 minutes, until the peas and carrots are softened. Add the cooked rice, the eggs, ¼ cup of the green onions, the soy sauce, lime juice, sesame oil, and red pepper flakes and stir to combine. Cook, undisturbed, for 2 minutes, then stir the fried rice, scraping up any crispy bits from the bottom of the pan, and cook, stirring occasionally, for 2 minutes more. Remove from the heat.

5. Garnish the fried rice with the remaining 2 tablespoons green onions and the sesame seeds, then serve.

CALORIES: 486   FAT: 22.9G   CARBS: 48.7G   PROTEIN: 22.5G

Roasted Garlic Turkey Breast

WITH LEMON-DILL QUINOA

/ RECIPE PAGE 74 /

ABOUT

Turkey breast is an unsung hero of the "make dinner easier" challenge. Less intimidating than a whole holiday-dinner-style bird, turkey breast is easy to prepare, especially if you let the oven do all the work, and yields a large quantity of meat that can be used in a wide variety of dishes. The first dinner in this series features the roasted turkey breast fresh out of the oven, with a delightful lemon-dill quinoa alongside. The leftovers are transformed into the most wonderful spiced turkey potato soup. I love to make this dinner series as summer turns to fall or winter gives way to spring; the garlic turkey and fresh-herb-spiked quinoa keep me thinking of warm weather, and the soup reminds me of the cozy feelings the colder seasons bring.

- $$
- DAIRY-FREE OPTION
- EGG-FREE
- GLUTEN-FREE
- GRAIN-FREE OPTION
- NUT-FREE
- FREEZER-FRIENDLY

Spiced Turkey Potato Soup

/ RECIPE PAGE 75 /

SUBSTITUTIONS

Make It Dairy-Free:

- **MEAL 1:** Substitute olive oil for the butter on the roasted turkey.

Make It Grain-Free:

- **MEAL 1:** Substitute 4 cups cooked cauliflower rice for the quinoa in the lemon-dill quinoa.

ROASTED GARLIC TURKEY BREAST WITH LEMON-DILL QUINOA

Serves 4

Active time: 15 MINUTES **Total time:** 1 HOUR 15 MINUTES

For the Roasted Garlic Turkey Breast

3 tablespoons salted butter, at room temperature

3 garlic cloves, grated

2 bone-in split turkey breasts (about 2 pounds each)

1 teaspoon fine sea salt

½ teaspoon ground black pepper

For the Lemon-Dill Quinoa

1 cup uncooked quinoa, rinsed

1 tablespoon salted butter or extra-virgin olive oil

½ teaspoon fine sea salt

3 tablespoons chopped fresh dill

3 tablespoons fresh lemon juice (from 1 lemon)

2 tablespoons extra-virgin olive oil

¼ teaspoon ground black pepper

1 tablespoon chopped fresh dill, for garnish

1. Roast the turkey breasts: Preheat the oven to 325°F.

2. In a small bowl, mix together the butter and garlic until well combined.

3. Pat the turkey breasts dry with a paper towel. Massage the garlic butter over the entire surface of both turkey breasts.

4. Place the turkey skin side up in a baking pan or roasting pan. Season with the salt and pepper. Cover the pan loosely with aluminum foil and bake for 40 minutes, then raise the oven temperature to 400°F, remove the foil, and roast the turkey for 15 minutes more, or until the skin looks golden brown and an instant-read thermometer inserted into the thickest portion of each breast registers 165°F.

5. Meanwhile, make the quinoa: Rinse the quinoa in a fine-mesh sieve for 1 minute, until the water runs clear, then transfer it to a medium saucepan and add the butter, salt, and 1½ cups water. Bring to a boil over high heat, then whisk the quinoa, reduce the heat to low, cover, and cook for 15 minutes.

6. Transfer the cooked quinoa to a medium bowl and add the dill, lemon juice, olive oil, and pepper. Stir to combine.

7. Remove the turkey from the oven. Let rest for 10 minutes. Carve the meat from one breast off the bone, discard the bone and skin, and chop the meat into ½-inch pieces (you should have about 1½ cups); transfer to an airtight container and refrigerate to use for Meal 2 (it will keep for up to 5 days). Thinly slice the meat from the second turkey breast and divide it among four plates.

8. Serve the sliced turkey with the quinoa, garnished with the dill.

TIP

- Start the quinoa when the turkey has about 10 minutes left to cook.

CALORIES: 468   FAT: 16.2G   CARBS: 30.4G   PROTEIN: 49.4G

MEAL 2

SPICED TURKEY POTATO SOUP

Serves 5

Active time: 25 MINUTES   **Total time:** 45 MINUTES

1 pound bratwurst, casing removed

½ white onion, finely chopped

2 tablespoons minced garlic

4 celery stalks, finely chopped

1½ pounds Yukon Gold potatoes, cut into ½-inch pieces

4 cups chicken broth or vegetable broth

1½ cups diced (½-inch pieces) cooked turkey breast (reserved from Meal 1; see page 74)

¼ cup Dijon mustard

1 tablespoon dried thyme

1½ teaspoons fine sea salt, plus more if needed

½ teaspoon ground black pepper

¼ cup fresh lemon juice (from about 2 lemons)

2 tablespoons chopped fresh chives, for garnish

1. In a large pot, brown the bratwurst over medium heat, breaking it up with a spatula as it cooks, until no pink remains, 5 to 7 minutes.

2. Add the onion, garlic, and celery and stir to combine. Cook, stirring occasionally, for 3 minutes, or until the onion starts to soften.

3. Add the potatoes and broth. Cover and bring to a low boil. Boil for 15 to 20 minutes, until the potatoes are easily pierced with a fork.

4. Add the turkey, mustard, thyme, salt, and pepper and stir to combine. Bring the soup back to a low boil.

5. Add the lemon juice and stir. Taste the soup and add more salt if needed. Remove from the heat.

6. Ladle the soup into bowls, garnish with the chives, and serve.

CALORIES: 577   FAT: 28.9G   CARBS: 32.1G   PROTEIN: 42.9G

Chipotle-Maple Turkey Bake

WITH SWEET POTATOES

/ RECIPE PAGE 78 /

ABOUT

This is a fun dinner series! Because turkey is such a mild-tasting protein, it takes on other flavors incredibly well. To play with this concept, the turkey is first baked in a chipotle-maple marinade, then served alongside roasted sweet potatoes for a full dinner experience. The leftover turkey is chopped and layered high with southwestern ingredients—corn, beans, and cheese—for a robust southwestern turkey casserole.

▧ $$
▧ DAIRY-FREE OPTION
▧ EGG-FREE OPTION
▧ GLUTEN-FREE
▧ GRAIN-FREE OPTION
▧ NUT-FREE
▧ FREEZER-FRIENDLY

MEAL 2

Southwestern Turkey Casserole

/ RECIPE PAGE 79 /

SUBSTITUTIONS

Make It Dairy-Free:

- **MEAL 2:** Omit the cheese from the turkey casserole or use a vegan shredded cheese. Replace the sour cream with ¼ cup coconut cream from full-fat coconut milk.

Make It Egg-Free:

- **MEALS 1 AND 2:** Use vegan mayo or olive oil in place of the mayonnaise in the turkey bake.

Make It Grain-Free:

- **MEAL 2:** Omit the corn from the turkey casserole.

CHIPOTLE-MAPLE TURKEY BAKE WITH SWEET POTATOES

Serves 4

Active time: 15 MINUTES

Total time: 1 HOUR 10 MINUTES

For the Chipotle-Maple Turkey Bake

¼ cup pure maple syrup

¼ cup extra-virgin olive oil

2 tablespoons paprika

1 teaspoon fine sea salt

½ teaspoon chipotle chile powder

3 pounds boneless, skinless turkey breast tenderloins

¼ cup mayonnaise

2 tablespoons fresh lime juice (from 1 lime)

For the Baked Sweet Potatoes

1 pound sweet potatoes, scrubbed and dried

1 teaspoon extra-virgin olive oil

½ teaspoon fine sea salt

2 tablespoons chopped fresh cilantro, for garnish

1. Preheat the oven to 350°F.

2. Bake the turkey: In a small bowl, whisk together the maple syrup, olive oil, paprika, salt, and chipotle chile powder.

3. Place the turkey breasts in a baking dish. Pour half the chipotle-maple sauce over the breasts and turn them to coat on all sides. Add the mayonnaise and lime juice to the bowl with the remaining chipotle-maple sauce and whisk until well combined; set aside until ready to serve.

4. Bake the turkey breasts, uncovered, for 45 to 50 minutes, until the tops have darkened in color and an instant-read thermometer inserted into the thickest portion of each breast registers 165°F.

5. Meanwhile, bake the sweet potatoes: If your sweet potatoes are larger than 2 inches in diameter, cut them into roughly 2-inch-thick disks. Rub the sweet potatoes with the olive oil and spread them out on a rimmed baking sheet. Season with the salt. Bake for 35 to 45 minutes, until they're easily pierced with a fork.

6. Remove the turkey from the oven. Let rest for 10 minutes. Chop half the breasts into ½-inch pieces (you should have about 3 cups), transfer to an airtight container, and refrigerate to use for Meal 2 (it will keep for up to 5 days). Thinly slice the remaining turkey and divide it among four plates.

7. Serve the turkey with the sweet potatoes alongside, topped with the creamy chipotle-maple sauce and garnished with the cilantro.

TIP

- Bake the sweet potatoes on the bottom rack of the oven while the turkey bakes on the top rack. The potatoes will be done by the time you've finished making the sauce and slicing the turkey.

CALORIES: 589	FAT: 30.5G	CARBS: 38.8G	PROTEIN: 40.7G

MEAL 2

SOUTHWESTERN TURKEY CASSEROLE

Serves 5

Active time: 30 MINUTES   **Total time:** 50 MINUTES

2 tablespoons extra-virgin olive oil

1 red bell pepper, chopped

1 orange bell pepper, chopped

½ medium onion, chopped

1 garlic clove, minced

1 (15-ounce) can black beans, drained and rinsed

1½ cups frozen corn kernels

1 teaspoon fine sea salt

About 3 cups chopped cooked turkey breast

(reserved from Meal 1; see page 78)

½ teaspoon ground cumin

1½ cups shredded Mexican-style cheese blend

½ cup plus 2 tablespoons chopped fresh cilantro

¼ cup sour cream

2 tablespoons fresh lime juice (from 1 lime)

1 jalapeño, thinly sliced, for garnish

1. Preheat the oven to 350°F.

2. In a large skillet, heat the olive oil over medium heat. Add the bell peppers, onion, and garlic and cook, stirring occasionally, for 4 to 5 minutes, until the onion is softened and starting to look translucent.

3. Transfer the sautéed peppers and onion to a 9 x 13-inch casserole dish, add the black beans, corn, and ½ teaspoon of the salt, and stir to combine. Spread the mixture in an even layer over the bottom of the casserole.

4. In a large bowl, combine the turkey, cumin, and remaining ½ teaspoon salt. Toss to combine, then spread the turkey over the bean mixture in the casserole and top evenly with the cheese. Bake for 30 minutes, or until the cheese is bubbling.

5. Meanwhile, in a blender, combine ½ cup of the cilantro, the sour cream, lime juice, and 2 tablespoons water. Blend until the sauce is smooth; set aside until ready to serve.

6. Drizzle the sauce over the casserole, garnish with the jalapeño and remaining 2 tablespoons cilantro, and serve.

CALORIES: 466   FAT: 20.9G   CARBS: 28.5G   PROTEIN: 41.8G

Asian-Inspired Lettuce Wraps

WITH RICE NOODLES

/ RECIPE PAGE 82 /

ABOUT

Ground turkey is the star of this dinner series show. A big batch of ground turkey is cooked in a large pot or skillet and then divided in two. The first portion is seasoned with a blend of soy sauce, lime, and spices for restaurant-style Asian lettuce wraps. These wraps are so delicious—they're a wonderful low-carb dinner as is, or you can do as I do and plate them with a bowl of seasoned rice noodles alongside. The second portion of prepared ground turkey is used to make a turkey taco casserole. This taco casserole is essentially my favorite taco-night fillings—beans, seasoned meat, cheese, and all the fresh toppings—turned into one big dish.

- $$
- DAIRY-FREE OPTION
- EGG-FREE
- GLUTEN-FREE OPTION
- GRAIN-FREE OPTION
- NUT-FREE
- FREEZER-FRIENDLY

Turkey Taco Casserole

/ RECIPE PAGE 83 /

SUBSTITUTIONS

Make It Dairy-Free:

- **MEAL 2:** Substitute ½ cup coconut cream from full-fat coconut milk for the sour cream in the taco casserole and omit the shredded cheese or use a vegan shredded cheese.

Make It Gluten-Free:

- **MEAL 1:** Substitute gluten-free soy sauce or tamari for the soy sauce in the lettuce wraps.

Make It Grain-Free:

- **MEAL 1:** Omit the rice noodles served with the lettuce wraps. Use tamari or coconut aminos in place of the soy sauce in the lettuce wraps.

MEAL 1

ASIAN-INSPIRED LETTUCE WRAPS WITH RICE NOODLES

Serves 4

Active time: 25 MINUTES   **Total time:** 30 MINUTES

For the Filling

1 tablespoon extra-virgin olive oil

3 pounds ground turkey

½ cup shredded carrots

¼ cup soy sauce

2 tablespoons coconut aminos

2 tablespoons fresh lime juice (from 1 lime)

½ teaspoon ground ginger

½ teaspoon garlic powder

½ teaspoon toasted sesame oil

¼ cup sliced green onions

For the Rice Noodles (optional)

1 (8.8-ounce) package thin rice noodles

2 tablespoons fresh lime juice (from 1 lime)

½ teaspoon toasted sesame oil

To Serve

6 large butter lettuce leaves

1 tablespoon white sesame seeds, for garnish

1 teaspoon red pepper flakes, for garnish

1. If you plan to serve the lettuce wraps with rice noodles, bring a 3-quart pot of water to a boil.

2. Make the filling: In a large skillet, heat the olive oil over medium heat. Add the ground turkey and cook, breaking up the meat with a spatula as it cooks, for 6 minutes, or until the turkey is cooked through and starting to brown. Remove from the heat. Transfer half the cooked turkey (about 3½ cups) to an airtight container and refrigerate to use for Meal 2 (it will keep for up to 5 days).

3. Return the skillet to medium heat. Add the carrots and stir to combine with the turkey. Cook, stirring occasionally, for 5 to 7 minutes, until the carrots start to soften.

4. Add the soy sauce, coconut aminos, lime juice, ginger, garlic powder, sesame oil, and green onions and stir to combine. Cook, stirring occasionally, for 2 to 3 minutes, until the green onions are wilted.

5. Meanwhile, make the rice noodles (if using): Add the rice noodles to the boiling water and cook according to the package instructions. Drain and transfer to a medium bowl.

6. Add the lime juice and sesame oil to the noodles and toss to combine.

7. Divide the lettuce leaves among four plates and top each with some of the filling. Serve with the rice noodles alongside, garnished with the sesame seeds and red pepper flakes.

TIP

- Rice noodles cook quickly, and as they cool, they will stick together and become hard to work with, so don't start them too early. Put the water on to boil before you start the filling, but wait until it is nearly finished before adding the rice noodles.

CALORIES: 575   FAT: 19.4G   CARBS: 60G   PROTEIN: 39.6G

MEAL 2

TURKEY TACO CASSEROLE

Serves 5

Active time: 15 MINUTES   **Total time:** 45 MINUTES

1 (16-ounce) can refried beans or whole black beans (drained and rinsed, if using black beans)

About 3½ cups cooked ground turkey (reserved from Meal 1; see page 82)

2 teaspoons mild chili powder

1 teaspoon ground cumin

½ teaspoon dried oregano

½ teaspoon fine sea salt

¼ teaspoon ground black pepper

½ cup sour cream

¼ cup chicken broth

2 tablespoons fresh lime juice (from 1 lime)

2 cups shredded iceberg lettuce

1 cup finely shredded Monterey Jack cheese

1 large tomato, chopped

1 (2.25-ounce) can sliced black olives, drained

1. Preheat the oven to 350°F.

2. Spread the beans evenly over the bottom of a 9 x 13-inch baking dish.

3. In a large bowl, combine the cooked turkey, chili powder, cumin, oregano, salt, and pepper. Toss to combine, then spread the turkey mixture over the beans in the casserole.

4. In the same bowl you used for the turkey mixture (no reason to dirty another one!), whisk together the sour cream, broth, and lime juice until evenly combined. Pour the sour cream mixture over the turkey mixture.

5. Bake the casserole for 30 minutes, or until the top starts to look golden brown. Remove from the oven and sprinkle with the lettuce, cheese, tomato, and olives. Scoop onto plates, and serve.

TIP

- Think of this recipe as a template you can customize to your liking! You could add rice, swap out for any bean you like, omit entire layers, use salsa instead of the sour cream mixture, omit cheese, add more cheese, and customize the fresh toppings to exactly your liking.

CALORIES: 437G   FAT: 22.5G   CARBS: 20.3G   PROTEIN: 40.1G

beef

MEAL 1

Dry-Rubbed Barbecue Brisket

WITH ZESTY CABBAGE SLAW

/ RECIPE PAGE 88 /

ABOUT

You are in for a treat with these two meals. If you have a hankering for a soul-lifting barbecue dinner, this dry-rubbed brisket will hit the spot. It's served exactly how I prefer: with a side of cheesy polenta and a zesty cabbage slaw. For the second meal, the tender, perfectly cooked brisket is transformed into a Philly cheesesteak–inspired stuffed pepper. The flavors are spot-on, and the side of wild rice helps balance out the meal.

- $$
- DAIRY-FREE OPTION
- EGG-FREE
- GLUTEN-FREE
- GRAIN-FREE OPTION
- LOW-CARB OPTION
- NUT-FREE
- FREEZER-FRIENDLY

Cheesesteak-Stuffed Peppers

WITH WILD RICE

/ RECIPE PAGE 89 /

SUBSTITUTIONS

Make It Dairy-Free:

- **MEAL 1:** Omit the cheese from the polenta.

- **MEAL 2:** Omit the provolone cheese from the stuffed peppers or substitute your favorite vegan cheese.

Make It Grain-Free:

- **MEAL 1:** Skip the polenta; replace it with the mashed potatoes on page 92, if you like.

- **MEAL 2:** Substitute 4 cups cooked cauliflower rice for the wild rice.

Make It Low-Carb:

- **MEAL 1:** Skip the polenta.

- **MEAL 2:** Substitute 4 cups cooked cauliflower rice for the wild rice.

Tip

- If you're using the Instant Pot cooking method, sear the beef in two batches. Searing the beef all at once will cause overcrowding and will prevent it from browning nicely.

MEAL 1

DRY-RUBBED BARBECUE BRISKET WITH ZESTY CABBAGE SLAW

Serves 5

Active time: 35 MINUTES

Total time: 4 HOURS 20 MINUTES

For the Dry-Rubbed Barbecue Brisket

1 tablespoon fine sea salt

1 tablespoon brown sugar or coconut sugar

1 tablespoon chili powder

2 teaspoons ground cumin

1 teaspoon garlic powder

½ teaspoon ground black pepper

1 (5-pound) beef brisket, trimmed

1 tablespoon olive oil (if using Instant Pot method)

For the Zesty Cabbage Slaw

¼ cup mayonnaise

2 tablespoons fresh lime juice (from 1 lime)

½ teaspoon fine sea salt

¼ teaspoon ground black pepper

½ head green cabbage, thinly sliced

½ cup fresh cilantro, coarsely chopped, plus more for garnish

1 jalapeño, seeded and minced

For the No-Stir Cheesy Polenta

4 cups chicken broth

½ teaspoon fine sea salt, plus more if needed

1 cup coarse cornmeal

¾ cup shredded cheddar cheese

2 tablespoons salted butter

¼ teaspoon cracked black pepper

1. Make the brisket: Preheat the oven to 325°F.

2. In a small bowl, whisk together the salt, brown sugar, chili powder, cumin, garlic powder, and pepper. Rub this mixture over the brisket.

3. Put the brisket in a Dutch oven and pour in ½ cup water. Cover the pot with its lid, transfer to the oven, and bake for 4 hours, until the brisket pulls apart easily with a fork.

4. Meanwhile, make the slaw: In a medium bowl, whisk together the mayonnaise, lime juice, salt, and pepper. Add the cabbage, cilantro, and jalapeño and toss to coat evenly in the dressing.

5. Make the polenta: About 30 minutes before the brisket is done, combine the broth and salt in a large saucepan and bring to a boil over high heat.

6. Reduce the heat to low, then, while whisking continuously, pour in the cornmeal and whisk until combined. Bring the mixture back to a simmer, then cover and cook for 10 minutes. Uncover and whisk the cornmeal, making sure to scrape up anything stuck to the bottom of the pan, then cover and cook for 15 minutes more.

7. Add the cheese, butter, and pepper and stir until the cheese and butter have melted. Taste and season with additional salt, if needed.

8. When the brisket is done, remove the pot from the oven and transfer the brisket to a cutting board. Let rest for 10 minutes before slicing. Using a sharp knife, cut the brisket across the grain into ¼-inch-thick slices. Transfer 3 cups of the sliced brisket to an airtight container and refrigerate to use for Meal 2 (it will keep for up to 5 days).

9. Spoon the polenta into bowls and top with the remaining sliced brisket and the slaw. Garnish with the cilantro and serve.

TIPS

- Save time by buying 8 cups preshredded cabbage or coleslaw mix in place of the head of cabbage used to make the zesty slaw.

- Bake the bell peppers and onion for Meal 2 with the brisket: Prep the peppers and onion as directed on page 89, bake for 25 minutes, then let cool.

CALORIES: 698   FAT: 35G   CARBS: 30.2G   PROTEIN: 58.6G

VARIATION: INSTANT POT METHOD

1. In a small bowl, whisk together the barbecue rub ingredients. Rub this mixture over the brisket. Cut the brisket into 4 equal pieces.

2. Set your Instant Pot to "Sauté" and pour the olive oil into the pot. Working in two batches, add the brisket to the pot and sear for 2 to 3 minutes on each side, until browned. Transfer the brisket to a plate and repeat to brown the remaining pieces.

3. Once all the brisket is browned, return all the pieces to the pot and add ½ cup water. Lock on the lid, making sure the valve is set to "Sealing" rather than "Venting." Press the "Meat/Stew" button and adjust to cook at high pressure for 1 hour 10 minutes. When the brisket is finished cooking, allow the pressure to release naturally until the lid opens easily, about 15 minutes.

4. Transfer the brisket to a cutting board and let rest for 10 minutes before slicing.

MEAL 2

CHEESESTEAK-STUFFED PEPPERS WITH WILD RICE

Serves 4

Active time: 25 MINUTES   **Total time:** 1 HOUR 10 MINUTES

For the Wild Rice (optional)

1 cup uncooked wild rice, rinsed

1 tablespoon salted butter

For the Cheesesteak-Stuffed Peppers

4 green bell peppers

½ small onion, cut into slivers

1 tablespoon extra-virgin olive oil

½ teaspoon fine sea salt

3 cups sliced cooked brisket (reserved from Meal 1; see page 88)

4 slices provolone cheese

2 tablespoons chopped fresh parsley, for garnish

1. Make the wild rice (if using): Cook the rice according to the package instructions. Add the butter and stir to combine. Keep warm until ready to serve, if necessary.

2. Meanwhile, make the stuffed peppers: Preheat the oven to 375°F.

3. Slice the tops off the bell peppers and remove the seeds; discard the tops. Place the bell peppers and onion in a baking dish, drizzle with the olive oil, and sprinkle with the salt.

4. Bake for 25 minutes, or until the peppers are slightly wilted. Remove from the oven; keep the oven on.

5. In a medium bowl, combine the onion and sliced brisket.

6. Stand the peppers upright in the baking dish and divide the brisket and onion evenly among them. Place one slice of provolone over the top of each pepper. Bake for 20 minutes, or until the cheese is bubbling.

7. Serve the stuffed peppers with the warm wild rice alongside, garnished with the parsley.

CALORIES: 562   FAT: 23.3G   CARBS: 38.7G   PROTEIN: 50.9G

ABOUT

This may very well be my husband's most favorite dinner series out of this entire book! Don't let the words "classic brisket" fool you into thinking this isn't an exciting meal. This brisket and the savory gravy accompanying it are jaw-droppingly delicious. Balsamic vinegar is my secret ingredient for making this a gravy like no other. For the second meal, we transform half the prepared brisket into the most tender Mongolian beef bowls with a perfect sticky brown sauce and serve it all over fluffy white rice.

▦ $$$
▦ DAIRY-FREE OPTION
▦ EGG-FREE
▦ GLUTEN-FREE OPTION
▦ GRAIN-FREE OPTION
▦ NUT-FREE

Classic Brisket

WITH GRAVY, MASHED POTATOES, AND ASPARAGUS

/ RECIPE PAGE 92 /

Mongolian Beef Bowls

/ RECIPE PAGE 93 /

SUBSTITUTIONS

Make It Dairy-Free:

- **MEAL 1:** For the mashed potatoes, use full-fat coconut milk in place of the sour cream and olive oil in place of the butter.

- **MEAL 2:** Use avocado oil in place of the butter in the beef bowls.

Make It Gluten-Free:

- **MEAL 1:** Use cup-for-cup gluten-free flour in place of the all-purpose flour in the gravy.

Make It Grain-Free:

- **MEAL 1:** Use 1 tablespoon arrowroot starch in place of the all-purpose flour in the gravy.

- **MEAL 2:** Substitute 4 cups cooked cauliflower rice for the white rice in the beef bowls.

CLASSIC BRISKET WITH GRAVY, MASHED POTATOES, AND ASPARAGUS

Serves 5

Active time: 45 MINUTES **Total time:** 4 HOURS 40 MINUTES

For the Classic Brisket

2 tablespoons extra-virgin olive oil

1 tablespoon fine sea salt

1 (5-pound) beef brisket, trimmed

For the Garlic Mashed Potatoes

1½ pounds Yukon Gold potatoes, peeled and cut into 1-inch cubes

¼ cup sour cream

3 tablespoons salted butter

1 teaspoon garlic powder

½ teaspoon fine sea salt

¼ teaspoon ground black pepper

For the Roasted Asparagus

1 bunch asparagus, rinsed and patted dry, bottom 1 to 2 inches trimmed

1 teaspoon extra-virgin olive oil

½ teaspoon fine sea salt

¼ teaspoon ground black pepper

For the Balsamic Gravy

2 tablespoons all-purpose flour

½ cup beef broth or water

¼ cup balsamic vinegar

1 tablespoon fresh lemon juice (from about ½ lemon)

Fine sea salt and ground black pepper if needed

1. Make the brisket: Preheat the oven to 325°F.

2. In a Dutch oven large enough to fit the brisket lying flat, heat the olive oil over high heat. Rub the salt over the brisket, place the seasoned brisket in the pot, and sear, undisturbed, for 2 to 3 minutes, until a crust forms on the bottom. Flip the brisket and sear for 2 to 3 minutes on the second side.

3. Pour ½ cup water into the pot, cover with the lid, and transfer to the oven. Bake for 4 hours.

4. Meanwhile, make the mashed potatoes: Put the potatoes in a medium saucepan and add water to cover. Cover the pot and bring to a boil over medium-high heat, and cook for 15 to 20 minutes, until the potatoes are easily pierced with a fork. Drain the potatoes and return them to the pot.

5. Add the sour cream, butter, garlic powder, salt, and pepper to the pot with the potatoes. Using a potato masher or a handheld mixer, mash the potatoes until smooth and well combined with the other ingredients. Keep warm until ready to serve.

6. When the brisket is done, remove the pot from the oven and transfer the brisket to a cutting board; raise the oven temperature to 350°F. Reserve 2 cups of the drippings from the pot to use in the gravy. Let the brisket rest for 10 minutes before slicing. Using a sharp knife, cut the brisket across the grain into ¼-inch-thick slices. Transfer 3 cups of the sliced brisket to an airtight container and refrigerate to use for Meal 2 (it will keep for up to 5 days). Transfer the remaining brisket back to the pot and cover until ready to serve.

7. Roast the asparagus: On a rimmed baking sheet, toss the asparagus with the olive oil to coat. Season with the salt and pepper, then spread the stalks evenly over the baking sheet. Roast for 30 minutes, or until the asparagus look wilted but not overbrowned.

8. Make the gravy: In a bowl, whisk together the flour and broth until the flour has completely dissolved.

9. In a large skillet or pot, whisk together the flour-broth mixture, reserved brisket drippings, and the vinegar. Bring to a simmer over medium-high heat, then reduce the heat to low to keep the gravy warm until serving time. Add the lemon juice, then taste and season with salt and pepper, if needed.

10. Serve the brisket and the mashed potatoes with the gravy poured over the top and the roasted asparagus alongside.

CALORIES: 511   FAT: 20G   CARBS: 30.9G   PROTEIN: 53.1G

VARIATION: INSTANT POT OPTION

1. Set the Instant Pot to "Sauté" and pour the olive oil into the pot.

2. Rub the salt over the brisket. Cut the brisket into 4 equal pieces.

3. Working in two batches to avoid overcrowding the pot, add the brisket to the pot and sear for 2 to 3 minutes on each side, until browned. Transfer the brisket to a plate and repeat to brown the remaining pieces.

4. Once all the brisket is browned, return all the pieces to the pot and add ½ cup water. Lock on the lid, making sure the valve is set to "Sealing" rather than "Venting." Press the "Meat/Stew" button and cook at high pressure for 1 hour 10 minutes. When the brisket is finished cooking, allow the pressure to release naturally until the lid opens easily, about 15 minutes.

5. Transfer the brisket to a cutting board and let rest for 10 minutes before slicing.

MEAL 2

MONGOLIAN BEEF BOWLS

Serves 4

Active time: 15 MINUTES   **Total time:** 20 MINUTES

1 cup uncooked white rice, rinsed

4 tablespoons (½ stick) salted butter, or ¼ cup ghee or avocado oil

3 cups sliced cooked brisket (reserved from Meal 1; see page 92)

2 cups coconut aminos (from one 16.9-ounce bottle)

1 teaspoon toasted sesame oil

½ teaspoon fish sauce

½ teaspoon garlic powder

½ teaspoon ground ginger

½ teaspoon red pepper flakes

1 bunch green onions, cut on an angle into 1½-inch-long pieces

1 teaspoon white sesame seeds, for garnish (optional)

1. Cook the rice according to the package instructions.

2. Meanwhile, in a large skillet, melt the butter over medium heat. Working in batches, add the cooked brisket and sear on each side for about 2 minutes, until the slices become slightly crispy. Transfer to a bowl or plate and repeat with the remaining brisket.

3. In a separate large skillet (or in the same skillet after all the meat has been browned, to save on dishes), bring the coconut aminos to a low simmer over medium heat. Simmer for about 5 minutes, or until thick enough to coat the back of a spoon.

4. Add the sesame oil, fish sauce, garlic powder, ginger, and red pepper flakes to the coconut aminos and whisk to combine. Add the beef and green onions to the sauce and toss to combine. Cook over medium heat for about 3 minutes, until the green onions wilt.

5. Serve the beef with the rice, garnished with the sesame seeds, if desired.

| CALORIES: 708 | FAT: 24.9G | CARBS: 62G | PROTEIN: 59.4G |

Beef Taco Night

/ RECIPE PAGE 96 /

ABOUT

These two dinners are at the top of my family's favorites list. First up, taco night! Half of the browned ground beef is seasoned with my family's go-to Mexican flair, then it's presented with all the fixings, including a delicious Mexican rice and some simple refried beans. Serving dinner with all the components displayed in separate dishes is a fun way to allow each member of the family to build their own ideal taco plate. The second dinner is a fabulous rustic cottage pie. Mixed with the right amount of peas and carrots and then topped with a traditional mashed potato crust, this meal is truly special.

- $$$
- DAIRY-FREE OPTION
- EGG-FREE
- GLUTEN-FREE
- GRAIN-FREE OPTION
- NUT-FREE
- FREEZER-FRIENDLY

MEAL 2

Cottage Pie

/ RECIPE PAGE 97 /

SUBSTITUTIONS

Make It Dairy-Free:

- **MEAL 1:** Omit the sour cream from the tacos. Either omit the shredded cheddar or use a vegan shredded cheese.

- **MEAL 2:** For the mashed potatoes used to top the cottage pie, substitute full-fat coconut milk for the heavy cream and olive oil for the butter.

Make It Grain-Free:

- **MEAL 1:** Use grain-free taco shells or tortillas for the tacos.

Tip

- Ground beef reheats well, so even if you won't be making the meals on consecutive nights, go ahead and cook all the ground beef, then store half in the fridge so you'll have it ready to go later in the week.

<h1>MEAL 1</h1>

<h1>BEEF TACO NIGHT</h1>

Serves 4

Active time: 45 MINUTES   **Total time:** 45 MINUTES

For the Mexican Rice

1 cup uncooked white rice, rinsed

1 (10-ounce) can diced tomatoes and green chiles (such as Ro-Tel), drained

2 tablespoons fresh lime juice (from 1 lime)

1 tablespoon extra-virgin olive oil

1 teaspoon ground cumin

½ teaspoon fine sea salt

For the Beef Taco Filling

4 pounds ground beef

1 tablespoon extra-virgin olive oil

1 tablespoon chili powder

2 teaspoons ground cumin

1 teaspoon dried oregano

1 teaspoon garlic powder

1 teaspoon fine sea salt

¼ teaspoon ground black pepper

1 tablespoon fresh lime juice (from about ½ lime)

For the Refried Beans

1 (16-ounce) can refried beans

½ teaspoon fine sea salt

½ teaspoon ground cumin

To Serve

8 hard taco shells

1 cup shredded lettuce

1 large tomato, chopped

1 cup shredded cheddar cheese

½ cup chopped red onion

½ cup sliced pickled jalapeños

½ cup sour cream

½ cup guacamole

1 lime, cut into wedges

1. Start the rice: Cook the rice according to the package instructions.

2. Make the taco filling: In a large skillet, cook the ground beef over medium heat, breaking up the meat with a spoon as it cooks, for about 10 minutes, until browned. Drain the fat from the cooked beef, then transfer half the beef (about 4 cups) to an airtight container and refrigerate to use for Meal 2 (it will keep for up to 5 days). Transfer the remaining beef to a bowl and set aside.

3. In the same skillet, heat the olive oil over medium heat. Return the cooked ground beef to the skillet and stir to break it up. Add the chili powder, cumin, oregano, garlic powder, salt, and pepper and stir to combine. Cook for 5 minutes, until the beef is heated through. Turn off the heat and stir in the lime juice.

4. Finish the rice: Add the tomatoes and green chiles, lime juice, olive oil, cumin, and salt and stir to combine.

5. Make the refried beans: In a small saucepan, stir together the refried beans, salt, and cumin and heat over medium heat for 5 to 10 minutes, until warmed through.

6. Plate the taco shells, beef filling, lettuce, tomato, cheese, onion, jalapeños, sour cream, and guacamole separately so that each person can build and fill their taco as they like. Serve the tacos with the rice, refried beans, and lime wedges alongside.

CALORIES: 752   FAT: 35.5G   CARBS: 63.3G   PROTEIN: 46G

MEAL 2

COTTAGE PIE

Serves 6

Active time: 45 MINUTES

Total time: 1 HOUR 15 MINUTES

1½ pounds Yukon Gold potatoes, peeled and quartered

¼ cup heavy cream or milk

2 tablespoons salted butter

½ teaspoon fine sea salt

1 tablespoon extra-virgin olive oil

About 4 cups cooked ground beef (reserved from Meal 1; see page 96)

1 (10-ounce) package frozen peas and carrots

2 tablespoons tomato paste

½ cup red wine

2 teaspoons Italian seasoning

½ teaspoon garlic powder

½ teaspoon fine sea salt

¼ teaspoon ground black pepper

1 tablespoon chopped fresh parsley, for garnish

1. Preheat the oven to 375°F.

2. Put the potatoes in a medium saucepan and add water to cover. Cover the pot and bring to a boil over medium-high heat. Cook for 15 to 20 minutes, until the potatoes are easily pierced with a fork. Drain the potatoes and return them to the pot.

3. Add the cream, butter, and salt to the pot with the potatoes. Using a potato masher or handheld mixer, mash the potatoes until smooth and well combined with the other ingredients.

4. In a large heavy-bottomed oven-safe pot or Dutch oven, heat the olive oil over medium heat. Add the cooked ground beef, peas and carrots, tomato paste, wine, Italian seasoning, garlic powder, salt, and pepper and stir to combine. Cook for about 5 minutes, until everything is well combined, then spread the mixture evenly over the bottom of the oven-safe pot. Spoon the mashed potatoes on top of the beef mixture and spread them into an even layer.

5. Bake for 30 minutes, or until the top is lightly browned. Garnish with the parsley and serve.

CALORIES: 435   FAT: 14G   CARBS: 27.4G   PROTEIN: 45.9G

Beef Enchilada Casserole

/ RECIPE PAGE 100 /

ABOUT

These two dinners pair flavors that I return to again and again: Tex-Mex and Asian inspired. This beef enchilada casserole is like a love letter from my Garcia heritage heart. It has all the good things: layers of tortillas, cheese, perfectly seasoned ground beef, and the opportunity to top your portion with all the avocado and sour cream you like. Then the teriyaki stir-fry is a delicious way to up the veggie content of your dinner by adding broccoli, peppers, carrots, and mushrooms. Serve it over white rice and garnish with fresh lime and spicy sauce for a satisfying meal.

- $$$
- DAIRY-FREE OPTION
- EGG-FREE
- GLUTEN-FREE
- GRAIN-FREE OPTION
- NUT-FREE
- FREEZER-FRIENDLY

Teriyaki Ground Beef Stir-Fry

WITH WHITE RICE

/ RECIPE PAGE 101 /

SUBSTITUTIONS

Make It Dairy-Free:

- **MEAL 1:** Omit the cheese from the enchilada casserole or replace it with vegan cheese. Skip the sour cream garnish.

Make It Grain-Free:

- **MEAL 1:** Use grain-free tortillas in place of the corn tortillas for the enchilada casserole.

- **MEAL 2:** Substitute 4 cups cooked cauliflower rice in place of the white rice for the stir-fry.

BEEF ENCHILADA CASSEROLE

Serves 5

Active time: 30 MINUTES   **Total time:** 1 HOUR

3 pounds ground beef

1 (15-ounce) can red enchilada sauce

1 cup beef broth

1 teaspoon dried oregano

½ teaspoon garlic powder

½ teaspoon onion powder

½ teaspoon fine sea salt

¼ teaspoon ground black pepper

12 corn tortillas

3 cups shredded cheddar cheese

¼ cup sour cream, for garnish

1 avocado, sliced, for garnish

2 tablespoons chopped fresh cilantro leaves, for garnish

1. Preheat the oven to 350°F.

2. In a large skillet, cook the ground beef over medium heat, breaking up the meat with a spoon as it cooks, until browned, about 10 minutes. Drain the excess fat from the cooked beef, then transfer half the beef (about 3½ cups) to an airtight container and refrigerate to use for Meal 2 (it will keep for up to 5 days). Transfer the remaining beef to a large bowl.

3. Add the enchilada sauce, broth, oregano, garlic powder, onion powder, salt, and pepper to the bowl with the ground beef and stir to combine.

4. Arrange a layer of tortillas over the bottom of an 8-inch square baking dish (breaking them as needed to fit), then spoon about 1 cup of the beef mixture over the tortilla layer. Top evenly with ½ cup of the cheese, then repeat the layers until all of the ingredients except the last cup of cheese are used. Top evenly with the remaining 1 cup cheese.

5. Bake for 30 minutes, or until the top is bubbling. Top with the sour cream and avocado, garnish with the cilantro, and serve.

CALORIES: 625   FAT: 34G   CARBS: 34.4G   PROTEIN: 45.9G

MEAL 2

TERIYAKI GROUND BEEF STIR-FRY WITH WHITE RICE

Serves 4

Active time: 35 MINUTES   **Total time:** 35 MINUTES

1 cup uncooked white rice, rinsed

1 cup coconut aminos

1 teaspoon ground ginger

1 teaspoon toasted sesame oil

1 tablespoon extra-virgin olive oil

2 cups shredded carrots

8 ounces mushrooms, diced

1 yellow bell pepper, sliced into thin strips

½ red onion, thinly sliced

4 cups broccoli florets

About 3½ cups cooked ground beef (reserved from Meal 1; see page 100)

1 tablespoon white sesame seeds, for garnish

1. Cook the rice according to the package instructions.

2. Meanwhile, in a medium skillet, bring the coconut aminos to a simmer over medium heat. Cook for 5 to 7 minutes, until reduced enough to coat the back of a spoon. Remove from the heat, stir in the ginger and sesame oil, and set aside.

3. In a large skillet, heat the olive oil over medium-high heat. Add the carrots, mushrooms, bell pepper, onion, and broccoli and cook, stirring, for 6 to 7 minutes, until the vegetables are soft.

4. Add the cooked ground beef and the coconut aminos teriyaki sauce. Stir to combine. Cook for 5 minutes, until the ground beef is heated through, then remove from the heat.

5. Garnish with the sesame seeds and serve with the rice.

TIPS

- Omit the coconut aminos, ground ginger, and sesame oil and substitute ½ cup of your favorite store-bought teriyaki sauce. Just add it in step 4 with the ground beef.

- Buy preshredded carrots and precut fresh or frozen broccoli florets to reduce the prep time.

CALORIES: 588   FAT: 11.9G   CARBS: 74.1G   PROTEIN: 46.3G

Classic Meatball Boats

/ RECIPE PAGE 104 /

ABOUT

You are in for a serious treat with these two meatball-centric dinners! Simply seasoned (and therefore versatile) baked meatballs are used to make a classic meatball boat and a Greek-flavored spin on Italian wedding soup. For the boats, meatballs are nestled into hollowed-out baguettes, topped liberally with marinara, and covered with melted cheese. The wedding soup is packed with orzo, spinach, carrots, and a creamy, lemony soup base, making it a full meal in itself.

▧ $$
▧ DAIRY-FREE OPTION
▧ EGG-FREE
▧ GLUTEN-FREE OPTION
▧ NUT-FREE
▧ FREEZER-FRIENDLY

Wedding Soup

WITH ORZO

/ RECIPE PAGE 105 /

SUBSTITUTIONS

Make It Dairy-Free:

- **MEAL 1:** Either omit the cheese on the meatball boats or use your favorite vegan cheese.

- **MEAL 2:** Substitute full-fat coconut milk for the heavy cream in the soup.

Make It Gluten-Free:

- **MEAL 1:** Use gluten-free rolls or baguettes for the meatball boats.

- **MEAL 2:** Use gluten-free orzo or rice.

Tip

- To save even more time, buy premade meatballs from your grocery store's freezer section and use those in place of the homemade meatballs in either recipe.

MEAL 1

CLASSIC MEATBALL BOATS

Serves 4

Active time: 20 MINUTES   **Total time:** 55 MINUTES

3 pounds ground beef

1 tablespoon fine sea salt

1 teaspoon garlic powder

1 teaspoon ground black pepper

1 (25-ounce) jar marinara sauce

2 baguettes, cut into thirds, then split in half lengthwise, insides scooped out

1½ cups shredded mozzarella cheese

2 tablespoons chopped fresh parsley, for garnish

1. Preheat the oven to 400°F.

2. In a large bowl, combine the ground beef, salt, garlic powder, and ½ teaspoon of the pepper. Roll the mixture into roughly tablespoon-size balls and place them on a rimmed baking sheet, spacing them evenly.

3. Bake for 20 minutes, or until browned. Remove the meatballs from the oven; keep the oven on. Transfer half the meatballs (about 18) to an airtight container and refrigerate to use in Meal 2 (it will keep for up to 5 days). Put the remaining meatballs in a large bowl.

4. Add the marinara to the meatballs and toss to coat. Spoon an equal number of meatballs (2 to 3) into each piece of baguette. Spoon additional marinara on top, then cover with the cheese.

5. Set the sandwiches on a baking sheet and bake for 15 minutes, or until the top is bubbling and starting to brown.

6. Season with the remaining ½ teaspoon pepper, garnish with the parsley, and serve.

TIP

- For an alternative way to serve these meatballs, bake in individual ramekins or in a small casserole dish without the bread. Keep your baguettes whole and serve them alongside to dip into the marinara at mealtime.

CALORIES: 505   FAT: 17.8G   CARBS: 41.9G   PROTEIN: 42.5G

MEAL 2

WEDDING SOUP WITH ORZO

Serves 4

Active time: 15 MINUTES	**Total time:** 30 MINUTES

1 tablespoon extra-virgin olive oil

3 garlic cloves, minced

3 carrots, cut into ¼-inch-thick rounds

About 18 cooked meatballs (reserved from Meal 1; see page 104)

6 cups chicken broth

1 teaspoon fine sea salt

½ teaspoon ground black pepper

1 cup dried orzo

3 cups fresh spinach

¼ cup fresh mint, finely chopped

1 tablespoon fresh oregano or 1 teaspoon dried, plus more for garnish

1 tablespoon grated lemon zest

¼ cup fresh lemon juice (from about 2 lemons)

¼ cup heavy cream

1 lemon, cut into wedges, for serving

TIPS

- This soup is very forgiving if you don't have one, or several, of the ingredients. Though the final product will be different, you'll still have a lovely soup if you omit the mint, oregano, or cream.

- You can swap kale, Swiss chard, or even collard greens for the spinach.

1. In a large pot, heat the olive oil over medium heat. Add the garlic and cook, stirring, for 3 to 5 minutes, until lightly browned and fragrant.

2. Add the carrots, meatballs, broth, salt, and pepper to the pot. Bring to a low boil and cook, stirring occasionally, for about 5 minutes, until the carrots are starting to soften.

3. Add the orzo and cook, stirring occasionally, for 10 minutes, until the orzo is tender.

4. Add the spinach, mint, oregano, lemon zest, lemon juice, and cream. Cook for about 3 minutes, until the spinach is completely wilted.

5. Ladle the soup into bowls and serve warm, garnished with oregano, with the lemon wedges alongside for squeezing over the top.

CALORIES: 523	FAT: 20.3G	CARBS: 43.6G	PROTEIN: 41.7G

Loaded Avocado Bacon Burgers

WITH WEDGE SWEET POTATO FRIES AND CHIPOTLE-LIME MAYO

/ RECIPE PAGE 108 /

ABOUT

This is such a fun dinner series! You'll start off with the most epic loaded avocado bacon burgers, complete with perfectly cooked wedge sweet potato fries and an easy chipotle-lime mayo. Then you're going to feel like an efficient kitchen genius as you transform half the already prepared burger patties into the easiest, most flavorful crispy hash. Because the hash is made from precooked burger patties, the dish takes on new flavors and recrisps really easily.

▧ $$$

▧ DAIRY-FREE OPTION

▧ EGG-FREE OPTION

▧ GLUTEN-FREE OPTION

▧ GRAIN-FREE OPTION

▧ LOW-CARB OPTION

▧ NUT-FREE

Crispy Beef Hash

WITH SIMPLE TZATZIKI

/ RECIPE PAGE 109 /

SUBSTITUTIONS

Make It Dairy-Free:

- **MEAL 1:** Omit the cheddar cheese from the burgers.

- **MEAL 2:** Omit the feta from the hash, and either omit the tzatziki or prepare it using a dairy-free Greek-style yogurt.

Make It Egg-Free:

- **MEAL 1:** Use your favorite vegan mayo to make the chipotle-lime mayo for the burgers.

Make It Gluten-Free:

- **MEAL 1:** Use gluten-free buns for the burgers.

Make It Grain-Free:

- **MEAL 1:** Serve the burgers over a bed of greens or lettuce-wrap style.

Make It Low-Carb:

- **MEAL 1:** Serve the burgers lettuce-wrap style and make the roasted asparagus on page 92 in place of the sweet potato fries.

- **MEAL 2:** Omit the potatoes from the hash.

LOADED AVOCADO BACON BURGERS WITH WEDGE SWEET POTATO FRIES AND CHIPOTLE-LIME MAYO

Serves 4

Active time: 50 MINUTES   **Total time:** 50 MINUTES

For the Wedge Sweet Potato Fries

1 pound sweet potatoes, cut into ½-inch-thick wedges

2 tablespoons extra-virgin olive oil

½ teaspoon paprika

½ teaspoon fine sea salt

¼ teaspoon ground black pepper

For the Loaded Avocado Bacon Burgers

3 pounds ground beef

1 tablespoon fine sea salt

1 teaspoon garlic powder

½ teaspoon ground black pepper

2 tablespoons extra-virgin olive oil (or olive oil spray, if using a grill)

For the Chipotle-Lime Mayo

½ cup mayonnaise

2 tablespoons fresh lime juice

1 tablespoon chipotle chile powder

To Assemble and Serve

4 burger buns, toasted 4 slices white cheddar cheese

1 avocado, sliced

4 slices bacon, cooked until crisp

4 lettuce leaves

1 tomato, thickly sliced

½ red onion, sliced

1. Make the sweet potato fries: Preheat the oven to 400°F. Line a rimmed baking sheet with parchment paper.

2. Toss the sweet potatoes with the olive oil, then spread them out over the prepared baking sheet in an even layer. Sprinkle with the paprika, salt, and pepper.

3. Bake the sweet potato fries for 35 minutes, or until they're cooked through and starting to crisp, tossing them once halfway through. Remove from the oven; keep the oven on.

4. Meanwhile, make the burgers: In a large bowl, mix together the ground beef, salt, garlic powder, and pepper until just combined. Form the meat mixture into 8 large, flat patties.

5. *To grill the burgers,* heat a grill to 450°F. Once hot, grease the grill grates with the olive oil or spray them with olive oil spray. Place all the burgers on the grill, close the lid, and grill for 4 to 5 minutes, then flip and grill for 3 to 4 minutes on the second side for medium-well.

To cook the burgers on the stovetop, in a large skillet, heat the olive oil over medium-high heat. Working in batches, add enough burgers to fit the skillet in a single layer. Cook for 4 to 5 minutes on the first side, then flip and cook on the second side for 3 to 4 minutes, until browned. Transfer the burgers to a plate and repeat to cook the remaining patties.

6. Make the chipotle-lime mayo: In a small bowl, whisk together the mayonnaise, lime juice, and chipotle chile powder.

7. To assemble the burgers, spread about 1 teaspoon of the chipotle mayo over each bottom half of the burger buns. Place on a rimmed baking sheet. Top 4 of the bun halves with a burger patty and a slice of cheddar cheese. Transfer the remaining burgers to an airtight container and refrigerate to use for Meal 2 (it will keep for up to 5 days).

8. Bake the burgers for 5 minutes, or until the cheese has melted.

9. Top each burger patty with a couple of slices of avocado, 1 slice of bacon, a lettuce leaf, and some tomato and onion. Set the other half of the bun on top and enjoy with the warm sweet potato fries and the remaining chipotle-lime mayo on the side.

CALORIES: 875   FAT: 49.2G   CARBS: 54.2G   PROTEIN: 55.3G

CRISPY BEEF HASH WITH SIMPLE TZATZIKI

Serves 4

Active time: 25 MINUTES

Total time: 1 HOUR 10 MINUTES

For the Crispy Beef Hash

1 pound baby Yukon Gold potatoes

4 tablespoons extra-virgin olive oil

¾ teaspoon fine sea salt

4 cooked burger patties (reserved from Meal 1; see page 108)

2 tablespoons fresh lemon juice (from 1 lemon)

1 tablespoon dried oregano

½ teaspoon garlic powder

For the Simple Tzatziki

1 cup plain full-fat Greek yogurt

¼ cup drained grated cucumber (water squeezed out; about ½ cucumber)

2 garlic cloves, finely grated

¼ teaspoon fine sea salt

To Serve

½ cup pitted kalamata olives

½ cucumber, coarsely chopped

1 tomato, cut into ½-inch-thick wedges

½ red onion, thinly sliced

¼ cup crumbled feta cheese

2 tablespoons chopped fresh parsley, for garnish

1. Make the beef hash: Preheat the oven to 400°F.

2. Toss the potatoes with 1 tablespoon of the olive oil and ¼ teaspoon of the salt and spread them over a rimmed baking sheet in an even layer. Bake for 25 to 30 minutes, until easily pierced with a fork.

3. Using the bottom of a large spatula, smash the potatoes to about 1 inch thick, then coarsely crumble the burger patties (into roughly 1-inch pieces) onto the baking sheet. Drizzle the potatoes and crumbled burgers with the remaining 3 tablespoons olive oil and the lemon juice, then sprinkle with the oregano, garlic powder, and remaining ½ teaspoon salt.

4. Bake for 30 minutes, or until the potatoes start to look crispy.

5. Meanwhile, make the tzatziki: In a small bowl, whisk together the yogurt, cucumber, garlic, and salt until smooth and well combined. Cover and refrigerate until the hash is ready to serve.

6. Top the hash with the olives, cucumber, tomato, onion, and feta, then garnish with the parsley. Serve warm, with the tzatziki on the side.

TIPS

- If you want to speed up the cooking time for the potatoes, wrap them in paper towels and microwave for 3 to 4 minutes, until they are tender when squeezed, then proceed to step 3.

- Get a head start on your Meal 2 prep by roasting the baby Yukon Gold potatoes at the same time the sweet potato fries for Meal 1 are in the oven. Just follow the prep and cooking time in step 2 on this page, then store in an airtight container in the refrigerator.

- In Meal 1, use frozen sweet potato fries instead of making them from scratch.

CALORIES: 606   FAT: 37.2G   CARBS: 25.2G   PROTEIN: 44.6G

Beef Burrito Bowls

WITH CILANTRO-LIME RICE, BLACK BEANS, AND CORN SALSA

/ RECIPE PAGE 112 /

ABOUT

Dinner this week is designed to feed your inner child. Enough ground beef for both dinners is simply seasoned then browned, but takes off in exciting directions from there. Half is used in hunger-busting burrito bowls that are complete with an easy cilantro-lime rice, wholesome black beans, and a zesty corn salsa. Then, for the second meal, we make hamburger dreams come to life with the cheeseburger pie. The ground beef is boldly flavored then poured on top of french fries. The whole dish is topped with cheese and bacon, then heads into the oven to melt into perfection. Serve it with your favorite burger toppings and an extra side of ketchup.

- $$$
- DAIRY-FREE OPTION
- EGG-FREE
- GLUTEN-FREE
- GRAIN-FREE OPTION
- NUT-FREE
- FREEZER-FRIENDLY

Cheeseburger Pie

/ RECIPE PAGE 113 /

SUBSTITUTIONS

Make It Dairy-Free:

- **MEAL 1:** Omit the cheese from the burrito bowls, or substitute a vegan cheese.

- **MEAL 2:** Omit the cheese from the cheeseburger pie, or substitute a vegan cheese.

Make It Grain-Free:

- **MEAL 1:** Substitute 4 cups cooked cauliflower rice for the white rice in the burrito bowls.

BEEF BURRITO BOWLS WITH CILANTRO-LIME RICE, BLACK BEANS, AND CORN SALSA

Serves 5

Active time: 40 MINUTES   **Total time:** 40 MINUTES

For the Ground Beef

3 pounds ground beef

1 teaspoon extra-virgin olive oil

1 tablespoon chili powder

1 teaspoon ground cumin

½ teaspoon dried oregano

½ teaspoon garlic powder

½ teaspoon fine sea salt

¼ teaspoon ground black pepper

For the Cilantro-Lime Rice

1 cup uncooked white rice, rinsed

1 tablespoon salted butter or extra-virgin olive oil

½ teaspoon fine sea salt

2 tablespoons fresh lime juice (from 1 lime)

2 tablespoons chopped fresh cilantro

For the Corn Salsa

1 cup thawed frozen corn kernels

1 red bell pepper, chopped

1 jalapeño, seeded and diced

2 tablespoons chopped red onion

2 tablespoons chopped fresh cilantro

2 tablespoons fresh lime juice (from 1 lime)

½ teaspoon fine sea salt

For the Black Beans

1 (16-ounce) can black beans, undrained

½ teaspoon fine sea salt

½ teaspoon ground cumin

To Serve

1 cup guacamole

1 cup pico de gallo or salsa

1 cup shredded Monterey Jack cheese

1½ cups shredded romaine lettuce

¼ cup chopped fresh cilantro, for garnish

1 lime, cut into quarters

1. Make the beef: In a large skillet, cook the ground beef over medium heat, breaking up the meat with a spoon as it cooks, until browned, about 10 minutes. Drain the fat from the cooked beef, then transfer half the beef (about 3½ cups) to an airtight container and refrigerate to use for Meal 2 (it will keep for up to 5 days).

2. In the same skillet, heat the olive oil over medium-high heat. Add the remaining cooked ground beef, then add the chili powder, cumin, oregano, garlic powder, salt, and pepper and stir to combine. Cook for 5 to 7 minutes, until the beef is completely warmed through.

3. Make the rice: Cook the rice according to the package instructions. Add the butter and salt to the cooked rice and stir to melt the butter. Stir in the lime juice and cilantro. Keep warm until ready to serve.

4. Make the corn salsa: In a small bowl, stir together the corn, bell pepper, jalapeño, onion, cilantro, lime juice, and salt. Cover and refrigerate until ready to serve. (The salsa is best served chilled.)

5. Make the black beans: In a small saucepan, combine the black beans (and the liquid from the can), salt, and cumin and cook over medium heat for 5 to 10 minutes, until warmed through. Keep warm until ready to serve.

6. Divide the rice, black beans, and corn salsa among five bowls and top with the beef. Top as you like with guacamole, pico de gallo, cheese, and lettuce, garnish with the cilantro, and serve with the lime wedges alongside for squeezing over the top.

TIP

- Burrito bowls are an "all toppings approved" situation. If you want to save time on this dish, simply grab whatever sauces and condiments you want in your bowl from the store.

CALORIES: 638   FAT: 23.3G   CARBS: 63G   PROTEIN: 46.8G

CHEESEBURGER PIE

Serves 5

Active time: 20 MINUTES   **Total time:** 45 MINUTES

1 (20- to 28-ounce) bag frozen french fries, thawed

About 3½ cups cooked ground beef (reserved from Meal 1; see page 112)

½ cup ketchup

½ teaspoon fine sea salt

¼ teaspoon ground black pepper

1½ cups shredded cheddar cheese

8 ounces slice bacon, for garnish

1 jalapeño, thinly sliced, for garnish

1. Preheat the oven to 350°F.

2. Press the fries into an even layer over the bottom of a 2-quart casserole dish.

3. In a large bowl, stir together the cooked ground beef, ketchup, salt, and pepper. Spread the beef mixture evenly over the french fries. Sprinkle the top evenly with the cheese. Cover the casserole dish with a lid and bake for 30 minutes, until the cheese has melted and the beef is warmed through.

4. Meanwhile, place the bacon in a large skillet and cook over medium-high heat, flipping the slices about every 3 minutes, until crispy, 5 to 10 minutes. Transfer the bacon to a paper towel to drain and cool slightly, then coarsely chop.

5. Uncover the casserole dish and bake for 10 minutes more, until the cheese is browned and bubbling. Remove from the oven.

6. Garnish the casserole with the bacon and jalapeños and serve.

TIPS

- If you want to avoid the splatter that results from cooking bacon on the stove-top, lay it on a rimmed baking sheet and bake on the lower rack of the oven, while the cheeseburger pie cooks on the top rack, for about 15 minutes, until crisp.

- Pull the fries out of the freezer 30 minutes before you plan to cook them to make sure they have time to thaw. If you're short on time, you can microwave them on the defrost setting for 2 to 3 minutes, until they are soft enough to press into the bottom of the pan.

CALORIES: 822   FAT: 50.3G   CARBS: 45.1G   PROTEIN: 46.6G

MEAL 1

Balsamic Beef Roast

WITH RED WINE MUSHROOMS AND PURPLE POTATOES

/ RECIPE PAGE 116 /

ABOUT

I adore this dinner series because it really showcases the versatility of a beef roast. The first dinner is a beautiful preparation that leans on the bold and subtly sweet flavors of balsamic vinegar. The roast is served with purple potatoes and luscious sautéed mushrooms. Then, for the second dinner, the remaining roast is cleverly incorporated into a flavorful French-style onion soup. The soup gets the classic topping treatment with a slice of bread and bubbling Gruyère cheese and is served alongside a fresh lemon-dill salad.

▓ $$$
▓ DAIRY-FREE OPTION
▓ EGG-FREE
▓ GLUTEN-FREE OPTION
▓ GRAIN-FREE OPTION
▓ NUT-FREE

Onion and Roast Beef Soup

WITH LEMON-DILL SALAD

/ RECIPE PAGE 117 /

SUBSTITUTIONS

Make It Dairy-Free:

- **MEAL 2:** Omit the Gruyère cheese used for topping the soup, and simply broil until the bread is lightly toasted. Use olive oil instead of butter.

Make It Gluten-Free:

- **MEAL 2:** Use a gluten-free baguette or the best crusty gluten-free bread you have available for topping the soup.

Make It Grain-Free:

- **MEAL 2:** Omit the bread used for topping the soup and simply stir the cheese into the soup, if desired, rather than melting it under the broiler, or skip the cheese entirely.

BALSAMIC BEEF ROAST WITH RED WINE MUSHROOMS AND PURPLE POTATOES

Serves 4

Active time: 35 MINUTES

Total time: 3 HOURS 45 MINUTES

For the Balsamic Beef Roast and Purple Fingerling Potatoes

¼ cup balsamic vinegar

3 tablespoons extra-virgin olive oil

2 tablespoons fresh lemon juice (from 1 lemon)

1 tablespoon Italian seasoning

1¼ teaspoons fine sea salt

1 (3-pound) beef chuck or shoulder roast

1 pound purple fingerling potatoes

For the Red Wine Mushrooms

2 tablespoons salted butter or extra-virgin olive oil

16 ounces baby bella mushrooms, sliced

¼ cup red wine

1 tablespoon balsamic vinegar

½ teaspoon fine sea salt

¼ teaspoon ground black pepper

1. Roast the beef and potatoes: Preheat the oven to 350°F.

2. In a small bowl, whisk together the vinegar, 2 tablespoons of the olive oil, the lemon juice, Italian seasoning, and 1 teaspoon of the salt.

3. Place the roast in a roasting pan or baking dish and pour one-third to one-half of the balsamic marinade over the top; set the remaining marinade aside.

4. Toss the potatoes with the remaining 1 tablespoon olive oil and sprinkle with the remaining ¼ teaspoon salt. Spread the potatoes around the beef (or roast them in their own pan).

5. Roast the beef and potatoes for 2½ to 3 hours, until the beef easily pulls apart with a fork and the potatoes are very tender.

6. Meanwhile, make the mushrooms: In a large skillet, melt the butter over high heat. Add the mushrooms and toss to coat in the butter. Cook for 5 to 7 minutes, until the mushrooms have reduced in size and browned.

7. Add the wine, vinegar, salt, and pepper. Bring to a low boil over medium-high heat, then reduce the heat to medium and simmer for about 10 minutes, until the liquid has reduced by half. Remove from the heat.

8. Remove the beef and potatoes from the oven. Transfer the beef to a cutting board and let rest for 10 minutes, then, using two forks, shred the beef. Transfer half the shredded beef (about 3 cups) to an airtight container and refrigerate to use for Meal 2 (it will keep for up to 5 days).

9. Serve the beef with the potatoes and mushrooms alongside and the reserved balsamic marinade drizzled over the top.

TIP

- Place the onions for the soup in Meal 2 in the oven at the same time as the roast. They keep well in the fridge and can easily be transformed into soup on another day.

CALORIES: 474   FAT: 27.1G   CARBS: 30G   PROTEIN: 27.8G

ONION AND ROAST BEEF SOUP WITH LEMON-DILL SALAD

Serves 4

Active time: 30 MINUTES **Total time:** 1 HOUR 50 MINUTES

For the Onion and Roast Beef Soup

3 pounds yellow onions, sliced

4 tablespoons (½ stick) salted butter, melted

½ teaspoon fine sea salt, plus more if needed

About 3 cups shredded cooked beef (reserved from Meal 1; see page 116)

4 cups beef broth

1 cup red wine, or ¼ cup balsamic vinegar

2 tablespoons chopped fresh thyme, plus more for garnish

¼ teaspoon ground black pepper

2 tablespoons fresh lemon juice (from 1 lemon)

1 baguette, sliced into ½-inch-thick rounds

1 cup grated Gruyère cheese

For the Lemon-Dill Salad

2 tablespoons fresh lemon juice (from 1 lemon)

2 tablespoons extra-virgin olive oil

1 teaspoon Dijon mustard

¼ teaspoon fine sea salt

¼ teaspoon ground black pepper

1 head butter lettuce, cored and chopped

2 tablespoons chopped fresh dill

1. Make the soup: Preheat the oven to 375°F.

2. In a large bowl, toss the onions with the melted butter and spread them out over one or two rimmed baking sheets. Sprinkle with the salt, then cover with foil and bake for 30 minutes. Remove from the oven, carefully take off the foil, stir, and return to the oven for an additional 30 to 40 minutes, until the onions have darkened in color and reduced in size.

3. Scrape the contents of the baking sheet(s) into a 6-quart pot. Add the shredded beef, broth, wine, thyme, and pepper and stir to combine. Bring to a simmer over medium heat. Cook for 20 minutes, then add the lemon juice. Taste and season with additional salt, if needed.

4. Preheat the broiler.

5. Spoon the soup into individual oven-safe soup bowls and set the bowls on a baking sheet. Place 2 baguette slices over the soup in each bowl and then sprinkle a generous amount of Gruyère over the top. Broil for 3 to 4 minutes, until the cheese is bubbling and darkened in color.

6. Make the salad: In a small bowl, whisk together the lemon juice, olive oil, mustard, salt, and pepper until fully combined.

7. In a large bowl, combine the lettuce and dill. Add the dressing and toss to coat.

8. Serve the soup hot garnished with thyme, with the lemon-dill salad alongside.

CALORIES: 783   FAT: 39.9G   CARBS: 45.8G   PROTEIN: 53.9G

Chipotle Beef Roast

WITH YUCA

/ RECIPE PAGE 120 /

ABOUT

If I could eat these two dinners on repeat, I absolutely would. Talk about *big* flavor! To start off, a beef roast is prepared with a spicy and smoky chipotle-in-adobo marinade. For the first dinner, sliced roast is served alongside roasted yuca and a cream sauce so delicious, I have a feeling you'll revisit that recipe on its own to keep in your refrigerator at all times. The rest of the beef roast is brilliantly transformed into the best barbacoa tacos. The roast is sliced, seared until crispy, and served in toasted corn tortillas with fresh avocado, lime, and cilantro, alongside simple Mexican pinto beans.

〰 $$

〰 DAIRY-FREE OPTION

〰 EGG-FREE

〰 GLUTEN-FREE

〰 GRAIN-FREE OPTION

〰 NUT-FREE

〰 FREEZER-FRIENDLY

MEAL 2

Barbacoa Tacos

WITH MEXICAN PINTO BEANS

/ RECIPE PAGE 121 /

SUBSTITUTIONS

Make It Dairy-Free:

- **MEAL 1:** Substitute mayonnaise for the sour cream in the beef roast, or use olive oil to make it both dairy- and egg-free.

- **MEAL 2:** Omit the cotija cheese garnish from the tacos.

Make It Grain-Free:

- **MEAL 2:** Use grain-free tortillas for the tacos.

Tips

- If you've never made yuca before, you're in for a treat! It's a starchy root vegetable with a waxy brown outer skin. You can typically find it in the tropical foods section of the produce aisle.

- For a milder sauce, skip using the chipotles and use 2 additional tablespoons of the adobo sauce from the can instead.

CHIPOTLE BEEF ROAST WITH YUCA

Serves 5

Active time: 30 MINUTES

Total time: 3 HOURS 30 MINUTES

2 canned chipotle chiles in adobo sauce, plus 2 tablespoons adobo sauce from the can

½ cup sour cream

¼ cup plus 1 tablespoon extra-virgin olive oil

¼ cup fresh lime juice (from about 2 limes)

1 teaspoon fine sea salt

1 (4-pound) beef chuck or shoulder roast

1 pound yuca, peeled and cut into 1-inch pieces

1. Preheat the oven to 350°F.

2. In a blender, combine the chipotles and adobo sauce, sour cream, ¼ cup of the olive oil, the lime juice, and the salt. Blend until smooth.

3. Spread one-third to one-half of the chipotle cream sauce over the beef roast and place the roast in a roasting pan or baking dish; reserve the remaining sauce for serving.

4. In a large bowl, toss the yuca with the remaining 1 tablespoon olive oil and spread the yuca around the beef (or roast them on their own pan).

5. Roast the beef and yuca for 2½ to 3 hours, until the beef easily pulls apart with a fork and the yuca is very tender.

6. Remove from the oven and transfer the beef to a cutting board. Let the beef rest for 10 minutes before slicing. Cut the beef in half; shred one half and transfer the meat to an airtight container and refrigerate to use for Meal 2 (it will keep for up to 5 days). Cut the remaining half across the grain into ½-inch-thick slices.

7. Serve the sliced beef with the yuca and the remaining cream sauce.

CALORIES: 667   FAT: 40.6G   CARBS: 37G   PROTEIN: 34.5G

BARBACOA TACOS WITH MEXICAN PINTO BEANS

Serves 4

Active time: 25 MINUTES   **Total time:** 25 MINUTES

For the Barbacoa Tacos

1 tablespoon extra-virgin olive oil

2 garlic cloves, minced

About 3 cups shredded cooked beef (reserved from Meal 1; see page 120)

½ teaspoon fine sea salt

1 teaspoon ground cumin

1 teaspoon chipotle chile powder

1 teaspoon dried oregano

¼ teaspoon ground cloves

2 tablespoons fresh lime juice (from 1 lime)

1 tablespoon apple cider vinegar

For the Mexican Pinto Beans

1 tablespoon extra-virgin olive oil

¼ cup finely chopped red onion, plus more for garnish

1 garlic clove, minced

1 (16-ounce) can pinto beans, undrained

2 tablespoons fresh lime juice (from 1 lime), plus more if needed

1 teaspoon ground cumin

½ teaspoon fine sea salt, plus more if needed

2 tablespoons chopped fresh cilantro, for garnish

2 tablespoons grated cotija cheese, for garnish

To Serve

6 to 10 corn tortillas, warmed

1 avocado, sliced

¼ cup chopped fresh cilantro, for garnish

1 lime, cut into wedges, for garnish

1. Make the taco filling: In a large skillet or pot, heat the olive oil over medium heat. Add the garlic and sauté for 2 to 3 minutes, until lightly browned and fragrant.

2. Add the beef, salt, cumin, chipotle chile powder, oregano, cloves, lime juice, and vinegar and stir to combine. Cover and simmer for 5 to 10 minutes, until the beef starts to crisp a bit on the bottom.

3. Make the pinto beans: In a small pot, heat the olive oil over medium heat. Add the onion and garlic and cook, stirring, for 3 minutes, or until the onion becomes slightly translucent and the garlic is fragrant.

4. Add the beans, lime juice, cumin, and salt and stir to combine. Bring to a low boil and cook, stirring occasionally, for about 5 minutes, until warmed through. Taste and season with more salt and lime juice, if needed. Just before serving, garnish with the cilantro, cotija, and additional red onion.

5. Uncover the beef and stir. Serve in the warmed tortillas, topped with the avocado, cilantro, and lime, with the pinto beans alongside.

CALORIES: 671   FAT: 33.8G   CARBS: 51G   PROTEIN: 45.2G

Garlic-Peppercorn Beef Roast

WITH ROASTED CARROTS AND MASHED POTATOES

/ RECIPE PAGE 124 /

ABOUT

If you're on the hunt for extremely comforting food, this meal series has you covered. A tender, perfectly cooked garlic-peppercorn roast is served with roasted carrots and velvety mashed potatoes. It's then topped with a simple but bold creamy horseradish sauce. The rest of the prepared roast is then put to good use in a rustic shredded beef ragout, served over buttered pappardelle pasta and topped with a liberal sprinkle of Parmesan cheese. Though these dinners remind me of special occasions, they're actually very easy to pull together.

- $$
- DAIRY-FREE OPTION
- EGG-FREE
- GLUTEN-FREE OPTION
- GRAIN-FREE OPTION
- LOW-CARB OPTION
- NUT-FREE
- FREEZER-FRIENDLY

Shredded Beef Ragout

OVER PAPPARDELLE PASTA

/ RECIPE PAGE 125 /

SUBSTITUTIONS

Make It Dairy-Free:

- **MEAL 1:** For the mashed potatoes, substitute ½ cup full-fat coconut milk for the sour cream and milk, and olive oil for the butter. Substitute mayo for the sour cream in the horseradish sauce.

- **MEAL 2:** Omit the Parmesan cheese.

Make It Gluten-Free:

- **MEAL 2:** Use a gluten-free pasta in place of the pappardelle (if you can find gluten-free pappardelle, even better!).

Make It Grain-Free:

- **MEAL 2:** Use zucchini noodles or cooked spaghetti squash in place of the pappardelle.

Make It Low-Carb:

- **MEAL 1:** Omit the mashed potatoes and make the fresh arugula salad on page 66 in their place.

- **MEAL 2:** Use zucchini noodles or cooked spaghetti squash in place of the pappardelle.

GARLIC-PEPPERCORN BEEF ROAST WITH ROASTED CARROTS AND MASHED POTATOES

Serves 4

Active time: 45 MINUTES

Total time: 3 HOURS 25 MINUTES

For the Garlic-Peppercorn Beef Roast

5 garlic cloves, minced

¼ cup extra-virgin olive oil

1 tablespoon fine sea salt

2 teaspoons coarsely cracked black peppercorns

1 (4-pound) beef chuck or shoulder roast

1 pound carrots, cut into 2-inch pieces

For the Mashed Potatoes

1 pound red or Yukon Gold potatoes, peeled and cut into 1-inch pieces

¼ cup sour cream

¼ cup milk or heavy cream

3 tablespoons salted butter

½ teaspoon fine sea salt

¼ teaspoon ground black pepper

For the Creamy Horseradish Sauce

½ cup sour cream

2 tablespoons prepared horseradish

1 tablespoon fresh lemon juice (from about ½ lemon)

½ teaspoon ground black pepper

1. Roast the beef: Preheat the oven to 350°F.

2. In a small bowl, stir together the garlic, olive oil, salt, and peppercorns.

3. Spread the garlic mixture over the beef roast. Place the beef in a roasting pan or baking dish and spread the carrots around it. Roast for 2½ to 3 hours, until the beef easily pulls apart with a fork and the carrots are tender.

4. Meanwhile, make the mashed potatoes: Put the potatoes in a medium saucepan and add water to cover. Cover the pot and bring to a boil over medium-high heat, then reduce the heat to maintain a low boil and cook for 10 to 15 minutes, until the potatoes are easily pierced with a fork. Drain the potatoes and return them to the pot.

5. Add the sour cream, milk, butter, salt, and pepper to the pot with the potatoes. Using a potato masher or a handheld mixer, mash the potatoes until smooth and well combined with the other ingredients. Keep warm until ready to serve.

6. Make the horseradish sauce: In a small bowl, stir together the sour cream, horseradish, lemon juice, and pepper. Stir in water 1 tablespoon at a time as needed to reach the desired consistency. Cover and refrigerate until ready to serve.

7. Remove the beef from the oven and transfer the meat to a cutting board. Let rest for 10 minutes. Cut the beef in half; shred one half (you should have about 3 cups), transfer to an airtight container, and refrigerate to use for Meal 2 (it will keep for up to 5 days). Cut the remaining beef across the grain into ½-inch-thick slices.

8. Serve the sliced beef topped with the creamy horseradish sauce, with the carrots and mashed potatoes alongside.

CALORIES: 595   FAT: 27.3G   CARBS: 37.1G   PROTEIN: 53.3G

SHREDDED BEEF RAGOUT OVER PAPPARDELLE PASTA

Serves 4

Active time: 15 MINUTES   **Total time:** 25 MINUTES

10 ounces dried pappardelle pasta

2 tablespoons salted butter

2 tablespoons extra-virgin olive oil

½ red onion, diced

2 garlic cloves, minced

1 (28-ounce) can crushed tomatoes

¼ cup red wine (or an additional 2 tablespoons balsamic vinegar)

2 tablespoons balsamic vinegar

1 tablespoon Italian seasoning

½ teaspoon fine sea salt

¼ teaspoon ground black pepper

About 3 cups shredded cooked beef (reserved from Meal 1; see page 124)

¼ cup shaved Parmesan cheese, for garnish

2 tablespoons chopped fresh parsley, for garnish

1. Bring a large pot of water to a boil. Add the pasta and cook according to the package instructions. Drain the pasta, return it to the pot, and add the butter right away; stir until the butter has melted (this helps prevent the noodles from sticking together).

2. In a medium pot, combine the olive oil, onion, and garlic. Cook over medium heat for about 5 minutes, until the onion is translucent and the garlic is fragrant.

3. Add the tomatoes, wine, vinegar, Italian seasoning, salt, pepper, and beef and stir to combine. Bring to a simmer and cook, stirring occasionally, for about 10 minutes, until the flavors have come together.

4. Serve the ragout over the buttered pasta, garnished with the Parmesan and parsley.

TIP

• Use your favorite pasta sauce in place of the homemade one for the shredded beef ragout.

CALORIES: 783   FAT: 34.1G   CARBS: 72G   PROTEIN: 47.7G

Herb-Crusted Beef Roast

WITH POTATOES AND CHOPPED VEGGIE SALAD

/ RECIPE PAGE 128 /

ABOUT

This dinner series takes me right back to my mom's kitchen, as these are two meals I grew up making and enjoying with her. The roast has a perfect herb crust and, for the first dinner, is served alongside some simply roasted potatoes and a bright and crunchy chopped veggie salad. The remaining roast is then transformed into my version of an incredibly satisfying beef stroganoff that's studded with just the right amount of mushrooms and served over egg noodles, exactly how Mom would do it.

▥ $$$

▥ DAIRY-FREE OPTION

▥ EGG-FREE OPTION

▥ GLUTEN-FREE OPTION

▥ GRAIN-FREE OPTION

▥ LOW-CARB OPTION

▥ NUT-FREE

Beef Stroganoff

WITH MUSHROOMS OVER EGG NOODLES

/ RECIPE PAGE 129 /

SUBSTITUTIONS

Make It Dairy-Free:

- **MEAL 1:** Omit the feta cheese from the chopped veggie salad.

- **MEAL 2:** Substitute full-fat coconut milk in place of the sour cream in the beef stroganoff.

Make It Egg-Free:

- **MEAL 2:** Use an egg-free pasta.

Make It Gluten-Free:

- **MEAL 2:** Serve the stroganoff over gluten-free tagliatelle or cooked rice in place of the egg noodles.

Make It Grain-Free:

- **MEAL 2:** Serve the stroganoff over zucchini noodles, cooked spaghetti squash, or mashed potatoes (see page 195) in place of the egg noodles.

Make It Low-Carb:

- **MEAL 1:** Omit the potatoes from the beef roast.

- **MEAL 2:** Serve the stroganoff over zucchini noodles or cooked spaghetti squash instead of the egg noodles.

HERB-CRUSTED BEEF ROAST WITH POTATOES AND CHOPPED VEGGIE SALAD

Serves 4

Active time: 40 MINUTES   **Total time:** 1 HOUR 20 MINUTES

For the Herb-Crusted Beef Roast

½ cup packed fresh herbs (rosemary, thyme, basil, dill—whatever is in season), finely chopped

4 tablespoons extra-virgin olive oil

1 teaspoon grated lemon zest

¼ cup fresh lemon juice (from about 2 lemons)

1 teaspoon garlic powder

1 tablespoon fine sea salt

½ teaspoon ground black pepper

1 (4-pound) beef round or sirloin roast

1 pound baby Yukon Gold potatoes

For the Chopped Veggie Salad

3 carrots, chopped

1 red bell pepper, chopped

1 yellow bell pepper, chopped

1 medium cucumber, chopped

½ red onion, chopped

½ cup crumbled feta cheese

¼ cup fresh lemon juice (from about 2 lemons)

2 tablespoons extra-virgin olive oil

½ teaspoon fine sea salt

¼ teaspoon ground black pepper

2 tablespoons chopped fresh dill, for serving

1 lemon, cut into wedges, for serving

1. Roast the beef: Preheat the oven to 350°F.

2. In a small bowl, stir together the chopped herbs, 2 tablespoons of the olive oil, the lemon zest, lemon juice, garlic powder, salt, and pepper.

3. Spread half the herb marinade over the beef roast and place the beef in a roasting pan or baking dish; reserve the remaining herb marinade for serving. Toss the potatoes with the remaining 2 tablespoons olive oil to coat and spread them around the beef.

4. Roast for about 1 hour, until an instant-read thermometer inserted into the beef reads 130°F for rare, 140°F for medium-rare, 150°F for medium, or 155° to 160°F for well done.

5. Meanwhile, make the salad: In a large bowl, combine the carrots, bell peppers, cucumber, onion, feta, lemon juice, olive oil, salt, and pepper. Toss to combine. Cover and refrigerate until ready to serve. Just before serving, garnish with the dill.

6. Remove the beef from the oven and transfer the meat to a cutting board. Let rest for 10 minutes. Cut the beef in half; thinly slice one half, then cut it into bite-size pieces (you should have about 4 cups), transfer to an airtight container, and refrigerate to use for Meal 2 (it will keep for up to 5 days). Cut the remaining beef across the grain into ½-inch-thick slices.

7. Divide the sliced beef among four plates and plate the potatoes and chopped veggie salad alongside. Drizzle the beef with the reserved herb marinade and serve, with the lemon wedges alongside for squeezing over the top.

TIP

- Substitute 2 tablespoons mixed dried herbs for the ½ cup packed fresh herbs.

CALORIES: 523   FAT: 22.8G   CARBS: 36.8G   PROTEIN: 47.3G

BEEF STROGANOFF WITH MUSHROOMS OVER EGG NOODLES

Serves 4

Active time: 30 MINUTES   **Total time:** 30 MINUTES

9 ounces uncooked wide egg noodles

4 tablespoons (½ stick) salted butter, or ¼ cup ghee or extra-virgin olive oil

1 white onion, diced

3 garlic cloves, minced

8 ounces baby bella mushrooms, sliced

About 4 cups bite-size pieces cooked beef (reserved from Meal 1; see page 128)

1½ cups beef broth

¾ cup sour cream

2 tablespoons fresh lemon juice (from 1 lemon)

2 tablespoons all-purpose flour

1 tablespoon coconut aminos

1 tablespoon Dijon mustard

1 teaspoon fine sea salt, plus more as needed

½ teaspoon ground black pepper, plus more as needed

Chopped fresh parsley, for garnish

1. Bring a large pot of water to a boil. Add the egg noodles and cook according to the package instructions.

2. In a large skillet, melt the butter over high heat. Add the onion and garlic, toss, and cook, stirring, for about 5 minutes, until the onion is translucent and the garlic is fragrant.

3. Add the mushrooms and cook until they have reduced in size, about 5 minutes.

4. Add the beef, broth, sour cream, lemon juice, flour, coconut aminos, mustard, salt, and pepper and stir to combine. Using a wooden spoon, scrape up any bits that are stuck to the bottom of the pan. Bring to a simmer and cook, stirring occasionally, for about 5 minutes, until the beef is heated through and the sauce has thickened. Taste and season with salt and pepper.

5. Serve the beef stroganoff over the egg noodles, garnished with parsley.

CALORIES: 522   FAT: 23.3G   CARBS: 29.9G   PROTEIN: 49.4G

Perfect Stovetop Steaks

WITH BAKED SWEET POTATOES AND SIMPLE SPINACH SALAD

/ RECIPE PAGE 132 /

ABOUT

This dinner series is right out of our family's regular meal rotation. I start by cooking about twice as many steaks as we need for one night. I serve half the steak fresh off the skillet, with a simple baked sweet potato and a fresh, crunchy spinach salad alongside. The rest of the steaks are then put to good use in the second dinner, a beef ramen noodle skillet. The steaks are thinly sliced and then tossed with noodles, crunchy veggies, and the most perfect sticky brown lo mein–style sauce. You are going to love these dinners!

$$

- $$$ — $$
- ▓ DAIRY-FREE OPTION
- ▓ EGG-FREE
- ▓ GLUTEN-FREE OPTION
- ▓ GRAIN-FREE OPTION
- ▓ LOW-CARB OPTION
- ▓ NUT-FREE

DINNER SERIES 26

MEAL 2

Beef Ramen Noodle Skillet

/ RECIPE PAGE 133 /

SUBSTITUTIONS

Make It Dairy-Free:

- **MEAL 1:** Omit the goat cheese from the spinach salad. For the sweet potatoes, substitute olive oil for the butter and omit the sour cream.

Make It Gluten-Free:

- **MEAL 2:** Use gluten-free ramen noodles or rice noodles.

Make It Grain-Free:

- **MEAL 2:** Use zucchini noodles (spiralized from about 4 medium zucchini) in place of the ramen noodles.

Make It Low-Carb:

- **MEAL 1:** Omit the apple from the simple spinach salad. Skip the baked sweet potatoes and make the roasted asparagus on page 92 to serve in their place.

- **MEAL 2:** Omit the coconut sugar from the sauce for the ramen skillet, and use zucchini noodles (spiralized from about 4 medium zucchini) in place of the noodles.

PERFECT STOVETOP STEAKS WITH BAKED SWEET POTATOES AND SIMPLE SPINACH SALAD

Serves 4

Active time: 30 MINUTES   **Total time:** 45 MINUTES

For the Baked Sweet Potatoes

2 teaspoons extra-virgin olive oil

4 small sweet potatoes

½ teaspoon fine sea salt

For the Perfect Stovetop Steaks

4 teaspoons ground coffee

4 teaspoons unsweetened cocoa powder

4 teaspoons coarse sea salt

1 teaspoon ground black pepper

2 tablespoons ghee or extra-virgin olive oil

3 pounds beef rib eye or strip steaks

For the Simple Spinach Salad

3 cups baby spinach

¼ cup thinly sliced red onion

1 apple, cored and cut into thin wedges

¼ cup crumbled goat cheese

¼ cup red wine vinegar

¼ cup extra-virgin olive oil

½ teaspoon fine sea salt

¼ teaspoon ground black pepper

To Serve

4 tablespoons (½ stick) salted butter, chilled

¼ cup sour cream

¼ teaspoon ground black pepper

1. Bake the sweet potatoes: Preheat the oven to 375°F.

2. Rub the olive oil over the sweet potatoes and spread them out on a rimmed baking sheet. Sprinkle with the salt. Roast for 45 minutes, or until they're soft when pinched.

3. Meanwhile, cook the steaks: In a small bowl, stir together the coffee, cocoa powder, salt, and pepper.

4. Pat the steaks dry and then coat each side with the coffee rub.

5. In a large cast-iron skillet or other pan, melt the ghee over high heat. Working in two batches, add the steaks, being careful not to let them touch each other in the pan. Cook the steaks for 3 to 4 minutes on the first side, until darkened, then flip them and cook for 3 to 4 minutes on the second side for medium-well. Transfer the steaks to a cutting board and let rest for 10 minutes before slicing. Cut the steaks across the grain into ½-inch-thick slices. Transfer half the sliced steak (1½ pounds) to an airtight container and refrigerate to use for Meal 2 (it will keep for up to 5 days). Set the remainder aside.

6. Make the salad: In a large bowl, combine the spinach, onion, apple, and goat cheese.

7. In a small bowl, whisk together the vinegar, olive oil, salt, and pepper. Pour the dressing over the salad and toss to combine.

8. To serve, divide the steak and sweet potatoes among four plates. Top each sweet potato with an equal amount of the butter and sour cream, and season with the pepper. Serve the steak and sweet potatoes with the salad alongside.

TIPS

- The steak used for the ramen skillet is best when reheated in a pan, so cook all the steak for both meals and use half later in the week.

- Microwave the sweet potatoes instead of waiting for them to bake! Just wrap them individually in damp paper towels and microwave for 5 to 7 minutes, until they're easily pierced with a fork.

CALORIES: 721   FAT: 46.1G   CARBS: 36.5G   PROTEIN: 44G

BEEF RAMEN NOODLE SKILLET

Serves 5

Active time: 20 MINUTES   **Total time:** 20 MINUTES

10 ounces dried ramen or lo mein noodles

¼ cup soy sauce or tamari

1 tablespoon coconut sugar or brown sugar

1 teaspoon toasted sesame oil

¼ teaspoon fish sauce

2 tablespoons extra-virgin olive oil

1½ pounds sliced cooked steak (reserved from Meal 1; see page 132)

4 ounces sliced baby bella mushrooms (about 1 cup)

1 red bell pepper, cut into thin strips

1 cup snow peas

½ cup shredded carrots

2 green onions, sliced on an angle, for garnish

1. Cook the noodles according to the package directions.

2. In a small jar, combine the soy sauce, sugar, sesame oil, and fish sauce. Seal the jar and shake to combine.

3. In a large skillet or wok, heat the olive oil over high heat. Add the steak, mushrooms, bell pepper, snow peas, and carrots. Cook, stirring continuously, until wilted, about 5 minutes.

4. Add the noodles and the sauce to the pan. Toss to combine.

5. Serve hot, garnished with the green onions.

CALORIES: 634   FAT: 16.9G   CARBS: 75G   PROTEIN: 49G

Tender Balsamic-Pepper Grilled Steaks

/ RECIPE PAGE 136 /

ABOUT

Whether it's actually summertime when you whip up this dinner series or you just want it to feel like summer in your kitchen, these meals will brighten your week. Steaks are marinated in a bold balsamic-pepper marinade and then served with grilled corn and our family's traditional bright, crunchy tomato and cucumber salad. Then the remaining steaks are cleverly transformed with street taco-inspired chipotle-in-adobo flavors. The beef is served on top of a crisp jicama-carrot slaw, all wrapped up in a corn tortilla. Don't forget chips and lime!

- $$
- DAIRY-FREE OPTION
- EGG-FREE
- GLUTEN-FREE
- GRAIN-FREE OPTION
- LOW-CARB OPTION
- NUT-FREE

Chipotle Beef Tacos

WITH JICAMA-CARROT SLAW

/ RECIPE PAGE 137 /

SUBSTITUTIONS

Make It Dairy-Free:

- **MEAL 1:** For the grilled corn, substitute olive oil for the butter.

Make It Grain-Free:

- **MEAL 1:** Omit the grilled corn served with the steaks.

- **MEAL 2:** Use grain-free tortillas or lettuce cups for the tacos.

Make It Low-Carb:

- **MEAL 1:** Omit the grilled corn served with the steaks.

- **MEAL 2:** Serve the chipotle beef and slaw in lettuce cups instead of tortillas.

TENDER BALSAMIC-PEPPER GRILLED STEAKS

Serves 4

Active time: 45 MINUTES

Total time: 45 MINUTES, PLUS 2 HOURS MARINATING TIME

For the Tender Balsamic-Pepper Grilled Steaks

3 pounds beef rib eye or strip steaks

½ cup balsamic vinegar

1 teaspoon ground black pepper, plus more as needed

2 teaspoons fine sea salt

Olive oil spray, for the grill

For the Lime-Butter Grilled Corn

Olive oil spray, for the grill

4 ears corn, husked

2 tablespoons salted butter, melted

2 tablespoons fresh lime juice (from 1 lime)

½ teaspoon fine sea salt

For the Fresh Tomato Salad

4 medium tomatoes

½ red onion, thinly sliced

1 large cucumber, halved lengthwise and cut into ½-inch-thick half-moons

¼ cup chopped fresh parsley, plus more for garnish

¼ cup apple cider vinegar

¼ cup extra-virgin olive oil

¼ teaspoon ground black pepper

¼ cup steak sauce, for serving

1 lime, cut into wedges, for serving

1. Cook the steaks: Place half the steaks in a large zip-top plastic bag, pour in the vinegar, and add the pepper. Seal the bag and marinate in the refrigerator for at least 2 hours or up to 24 hours.

2. When ready to cook the steaks, heat a grill to about 450°F.

3. Pull the steaks from the marinade. Season all the steaks including the unmarinated ones, with the salt and some pepper.

4. Spray the grill grates with olive oil spray. Place the steaks on the grill, with the balsamic-marinated steaks on one side and the unmarinated steaks on the other, close the lid and cook for about 4 minutes, then flip and cook for 3 to 4 minutes on the second side for medium-well.

5. Transfer the steaks to a cutting board and let rest for 10 minutes. Thinly slice the unmarinated steaks across the grain into ½-inch-thick slices (you should have about 3 cups), transfer to an airtight container, and refrigerate to use for Meal 2 (it will keep for up to 5 days). Slice the marinated steaks into four equal pieces and set aside until ready to serve.

6. Meanwhile, grill the corn: Spray the grill grates with olive oil spray.

7. Baste the corn with the melted butter and place it on the grill. Close the lid and grill for about 4 minutes, then flip the corn and cook for 3 to 4 minutes on the second side. Sprinkle with the lime juice and salt.

8. Make the salad: In a large bowl, mix the tomatoes, onion, cucumber, parsley, vinegar, olive oil, and pepper. Garnish with additional parsley, then cover and refrigerate until ready to serve.

9. Divide the steak among four plates and top with the steak sauce. Serve with the corn and salad on the side and the lime wedges for squeezing over the top.

CALORIES: 637   FAT: 33G   CARBS: 46.2G   PROTEIN: 45.4G

CHIPOTLE BEEF TACOS WITH JICAMA-CARROT SLAW

Serves 4

Active time: 30 MINUTES   **Total time:** 30 MINUTES

For the Jicama-Carrot Slaw

1 jicama, peeled and cut into thin matchsticks

1 cup shredded carrots

1 cup fresh cilantro, coarsely chopped

¼ cup fresh lime juice (from about 2 limes)

2 tablespoons extra-virgin olive oil

½ teaspoon fine sea salt

For the Chipotle Beef Tacos

1 canned chipotle chile in adobo sauce, plus 2 tablespoons adobo sauce from the can

¼ cup fresh lime juice (from about 2 limes)

About 3 cups sliced cooked steak (reserved from Meal 1; see page 136)

2 tablespoons extra-virgin olive oil

8 to 10 corn tortillas, warmed, for serving

1. Make the slaw: In a large bowl, combine the jicama, carrots, cilantro, lime juice, olive oil, and salt. Toss to combine, then cover and refrigerate until chilled before serving.

2. Make the tacos: In a blender, combine the chipotle chile, adobo sauce, and lime juice. Blend until smooth. Pour the marinade into a bowl and add the sliced steak; toss to coat.

3. In a large skillet, heat the olive oil over medium heat. Working in batches, add a layer of steak slices and cook for 3 to 4 minutes on one side, until it starts to crisp, then flip and cook for 2 to 3 minutes on the second side. Transfer to a bowl and repeat with the remaining steak.

4. Serve the steak in the warmed tortillas, topped with the slaw.

CALORIES: 533   FAT: 26.7G   CARBS: 33.8G   PROTEIN: 42.3G

Hearty Beef and Veggie Stew

/ RECIPE PAGE 140 /

ABOUT

If you've ever browned beef stew meat, you know that this flavor-building step is worth the work, but you might've wondered if there was a way to stretch your efforts. I cracked the code for you! These warming dinners are made from a single session spent browning beef, which then gets transformed in two totally different meals. The first is a rustic, filling beef and veggie stew. The second is a childhood favorite come to life in a whole new way: shredded beef tostadas. Refried beans are the base on the crispy flat tortilla, followed by the beef, cheese, then fresh toppings. You are going to love these two dinners.

▨ $$
▨ DAIRY-FREE OPTION
▨ EGG-FREE
▨ GLUTEN-FREE
▨ GRAIN-FREE
▨ NUT-FREE

Shredded Beef Tostadas

/ RECIPE PAGE 141 /

SUBSTITUTION

Make It Dairy-Free:

- **MEAL 2:** Omit the cheese on the tostadas, or substitute a vegan cheese.

Tip

- Stew meat is typically a cut of beef that gets more tender the longer it cooks, so cooking the beef for both meals means it will only get better when you use it for Meal 2.

HEARTY BEEF AND VEGGIE STEW

Serves 4

Active time: 45 MINUTES	**Total time:** 1 HOUR 40 MINUTES

2 tablespoons salted butter

3 pounds beef stew meat

½ yellow onion, finely chopped

4 garlic cloves, minced

3 cups beef broth

1 pound Yukon Gold potatoes, cut into 1-inch pieces

1 pound carrots, cut into 1-inch pieces

1 cup red wine, or ½ cup balsamic vinegar

1 (6-ounce) can tomato paste

2 sprigs rosemary

2 sprigs thyme

2 bay leaves

1 teaspoon fine sea salt, plus more as needed

¼ teaspoon ground black pepper, plus more as needed

1 cup frozen green peas

2 tablespoons fresh lemon juice (from 1 lemon)

¼ cup chopped fresh parsley, for garnish

1. In a large heavy-bottomed pot, melt 1 tablespoon of the butter over medium-high heat. Working in batches, add the beef and cook until browned on all sides, about 2 minutes per side. Transfer to a large bowl and repeat to brown the remaining beef. After the final batch, discard any excess fat in the pot. Melt the remaining 1 tablespoon butter in the same pot over medium heat. Add the onion and garlic and cook, stirring, for 3 to 5 minutes, until the onion is translucent and the garlic is fragrant. Transfer the cooked beef back to the pot along with the sautéed onion and garlic. Add the broth, then cover and cook for 1 hour, until the beef is tender and shreds easily with a fork. Remove half the beef (about 3 cups)

from the pot, transfer to a container, and refrigerate to use for Meal 2 (it will keep for up to 5 days).

2. Add the potatoes, carrots, wine, tomato paste, rosemary, thyme, bay leaves, salt, and pepper to the pot. Bring to a simmer, cover, and cook for 15 minutes, or until the potatoes are fork-tender.

3. Add the peas and lemon juice, bring back to a simmer, and cook for 5 minutes more. Taste and season with salt and pepper.

4. Serve the stew warm, garnished with the parsley.

VARIATION: INSTANT POT OPTION

Set your Instant Pot to the "Sauté" function and add the butter to the pot. Working in batches, add the beef and cook until browned on all sides, about 2 minutes per side. Transfer the meat to a large bowl and repeat to brown the remaining beef. Transfer the beef back to the pot along with the onion, garlic, and beef broth. Set to cook for 30 minutes on high pressure. Once the timer goes off, manually release the pressure, then remove half the beef (about 3 cups) from the pot and transfer to a container and refrigerate for Meal 2 (it will keep for up to 5 days). Continue to Step 2 in the recipe above.

CALORIES: 506	FAT: 10.7G	CARBS: 49.4G	PROTEIN: 46.7G

MEAL 2

SHREDDED BEEF TOSTADAS

Serves 4

Active time: 10 MINUTES **Total time:** 45 MINUTES

8 flour or corn tortillas

1 tablespoon extra-virgin olive oil

1 teaspoon fine sea salt

About 3 cups cooked beef stew meat (reserved from Meal 1; see page 140)

1 cup salsa verde

2 tablespoons fresh lime juice (from 1 lime)

½ teaspoon ground cumin

1 cup refried beans

¾ cup shredded Monterey Jack cheese

1 medium tomato, diced, for garnish

1 cup shredded lettuce, for garnish

1 avocado, diced, for garnish

¼ cup chopped fresh cilantro, for garnish

1. Preheat the oven to 400°F.

2. Place the tortillas on a rimmed baking sheet and brush on both sides with the olive oil, then sprinkle with ½ teaspoon of the salt. Bake for 5 minutes, then flip and bake the second side for 3 to 5 minutes, until browned and crisp.

3. In a large bowl, stir together the cooked beef, salsa, lime juice, cumin, and remaining ½ teaspoon salt.

4. Spread some refried beans evenly over each tostada, then top with the beef and shredded cheese. Bake for 5 minutes, until the cheese is melted.

5. Garnish with the diced tomato, shredded lettuce, avocado, and cilantro and serve.

TIP

- Save time by buying premade tostada shells instead of making your own.

CALORIES: 563   FAT: 29.1G   CARBS: 38.9G   PROTEIN: 40.7G

Beef Chili

WITH CHEDDAR CORN MUFFINS

/ RECIPE PAGE 144 /

ABOUT

Though you could absolutely make this dinner series all year long, to me it feels so appropriate for fall. It's exactly what I want during back-to-school season, when the temperatures just start to drop and tossing a football in the backyard with our kiddos consumes our afternoons. The first dinner is a hearty beef chili, a perfect canvas for all the toppings of your dreams, served alongside the most delicious corn bread muffins. If I weren't such a fan of the chili, I'd say that the corn bread muffins almost steal the show. The second dinner is my take on a hearty green curry that is served over fluffy white rice. The green curry sauce in this dinner is one of our household staples. It's just the right balance of creamy, spicy, briny, and bright from the citrus.

- $$$
- DAIRY-FREE OPTION
- EGG-FREE
- GLUTEN-FREE OPTION
- GRAIN-FREE OPTION
- LOW-CARB OPTION
- NUT-FREE
- FREEZER-FRIENDLY

Green Curry Beef Bowls

WITH WHITE RICE

/ RECIPE PAGE 145 /

/ RECIPE PAGE 145 /

SUBSTITUTIONS

Make It Dairy-Free:

- **MEAL 1:** Make the vegan corn bread on page 237 in place of the corn muffins and omit the sour cream topping for the chili.

Make It Gluten-Free:

- **MEAL 1:** Use a 1:1 gluten-free flour in the corn muffins.

Make It Grain-Free and Low-Carb:

- **MEAL 1:** Skip the corn muffins.

- **MEAL 2:** Substitute 4 cups cooked cauliflower rice for the white rice.

BEEF CHILI WITH CHEDDAR CORN MUFFINS

Serves 5

Active time: 30 MINUTES   **Total time:** 50 MINUTES

For the Beef Chili

1 tablespoon extra-virgin olive oil

4 pounds beef stew meat

1 cup beef broth

1 (15-ounce) can crushed tomatoes

2 tablespoons chili powder

1 tablespoon ground cumin

1 teaspoon onion powder

½ teaspoon fine sea salt

¼ teaspoon ground black pepper

For the Cheddar Corn Muffins

1½ cups finely ground cornmeal

1 cup all-purpose flour

1 tablespoon baking powder

1 teaspoon fine sea salt

1½ cups whole milk

⅓ cup salted butter, melted

¼ cup honey

1 large egg, beaten

1 cup shredded sharp cheddar cheese

½ cup finely chopped green onions

To Serve

¼ cup sour cream

¼ cup chopped green onions

¼ cup sliced pickled jalapeños

1. In a large heavy-bottomed pot, melt the olive oil over medium-high heat. Working in batches, add the beef and cook until browned on all sides, about 2 minutes per side. Transfer to a large bowl and repeat to brown the remaining beef. After the final batch, discard any excess fat in the pan. Transfer the cooked beef back to the pot along with the beef broth, then cover and cook for 1 hour, until the beef is tender and shreds easily with a fork. Remove half the beef (about 3 cups) from the pot, transfer to a container, and refrigerate for Meal 2 (it will keep for up to 5 days).

2. Meanwhile, make the corn muffins: Preheat the oven to 350°F. Line a standard muffin tin with paper liners.

3. In a large bowl, whisk together the cornmeal, flour, baking powder, and salt to combine.

4. Add the milk, melted butter, honey, and egg to the bowl and mix until a smooth batter forms. Stir in the cheese and green onions.

5. Distribute the batter evenly among the prepared muffin cups. Bake for 25 minutes, or until a toothpick inserted into the middle of a muffin comes out clean. Remove the corn muffins from the oven and let cool.

6. Return the remaining cooked beef to the pot and add the tomatoes, chili powder, cumin, onion powder, salt, and pepper. Stir to combine. Bring the mixture to a simmer, gently breaking up the pieces of stew meat with a spoon, and cook, stirring occasionally, for about 20 minutes, until slightly thickened.

7. Spoon the warm chili into bowls and top with the sour cream, green onions, and pickled jalapeños. Serve with the corn muffins alongside.

VARIATION: INSTANT POT OPTION

Set your Instant Pot to the "Sauté" function and add the olive oil to the pot. Working in batches, add the beef and cook until browned on all sides, about 2 minutes per side. Transfer to a large bowl and repeat to brown the remaining beef. Transfer the beef back to the pot along with the broth and set to cook for 30 minutes on high pressure. Once the timer goes off, manually release the pressure, then remove half the beef (about 3 cups) from the pot and transfer to a container and refrigerate for Meal 2. Then add the tomatoes, chili powder, cumin, onion powder, salt, and pepper. Cook on high pressure for 7 minutes, then manually release the pressure to remove the lid. Garnish and serve alongside the corn muffins.

CALORIES: 542   FAT: 21.9G   CARBS: 33G   PROTEIN: 57.4G

MEAL 2

GREEN CURRY BEEF BOWLS WITH WHITE RICE

Serves 4

Active time: 15 MINUTES   **Total time:** 25 MINUTES

1 cup uncooked white rice, rinsed

1 tablespoon ghee or extra-virgin olive oil

About 3 cups cooked beef stew meat (reserved from Meal 1; see page 144)

1 pound broccoli florets

1 (4-ounce) jar green curry paste

½ cup beef broth

1 (13.5-ounce) can full-fat coconut milk

2 tablespoons fresh lime juice (from 1 lime)

Fine sea salt, if needed

¼ cup chopped red onion, for garnish

¼ cup chopped fresh cilantro, for garnish

1. Cook the rice according to the package instructions.

2. Meanwhile, in a large saucepan, melt the ghee over medium heat. Add the cooked beef and the broccoli and stir to combine. Cook for about 5 minutes, until the broccoli starts to soften and the beef is warmed through.

3. Add the curry paste, broth, and coconut milk and stir to combine. Reduce the heat to medium-low, cover, and cook for 5 to 10 minutes to let the flavors combine. Add the lime juice, taste, and season with salt, if needed.

4. Serve the curry over the rice, garnished with the onion and cilantro.

TIPS

- If you want to simplify this meal, you can skip the rice altogether and enjoy a bowl of the green curry beef as is!
- Mix up your starches and try this green curry beef over quinoa or even rice noodles.

CALORIES: 681   FAT: 31.3G   CARBS: 54.8G   PROTEIN: 48G

pork

MEAL 1

Chorizo and Potato Taco Bake

WITH PINEAPPLE SALSA

/ RECIPE PAGE 150 /

ABOUT

Ground pork is center stage in this dinner series. What I love most about ground pork is its ability to take on big flavors with ease. After the pork needed for both dinners is browned, half is seasoned with my go-to chorizo spice blend and put to good use in a zesty and filling taco bake. Inspired by one of my favorite breakfast taco fillings, chorizo and potato, this taco-turned-casserole is rounded out with pineapple salsa, salty cotija cheese, and fresh cilantro. The second dinner is inspired by one of my favorite Thai salads: laab moo. Laab is a lime-forward ground meat salad that's freshened up with fresh mint, onion, cucumbers, and chile. Though I prefer to enjoy it with white rice, you can also serve it in lettuce cups.

- $$
- DAIRY-FREE OPTION
- EGG-FREE
- GLUTEN-FREE
- GRAIN-FREE OPTION
- NUT-FREE

Thai-Inspired Pork Salad Bowls

/ RECIPE PAGE 151 /

SUBSTITUTIONS

Make It Dairy-Free

- **MEAL 1:** Omit the cotija cheese from the chorizo potato bake.

Make It Grain-Free:

- **MEAL 2:** Substitute 4 cups cooked cauliflower rice for the salad bowls and omit the toasted rice powder.

CHORIZO AND POTATO TACO BAKE WITH PINEAPPLE SALSA

Serves 4

Active time: 40 MINUTES

Total time: 1 HOUR 15 MINUTES

For the Chorizo-Spiced Pork and Potato Bake

- 1½ pounds Yukon Gold potatoes, cut into ½-inch pieces
- 2 tablespoons extra-virgin olive oil
- 3 pounds ground pork
- 2 teaspoons fine sea salt
- 1 tablespoon chili powder
- 1 teaspoon paprika
- 1 teaspoon ground cumin
- 1 teaspoon dried oregano
- 2 tablespoons apple cider vinegar
- ¼ teaspoon ground black pepper

For the Pineapple Salsa

- 11 ounces fresh pineapple (about ⅓ whole small pineapple), peeled, cored, and cut into ¼-inch pieces
- ½ cup packed fresh cilantro leaves, coarsely chopped
- ¼ red onion, diced
- 1 large jalapeño, seeded and diced
- 1 garlic clove, minced
- 2 tablespoons fresh lime juice (from 1 lime)
- ½ teaspoon fine sea salt

To Serve

- 2 tablespoons grated cotija cheese
- ¼ cup chopped fresh cilantro, for garnish
- 1 lime, cut into wedges, for serving

1. Make the pork and potato bake: Preheat the oven to 375°F.

2. Spread the potatoes evenly over the bottom of a 2-quart baking dish. Drizzle with 1 tablespoon of the olive oil. Bake for 40 minutes, or until easily pierced with a fork.

3. Meanwhile, in a large skillet, combine the pork and 1 teaspoon of the salt. Cook over medium heat, breaking up the meat with a spoon as it cooks, for 10 to 15 minutes, until browned and crumbly. Transfer half the pork (about 3½ cups) to an airtight container and refrigerate to use for Meal 2 (it will keep for up to 5 days).

4. When the potatoes are finished baking, remove the baking dish from the oven and add the remaining cooked pork, remaining 1 tablespoon olive oil, the chili powder, paprika, cumin, oregano, vinegar, pepper, and remaining 1 teaspoon salt. Toss to combine. Return the baking dish to the oven and bake for 20 minutes more.

5. Meanwhile, make the pineapple salsa: In a small bowl, combine all the ingredients for the salsa and toss to combine. Set aside or cover and refrigerate until ready to serve.

6. Top the pork and potato bake with the pineapple salsa and cotija. Garnish with the cilantro and serve, with the lime wedges alongside for squeezing over the top.

TIP

- To save time, you can wrap the whole potatoes individually in wet paper towels and microwave them for 4 to 5 minutes to soften them, then dice them, transfer to a 2-quart baking dish, and proceed as directed in step 4.

CALORIES: 637   FAT: 36G   CARBS: 45.8G   PROTEIN: 36G

THAI-INSPIRED PORK SALAD BOWLS

Serves 4

Active time: 25 MINUTES   **Total time:** 25 MINUTES

¼ cup uncooked white rice, plus 1 cup for serving (optional)

1 tablespoon extra-virgin olive oil

About 3½ cups cooked ground pork (reserved from Meal 1; see page 150)

¼ cup thinly sliced red onion or shallots

2 tablespoons coarsely chopped fresh cilantro or basil leaves

2 tablespoons coarsely chopped fresh mint leaves, plus more for garnish

2 tablespoons fresh lime juice (from 1 lime)

2 tablespoons fish sauce

8 to 10 Bibb lettuce leaves, for serving (optional)

1 seedless cucumber, cut into thin rounds, for serving

1 lime, cut into wedges, for serving

1. If you'd like to serve the salad bowls with rice, rinse the 1 cup rice and cook it according to the package instructions.

2. In a large skillet, toast the remaining ¼ cup rice over medium heat, stirring continuously, for about 3 minutes, until lightly browned but not burned. Remove from the heat and transfer the rice to a coffee grinder or blender, and let sit for about 5 minutes, until cool. Grind the toasted rice into a fine powder and set aside.

3. In the same skillet, heat the olive oil over medium heat. Add the cooked pork and cook, stirring occasionally, for about 10 minutes, just until the pork is steaming hot again. Remove from the heat.

4. Add the onion, cilantro, mint, lime juice, fish sauce, and half the rice powder to the skillet with the pork and toss to combine.

5. Spoon the pork into bowls over the cooked rice, if using, or into lettuce cups and top with the cucumber slices. Garnish with the remaining toasted rice powder and additional fresh mint and serve with the lime wedges alongside for squeezing over the top.

TIPS

- Use ¼ cup store-bought toasted rice powder instead of toasting and grinding your own for the salad bowls. It can be found in most Asian markets or online.

- This recipe calls for a generous amount of fish sauce, which makes it distinctly Thai. If it's too much for your taste, you can reduce it to 1 tablespoon, or even less.

CALORIES: 634   FAT: 31.1G   CARBS: 52.8G   PROTEIN: 37.5G

ABOUT

This dinner series is another that hails directly from my own kitchen and dinner menu rotation. Ground pork is easy to flavor, so I've leaned on it to prepare a robust pork Bolognese for the first meal. I like to serve this fabulous sauce over buttered pasta, with an Italian-style salad alongside. The remaining pork is destined for my lemony sausage and veggie soup, the one soup I have made more times than any other. The name paints a clear picture of this refreshing soup. The broth is briny, with just enough lemon, the veggies are tender but not overcooked, and the pork offers flavor and filling protein. I love this series!

- ▨ $$
- ▨ DAIRY-FREE OPTION
- ▨ EGG-FREE
- ▨ GLUTEN-FREE OPTION
- ▨ GRAIN-FREE OPTION
- ▨ LOW-CARB OPTION
- ▨ NUT-FREE
- ▨ FREEZER-FRIENDLY

MEAL 1

Pork Bolognese Pasta

WITH ITALIAN SALAD

/ RECIPE PAGE 154 /

MEAL 2

Lemony Sausage

AND VEGGIE SOUP

/ RECIPE PAGE 155 /

SUBSTITUTIONS

Make It Dairy-Free:

- **MEAL 1:** Omit the Parmesan cheese from the Bolognese and substitute olive oil for the butter.

Make It Gluten- and Grain-Free:

- **MEAL 1:** Use a gluten-free spaghetti noodle for the Bolognese. You can also use 10 ounces of zucchini noodles or cooked spaghetti squash in place of the spaghetti noodles for the Bolognese.

Make It Low-Carb:

- **MEAL 1:** Use 10 ounces cooked zucchini noodles or a cooked spaghetti squash in place of the spaghetti noodles for the Bolognese.
- **MEAL 2:** Omit the potatoes from the soup.

MEAL 1

PORK BOLOGNESE PASTA WITH ITALIAN SALAD

Serves 4

Active time: 40 MINUTES	Total time: 40 MINUTES

3 pounds ground pork

1 teaspoon fine sea salt

12 ounces dried spaghetti

2 tablespoons salted butter

For the Bolognese Sauce

1 tablespoon extra-virgin olive oil

½ small red onion, diced

3 garlic cloves, minced

1 (28-ounce) can crushed tomatoes

½ cup red wine or beef broth

2 tablespoons Italian seasoning

½ teaspoon fine sea salt

¼ teaspoon ground black pepper

For the Italian Salad

¼ cup extra-virgin olive oil

¼ cup red wine vinegar

½ teaspoon fine sea salt

1 small head Bibb lettuce, cored and coarsely chopped

1 carrot, cut into thin rounds

½ red onion, thinly sliced

6 to 8 radishes, thinly sliced

¼ teaspoon ground black pepper

¼ cup shaved Parmesan cheese, for serving

1 tablespoon chopped fresh parsley, for garnish

1. Bring a large pot of water to a boil for the pasta.

2. In a large skillet, combine the pork and salt. Cook over medium heat, breaking up the meat with a spoon as it cooks, for 10 to 15 minutes, until browned and crumbly. Transfer half the pork (about 3½ cups) to an airtight container and refrigerate to use for Meal 2 (it will keep for up to 5 days).

3. Add the spaghetti to the boiling water and cook according to the package instructions. Drain the pasta and rinse it under cool water to stop it from sticking, then return it to the pot. Add the butter and lightly toss to coat the pasta, then set aside.

4. Meanwhile, make the Bolognese sauce: In a large saucepan, heat the olive oil over medium heat. Add the onion and garlic and cook, stirring, for 3 to 4 minutes, until the mixture is fragrant and the onion is translucent.

5. Add the tomatoes, wine, Italian seasoning, salt, and pepper. Bring to a simmer, then cook, stirring regularly, for 5 minutes. Add the cooked pork, stir to combine, and simmer for 5 minutes more.

6. Meanwhile, make the salad: In a small bowl, whisk together the olive oil, vinegar, and salt.

7. Divide the lettuce among four salad plates and top evenly with the carrot, onion, and radishes. Drizzle with the dressing and finish with the pepper.

8. Divide the pasta among four bowls or pasta plates and spoon the Bolognese sauce over the top. Top with the Parmesan, garnish with the parsley, and serve with the salad alongside.

TIP

- Instead of making the Bolognese from scratch, you can add the pork to your favorite premade spaghetti sauce, either store-bought or some homemade sauce you have on hand in the fridge or freezer. Just bring the sauce to a simmer, then stir in the pork and cook for 5 minutes, or until the pork is heated through.

CALORIES: 788	FAT: 38.1G	CARBS: 74.2G	PROTEIN: 39.7G

MEAL 2

LEMONY SAUSAGE AND VEGGIE SOUP

Serves 5

Active time: 20 MINUTES   **Total time:** 35 MINUTES

2 tablespoons extra-virgin olive oil

1 small onion, diced

4 garlic cloves, minced

About 3½ cups cooked ground pork (reserved from Meal 1; see page 154)

4 carrots, cut into rounds

1 pound Yukon Gold potatoes, cut into ½-inch pieces (optional)

1 red bell pepper, coarsely chopped

1 yellow bell pepper, coarsely chopped

6 cups chicken broth or beef broth

½ teaspoon fine sea salt, plus more if needed

1 bunch curly kale, leaves stemmed and coarsely chopped

¼ cup fresh lemon juice (from about 2 lemons)

½ teaspoon ground black pepper, for garnish

1 lemon, cut into wedges, for serving

1. In a large pot, heat the olive oil over medium heat. Add the onion and garlic and cook, stirring, for 3 to 5 minutes, until the mixture is fragrant and the onion is translucent.

2. Add the cooked pork, carrots, potatoes, bell peppers, broth, and salt and stir to combine. Bring to a simmer, then cook for 15 minutes, or until the potatoes are fork-tender.

3. Add the kale and lemon juice and cook, stirring occasionally, until the kale is bright green and wilted, about 3 minutes. Taste and season with more salt, if needed, then remove from the heat.

4. Ladle the soup into bowls. Garnish with the black pepper and serve with the lemon wedges alongside for squeezing over the soup.

CALORIES: 485   FAT: 28.4G   CARBS: 29.9G   PROTEIN: 29.9G

Madras-Inspired Curry Meatballs

/ RECIPE PAGE 158 /

ABOUT

For this ground pork-focused series, we're taking a peek at the versatility of meatballs. The pork is simply seasoned, formed into meatballs, and then baked. Half the meatballs will be used for an unexpected first dinner: Madras-inspired meatballs. The Indian-style curry powder in the dish is mild enough for the whole family, but makes these meatballs *sing* with so much fabulous flavor. The second dinner is a minestrone soup inspired by Little Italy, a restaurant my family frequented in my childhood. We always enjoyed a bowl of minestrone soup before our main course, and it was my favorite part of the meal. Packed with beautiful veggies and the most delicious broth, I recommend serving this soup with a hearty slice of crusty bread.

- $$
- DAIRY-FREE
- EGG-FREE
- GLUTEN-FREE OPTION
- GRAIN-FREE OPTION
- NUT-FREE
- FREEZER-FRIENDLY

MEAL 2

Minestrone Soup

/ RECIPE PAGE 159 /

Make It Gluten-Free:

- **MEAL 2:** Use gluten-free pasta shells in the minestrone.

Make It Grain-Free:

- **MEAL 2:** Omit the pasta shells in the minestrone.

MEAL 1

MADRAS-INSPIRED CURRY MEATBALLS

Serves 5

Active time: 40 MINUTES   **Total time:** 40 MINUTES

1 cup uncooked white rice, rinsed

For the Meatballs

3 pounds ground pork

1 tablespoon fine sea salt

½ teaspoon ground black pepper

For the Madras-Inspired Curry Sauce

1 tablespoon ghee or olive oil

1 small yellow onion, diced

1 tablespoon grated fresh ginger

3 garlic cloves, minced

1 tablespoon Madras curry powder (use regular curry powder for less spice)

2 teaspoons garam masala

1 teaspoon ground turmeric

1 teaspoon ground coriander

1 teaspoon ground cumin

½ teaspoon ground cinnamon

¼ to ½ teaspoon cayenne pepper, to taste

1 (15-ounce) can tomato sauce

1 (13.5-ounce) can full-fat coconut milk

½ teaspoon fine sea salt, plus more if needed

¼ cup fresh cilantro sprigs, for garnish

1. Preheat the oven to 400°F.

2. Cook the rice according to the package instructions.

3. Make the meatballs: In a large bowl, combine the ground pork, salt, and pepper. Roll the seasoned pork into roughly 1 tablespoon-size balls and place them on a rimmed baking sheet, spacing them evenly apart. (You should have about 36 meatballs.)

4. Bake for 20 minutes, or until the meatballs are browned but not burned. Remove from the oven. Transfer half the meatballs (about 18) to an airtight container and refrigerate to use for Meal 2 (it will keep for up to 5 days). Set the remainder aside.

5. Meanwhile, make the curry sauce: In a large skillet, melt the ghee over medium heat. Add the onion and cook, stirring, for 5 minutes, or until translucent. Add the ginger and garlic and cook, stirring, for 2 minutes more, or until fragrant.

6. Sprinkle the curry powder, garam masala, turmeric, coriander, cumin, cinnamon, and ¼ teaspoon of the cayenne over the onion-garlic mixture and stir to combine. Cook, stirring, for 1 to 2 minutes, until fragrant.

7. Add the tomato sauce, coconut milk, and salt and stir to combine, then taste the sauce and add more salt and/or cayenne, if desired. Add the meatballs to the sauce and cook for 5 minutes, or until the meatballs are warmed through.

8. Serve the meatballs and curry sauce over the rice, garnished with the cilantro.

CALORIES: 649   FAT: 41.5G   CARBS: 40.8G   PROTEIN: 30.3G

MEAL 2

MINESTRONE SOUP

Serves 5

Active time: 25 MINUTES   **Total time:** 45 MINUTES

2 tablespoons extra-virgin olive oil

1 small onion, diced

4 garlic cloves, minced

5 celery stalks, chopped

5 carrots, cut into rounds

1 (6-ounce) can tomato paste

1 (28-ounce) can diced tomatoes, drained

2 medium sweet potatoes, peeled and cut into ½-inch pieces (optional)

1 (15-ounce) can kidney beans, drained and rinsed

1 cup dried pasta shells

About 18 cooked meatballs (reserved from Meal 1; see page 158)

6 cups chicken broth or beef broth

1 pound green beans, trimmed and cut into 1-inch pieces

2 tablespoons fresh lemon juice (from 1 lemon)

½ teaspoon fine sea salt, plus more if needed

½ teaspoon ground black pepper, for garnish

2 tablespoons chopped fresh parsley, for garnish

1. In a large pot, heat the olive oil over medium heat. Add the onion and garlic and cook, stirring, for 3 to 5 minutes, until the mixture is fragrant and the onion is translucent.

2. Add the celery, carrots, tomato paste, diced tomatoes, sweet potatoes (if using), kidney beans, pasta, and meatballs and stir to combine. Pour in the broth and bring it to a simmer, then cook, stirring occasionally, for 15 minutes.

3. Add the green beans, lemon juice, and salt and stir to combine. Cook, stirring occasionally, for 3 minutes more, or until the green beans are tender and bright green. Taste and season with additional salt, if desired, then remove from the heat.

4. Ladle the soup into bowls, garnish with the pepper and parsley, and serve.

CALORIES: 644   FAT: 29.5G   CARBS: 61.8G   PROTEIN: 37.9G

Slow Cooker Balsamic Pork Roast

WITH SCALLOPED POTATOES AND EASY STEAMED BROCCOLI

/ RECIPE PAGE 162 /

ABOUT

While I love a pork roast dinner, roasts often yield so much more meat than my family can eat before food boredom sets in. As such, I've grown accustomed to creatively transitioning the leftover cooked pork into an entirely new and different dinner. In this meal series, I'm showcasing a pork roast flavored with balsamic vinegar. For the first meal, this roast is served alongside the easiest and most flavorful scalloped potatoes. The remaining pork roast is then used to make the most delicious pulled pork sandwiches, complete with a creamy coleslaw.

- $$
- DAIRY-FREE OPTION
- EGG-FREE OPTION
- GLUTEN-FREE OPTION
- GRAIN-FREE OPTION
- LOW-CARB OPTION
- NUT-FREE

Pulled Pork Sandwiches

WITH CLASSIC CREAMY SLAW

/ RECIPE PAGE 163 /

SUBSTITUTIONS

Make It Dairy-Free:

- **MEAL 1:** Omit the scalloped potatoes and serve with simple baked potatoes with toppings of choice (see page 43) instead.

Make It Egg-Free:

- **MEAL 2:** Use an equal amount of vegan mayonnaise or plain whole-milk Greek yogurt in place of the mayonnaise in the creamy coleslaw.

Make It Gluten-Free:

- **MEAL 2:** Use gluten-free buns for the pulled pork sandwiches.

Make It Grain-Free:

- **MEAL 2:** Omit the buns for the pulled pork sandwiches and make pulled pork bowls by serving the pork directly over the slaw.

Make It Low-Carb:

- **MEAL 1:** Omit the scalloped potatoes and serve with either a double quantity of steamed broccoli, or the side salad on page 51 instead.

MEAL 1

SLOW COOKER BALSAMIC PORK ROAST WITH SCALLOPED POTATOES AND EASY STEAMED BROCCOLI

Serves 4

Active time: 25 MINUTES

Total time: 4 HOURS 30 MINUTES

For the Slow Cooker Balsamic Pork Roast

1 tablespoon fine sea salt

½ teaspoon ground black pepper

1 (3- to 4-pound) pork loin roast

¼ cup balsamic vinegar

For the Scalloped Potatoes

1 pound Yukon Gold potatoes, thinly sliced

2 tablespoons salted butter, melted

1 teaspoon garlic powder

1 teaspoon fine sea salt

½ teaspoon dried thyme

½ teaspoon dried sage

½ teaspoon ground black pepper

½ cup heavy cream

1 cup shredded mozzarella cheese

For the Easy Steamed Broccoli

16 ounces broccoli florets (from about 3 small heads)

1 tablespoon salted butter

½ teaspoon fine sea salt

¼ teaspoon ground black pepper

1. Cook the pork: Rub the salt and pepper over the pork. Place the pork in a slow cooker and pour the vinegar over the top. Cover and cook on high for 4 hours.

2. About an hour before the pork is done, make the scalloped potatoes: Preheat the oven to 375°F.

3. In a 2-quart square baking dish, toss the potatoes with the melted butter, garlic powder, salt, thyme, sage, and pepper. Arrange the potato slices in even layers in the baking dish, overlapping the potatoes in each layer slightly, then pour the cream over the top. Cover with a lid or aluminum foil and bake for 30 minutes. Uncover the baking dish, top the potatoes evenly with the cheese, and bake, uncovered, for 15 minutes more, or until the cheese is bubbling.

4. Just before serving, steam the broccoli: Place the broccoli in a large glass bowl and add about ¼ cup water. Cover with a microwave-safe lid or plastic wrap and microwave on high for 5 minutes, or until the broccoli is tender. (Alternatively, place the broccoli in a medium pot and add ¼ cup water. Bring the water to a simmer over medium heat, then cover and cook the broccoli for 10 minutes, or until tender.) Drain the broccoli and transfer to a serving dish. Add the butter, salt, and pepper and gently toss to combine. Cover and keep hot until serving time.

5. When the pork is done cooking, baste it with the vinegar mixture in the slow cooker. Transfer the pork to a cutting board and cut it in half. Slice one portion and set it aside. Shred the remaining pork either with two forks or using a stand mixer (you should have about 3 cups), then transfer it to an airtight container and refrigerate to use for Meal 2 (it will keep for up to 5 days).

6. Serve the sliced pork with the scalloped potatoes and broccoli alongside.

TIP

- Use a mandoline or a food processor fitted with a slicing disk to quickly slice the potatoes for the scalloped potatoes.

CALORIES: 556   FAT: 25.7G   CARBS: 31.9G   PROTEIN: 49.6G

PULLED PORK SANDWICHES WITH CLASSIC CREAMY SLAW

Serves 4

Active time: 10 MINUTES   **Total time:** 15 MINUTES

For the Classic Creamy Slaw

½ cup mayonnaise

2 tablespoons fresh lemon juice (from 1 lemon)

1 tablespoon honey

½ teaspoon fine sea salt

¼ teaspoon ground black pepper

4 cups coleslaw mix (or a broccoli slaw mix)

For the Pulled Pork Sandwiches

1 cup barbecue sauce

About 3 cups shredded cooked pork (reserved from Meal 1; see page 162)

4 hamburger buns, toasted

¼ cup thinly sliced red onion, for garnish

Pickle spears, for serving

1. Make the slaw: In a medium bowl, whisk together the mayonnaise, lemon juice, honey, salt, and pepper until smooth. Add the coleslaw mix and toss to coat. Cover and refrigerate while you make the pulled pork sandwiches (the slaw is best served chilled, and can be prepared up to 3 days in advance and kept refrigerated).

2. Make the sandwiches: In a medium saucepan, combine the barbecue sauce and shredded pork. Cook over medium heat for 5 minutes, or until the pork is warmed through.

3. Serve the pork on the buns, topped with the onion, pickle spears, and creamy slaw.

TIPS

- You can use store-bought sauce for the pulled pork if you're short on time.
- Even if you're not looking for a low-carb meal option, this meal sans bun makes for a really fast and easy dinner. Just top a heaping serving of the slaw with the pulled pork filling for a satisfying dinner.

CALORIES: 649   FAT: 31.2G   CARBS: 43.5G   PROTEIN: 39.5G

Bacon-Wrapped Pork Roast

WITH PURPLE CABBAGE AND SWEET POTATOES

/ RECIPE PAGE 166 /

ABOUT

This dinner series is so delicious! The featured protein weaving the two dishes together is a bacon-wrapped pork roast. The bacon helps to infuse even more flavor into the roast and contributes great texture that both dinners benefit from. The first dinner showcases the roast as is, with a side of roasted purple cabbage (my favorite way to cook cabbage) and some classic sweet potatoes. The second dinner is an incredibly tasty crispy ginger pork stir-fry, complete with crunchy carrots and a side of fluffy white rice.

▧ $

▧ DAIRY-FREE

▧ EGG-FREE

▧ GLUTEN-FREE OPTION

▧ GRAIN-FREE OPTION

▧ LOW-CARB OPTION

▧ NUT-FREE

Crispy Ginger Pork Stir-Fry

/ RECIPE PAGE 167 /

SUBSTITUTIONS

Make It Gluten-Free:

- **MEAL 2:** Substitute gluten-free tamari for the soy sauce in the stir-fry.

Make It Grain-Free:

- **MEAL 2:** Substitute tamari or coconut aminos for the soy sauce in the stir-fry and use 4 cups cooked cauliflower rice in place of the white rice.

Make It Low-Carb:

- **MEAL 1:** Omit the sweet potatoes and double the amount of cabbage in their place.

- **MEAL 2:** Substitute 4 cups cooked cauliflower rice for the white rice.

Tip

- Avoid using thick-cut bacon on the pork roast. A more thinly sliced bacon is easier to wrap and crisps up better.

BACON-WRAPPED PORK ROAST WITH PURPLE CABBAGE AND SWEET POTATOES

Serves 4

Active time: 20 MINUTES

Total time: 1 HOUR 30 MINUTES

1 (3- to 4-pound) pork loin roast

1 pound thinly sliced bacon

2 tablespoons extra-virgin olive oil

½ head purple cabbage, cut into 4 large wedges

3 large sweet potatoes, peeled and cut into 3-inch pieces

1 teaspoon fine sea salt

½ teaspoon ground black pepper

2 tablespoons fresh lemon juice (from 1 lemon)

2 tablespoons chopped fresh parsley, for garnish

1 lemon, cut into wedges, for serving

1. Preheat the oven to 325°F.

2. Wrap the entire pork roast with the bacon slices, securing the bacon with toothpicks or by weaving the pieces together. Place the bacon-wrapped pork in a large (4-quart) baking dish.

3. Rub the olive oil over the cabbage wedges and sweet potato pieces. Arrange the cabbage and sweet potatoes around the pork, then season everything with the salt and pepper.

4. Cover the baking dish with its lid or tightly with aluminum foil and bake for 1 hour, until the bacon is crisped and the sweet potatoes and cabbage are tender. Remove from the oven and transfer the roast to a cutting board, tent it with foil, and let it rest for 10 minutes before slicing.

5. Slice the pork into ¼-inch-thick pieces. Then cut half the sliced pork into 2-inch-long pieces. Transfer the 2-inch-long pieces (3 cups) to an airtight container and refrigerate to use for Meal 2 (it will keep for up to 5 days).

6. Arrange the remaining sliced pork, the cabbage, and the sweet potatoes on a serving platter. Sprinkle the lemon juice over the meat, garnish with the parsley, and serve, with the lemon wedges alongside for squeezing over the top.

CALORIES: 614   FAT: 33.5G   CARBS: 32.4G   PROTEIN: 46.5G

CRISPY GINGER PORK STIR-FRY

Serves 4

Active time: 25 MINUTES   **Total time:** 25 MINUTES

1 cup uncooked white rice, rinsed

3 tablespoons soy sauce

1 tablespoon honey

1 tablespoon rice vinegar

½ teaspoon fish sauce

2 tablespoons ghee or salted butter

3 cups sliced cooked pork (reserved from Meal 1; see page 166; it's okay if the bacon is included)

1 teaspoon garlic powder

1 teaspoon ground ginger

1 cup matchstick-cut carrots

1 bunch green onions, cut into 2-inch-long pieces

1 teaspoon white sesame seeds, for garnish

1 lime, cut into wedges, for serving

1. Cook the rice according to the package instructions.

2. In a small bowl, whisk together the soy sauce, honey, vinegar, and fish sauce. Set aside.

3. In a large skillet, melt the ghee over high heat. Add the cooked pork, sprinkle with the garlic powder and ginger, and toss to combine. Arrange the pieces of pork in an even layer in the pan and sear for 2 to 3 minutes, until browned on the bottom, then flip and sear for 2 to 3 minutes on the second side.

4. Add the soy sauce mixture, carrots, and green onions and toss to combine with the pork. Cook for about 5 minutes, until the carrots are just slightly wilted, then remove from the heat.

5. Divide the rice among four plates or bowls and top with the stir-fry. Garnish with the sesame seeds and serve, with the lime wedges alongside for squeezing over the top.

CALORIES: 496   FAT: 13.5G   CARBS: 47.5G   PROTEIN: 43.3G

Butter-Garlic Pork Roast

WITH GOAT CHEESE PASTA AND SWISS CHARD SALAD

/ RECIPE PAGE 170 /

/ RECIPE PAGE 170 /

DINNER SERIES 35

ABOUT

This dinner series is an all-star. The protein that weaves the two dinners together is a perfectly cooked, incredibly flavorful butter-garlic pork roast. It's served with a goat cheese gravy (brace yourself, this gravy is *good*) over linguine in the first dinner. A fresh Swiss chard salad with a tangy, lemony dressing is served alongside. For the second dinner, the remaining pork gets a total makeover into my favorite tacos of all time: tacos al pastor. I've enjoyed a *lot* of these tacos over the years, and this marinade, these toppings, and these charro beans on the side are my favorite combination.

▒ $$
▒ EGG-FREE
▒ GLUTEN-FREE OPTION
▒ NUT-FREE

MEAL 2
Tacos al Pastor
WITH CHARRO BEANS
/ RECIPE PAGE 171 /

SUBSTITUTION

Make It Gluten-Free:

- **MEAL 1:** Use a gluten-free pasta for the goat cheese pasta.

BUTTER-GARLIC PORK ROAST WITH GOAT CHEESE PASTA AND SWISS CHARD SALAD

Serves 4

Active time: 35 MINUTES

Total time: 1 HOUR 20 MINUTES

For the Butter-Garlic Pork Roast

3 tablespoons salted butter, at room temperature

4 garlic cloves, minced

1 teaspoon fine sea salt

½ teaspoon ground black pepper

1 (3- to 4-pound) pork loin roast

For the Simple Lemony Swiss Chard Salad

1 bunch Swiss chard, leaves stemmed and coarsely chopped

2 tablespoons fresh lemon juice (from 1 lemon)

2 tablespoons extra-virgin olive oil

¼ teaspoon fine sea salt

¼ teaspoon ground black pepper

For the Goat Cheese Pasta

9 ounces dried linguine

2 tablespoons extra-virgin olive oil

4 ounces goat cheese

1 cup chicken broth

2 tablespoons fresh lemon juice (from 1 lemon)

2 tablespoons finely chopped fresh chives, for garnish

1. Cook the pork: Preheat the oven to 325°F.

2. In a small bowl, mix the butter, garlic, salt, and pepper. Spread the butter mixture over the pork. Place the pork in the center of a 4-quart Dutch oven with a heavy fitted lid. Cover and bake for 1 hour.

3. Meanwhile, make the salad: Place the chard in a large bowl. Drizzle with the lemon juice and olive oil and season with the salt and pepper. Toss to coat the chard, then set aside until ready to serve (or cover and refrigerate to serve chilled).

4. Make the goat cheese pasta: Bring a large pot of water to a boil. Add the linguine and cook according to the package instructions. Drain the pasta, return it to the pot, and toss with the olive oil to prevent sticking.

5. When the pork is done, remove the baking dish from the oven. Transfer the pork to a cutting board, tent it with aluminum foil, and let it rest for 10 minutes. Set the pot with the drippings on the stovetop over medium heat.

6. Add the goat cheese, broth, and lemon juice to the pot with the drippings and whisk until smooth, breaking up the cheese and scraping up the browned bits from the bottom of the pot. Bring to a simmer, then cook for 3 to 4 minutes, stirring occasionally, until the goat cheese is completely melted and the sauce is slightly thickened. Toss the linguine with the sauce.

7. Meanwhile, cut the pork in half; transfer one portion (about 3 cups) to an airtight container and refrigerate to use for Meal 2 (it will keep for up to 5 days). Slice the remaining portion.

8. Divide the linguine among four plates and top evenly with the sliced pork. Garnish with the chives and serve with the chard salad on the side.

CALORIES: 712   FAT: 32.4G   CARBS: 50.7G   PROTEIN: 53G

MEAL 2

TACOS AL PASTOR WITH CHARRO BEANS

Serves 5

Active time: 45 MINUTES   **Total time:** 45 MINUTES

For the Al Pastor Taco Filling

½ cup fresh orange juice

4 tablespoons (½ stick) salted butter, melted

3 tablespoons sauce from one 3.5-ounce can of chipotle chiles in adobo sauce

2 garlic cloves

1 tablespoon dried oregano

½ teaspoon fine sea salt

About 3 cups cooked pork (reserved from Meal 1; see page 170), cut into 1-inch-long, ¼-inch-thick pieces

1 cup chopped (½-inch pieces) fresh pineapple

For the Charro Beans

8 ounces sliced bacon, cut crosswise into 1-inch-wide pieces

½ small yellow onion, diced

2 garlic cloves, minced

1 jalapeño, seeded and diced

1 teaspoon ground cumin

½ teaspoon fine sea salt

½ teaspoon dried oregano

2 (15-ounce) cans pinto beans, drained and rinsed

4 cups chicken broth

To Serve

10 corn tortillas, warmed

¼ red onion, finely chopped

½ cup plus 2 tablespoons fresh cilantro sprigs, for garnish

1 lime, cut into wedges

1. Make the taco filling: Preheat the oven to 400°F.

2. Put the orange juice, melted butter, adobo sauce, garlic, oregano, and salt in a blender and blend until smooth. Pour the mixture into a large bowl, add the pork, and toss to coat. Spread the pork evenly over a rimmed baking sheet and sprinkle the pineapple over the pork. Bake for 25 minutes, or until the tops of the pork and pineapple pieces are starting to darken in color.

3. Meanwhile, make the charro beans: In a large pot, combine the bacon and onion and cook over medium heat, stirring occasionally, for 8 to 10 minutes, until the bacon is crispy and the onion has darkened in color. Add the garlic and cook, stirring, for 2 minutes more. Add the jalapeño, cumin, salt, oregano, beans, and broth and stir to combine. Bring to a simmer, then cook for 10 minutes, stirring occasionally, until the broth has thickened slightly. Keep warm until ready to serve.

4. Top the tortillas with the pork and pineapple, onion, and ½ cup of the cilantro and plate the charro beans on the side, garnished with the remaining 2 tablespoons cilantro. Serve with the lime wedges alongside for squeezing over the top.

TIP

• If desired, you can substitute simple black beans or pinto beans for the charro beans.

CALORIES: 656   FAT: 28.4G   CARBS: 53.6G   PROTEIN: 46.2G

MEAL 1

Perfect Carnitas

WITH ROASTED MEXICAN STREET CORN

/ RECIPE PAGE 174 /

ABOUT

I've boldly titled the first dinner in this series Perfect Carnitas because they really are perfect. Plenty of lime juice, butter, and salt are involved in cooking the pork, which gets shredded and served with roasted Mexican street corn, creamy salsa verde, and lots of fresh toppings. The remaining shredded pork is then tossed with a sticky honey-garlic sauce for a dinner that curbs any craving I ever have for Chinese takeout. I like to top the honey-garlic pork with sesame seeds and green onion and enjoy it with plenty of white rice. You'll notice that I use a pressure cooker, specifically the Instant Pot, to cook the pork shoulder because I have found that it saves tremendously on time.

$

DAIRY-FREE OPTION

EGG-FREE OPTION

GLUTEN-FREE OPTION

GRAIN-FREE OPTION

NUT-FREE

MEAL 2

Sticky Honey-Garlic Pork

WITH WHITE RICE

/ RECIPE PAGE 175 /

SUBSTITUTIONS

Make It Dairy-Free:

- **MEAL 1:** Substitute extra-virgin olive oil for the butter in the carnitas, ½ cup coconut cream for the sour cream in the salsa verde, and omit the cotija cheese.

- **MEAL 2:** Substitute extra-virgin olive oil for the butter.

Make It Egg-Free:

- **MEAL 1:** Substitute vegan mayo or extra-virgin olive oil for the mayonnaise on the Mexican street corn.

Make It Gluten-Free:

- **MEAL 2:** Substitute gluten-free tamari for the soy sauce.

Make It Grain-Free

- **MEAL 1:** Omit the street corn and make a tomato avocado salad (see page 35) instead. Use grain-free tortillas or lettuce wraps in place of the corn tortillas.

- **MEAL 2:** Substitute tamari for the soy sauce in the honey-garlic pork, and serve over 4 cups cooked cauliflower rice instead of white rice.

Pork **173**

MEAL 1

PERFECT CARNITAS WITH ROASTED MEXICAN STREET CORN

Serves 5

Active time: 40 MINUTES

Total time: 2 HOURS 20 MINUTES TO 8 HOURS 50 MINUTES, DEPENDING ON METHOD USED

For the Perfect Carnitas

1 (5-pound) pork shoulder, cut into 4 or 5 pieces

1 tablespoon plus 2 teaspoons fine sea salt

4 tablespoons (½ stick) salted butter, melted

¼ cup fresh lime juice (from about 2 limes)

½ teaspoon ground black pepper

For the Roasted Mexican Street Corn

¼ cup mayonnaise

2 tablespoons fresh lime juice (from 1 lime)

1 tablespoon chili powder

4 ears fresh corn, husked and halved crosswise

½ teaspoon fine sea salt

For the Creamy Salsa Verde

4 tomatillos, husked and rinsed well

½ cup packed fresh cilantro

1 jalapeño, seeded

2 tablespoons fresh lime juice

½ teaspoon fine sea salt

1 cup sour cream

To Serve

¼ cup grated cotija cheese

10 corn tortillas, warmed

1 bunch radishes, thinly sliced

¼ cup chopped fresh cilantro, for garnish

2 limes, cut into wedges

1. Make the carnitas: Place the pork in your Instant Pot. Sprinkle with 2 teaspoons of the salt and add ½ cup water. Lock on the lid, making sure the valve is set to "Sealing" rather than "Venting." Press "Manual" and cook on high pressure for 90 minutes.

2. About 20 minutes before the pork is done, preheat the oven to 400°F and position the racks in the upper and lower thirds.

3. When the pork is done, quick-release the pressure from the Instant Pot by turning the valve to "Venting"; when the pressure has dissipated, remove the lid.

4. To quickly shred the pork, transfer the meat to the bowl of a stand mixer fitted with the paddle attachment. Beat on low speed for about 30 seconds, until the meat is evenly shredded into 1-inch pieces. To shred the meat by hand, transfer the pork to a large bowl and use two forks to pull the meat apart into 1-inch pieces. Transfer half the shredded pork (about 4½ cups) to an airtight container and refrigerate to use for Meal 2 (it will keep for up to 5 days).

5. Add the melted butter, lime juice, pepper, and remaining 1 tablespoon salt to the pork remaining in the bowl and toss to combine. Spread the pork evenly over a rimmed baking sheet. Bake for 25 minutes on the upper oven rack, or until the pork is starting to look a little crispy.

6. About 15 minutes before the pork is done, make the roasted corn: In a small bowl, whisk together the mayonnaise, lime juice, and chili powder. Rub the mayo mixture all over the corn and place the ears on a rimmed baking sheet or in a 3-quart baking dish. Sprinkle the corn with the salt. Place the baking sheet on the lower rack in the oven with the pork and bake for 15 minutes, or until the tops of the ears start to look browned.

7. Meanwhile, make the creamy salsa verde: In a blender or food processor, combine the tomatillos, cilantro, jalapeño, and lime juice and pulse until evenly combined and mostly smooth. Pour the mixture into a bowl and stir in the salt and sour cream. Set aside until ready to serve.

8. When ready to serve, sprinkle the roasted corn with the cotija. Divide the carnitas among the tortillas

CALORIES: 721   FAT: 39.5G   CARBS: 54.1G   PROTEIN: 45.1G

and top with the creamy salsa verde and the radishes. Garnish the tacos with the cilantro and serve with the corn alongside, with lots of lime wedges for squeezing over it all.

VARIATION: SLOW COOKER METHOD

Place the pork in a 6-quart or larger slow cooker and sprinkle the top with the 2 teaspoons salt. Cover and cook on low for 8 hours, or until the pork shreds easily. Proceed as directed in step 4.

VARIATION: OVEN METHOD

1. Preheat the oven to 325°F.

2. Rub the pork with 2 tablespoons extra-virgin olive oil and place it in a 6-quart Dutch oven with a fitted lid. Sprinkle the top with the 2 teaspoons salt and cover. Bake for 4 hours, or until the pork shreds easily. Proceed as directed in step 4.

TIP

- Instead of making your own creamy salsa verde, buy your favorite standard salsa verde from the store and then mix 16 ounces with 1 cup sour cream.

STICKY HONEY-GARLIC PORK WITH WHITE RICE

Serves 4

Active time: 30 MINUTES   **Total time:** 30 MINUTES

1 cup uncooked white rice, rinsed

3 tablespoons salted butter

4½ cups shredded cooked pork (reserved from Meal 1; see page 174)

3 garlic cloves, minced

½ cup chicken broth

⅓ cup honey

2 tablespoons chili garlic sauce

2 tablespoons soy sauce

1 teaspoon toasted sesame oil

½ teaspoon red pepper flakes, for garnish

1. Cook the rice according to the package instructions.

2. In a large skillet, melt 2 tablespoons of the butter over medium-high heat. Add the shredded pork and press it into an even layer. Cook, undisturbed, for 4 to 5 minutes, until it starts to crisp on the bottom, then flip and cook for 4 to 5 minutes on the second side. Transfer the pork to a bowl and set aside.

3. In the same skillet, melt the remaining 1 table-spoon butter. Add the garlic and cook, stirring, for 2 to 3 minutes, until fragrant. Add the broth, honey, chili garlic sauce, soy sauce, and sesame oil and whisk to combine. Bring to a simmer, then cook for about 5 minutes, until the sauce has reduced slightly. Return the pork to the pan and toss to combine with the sauce.

4. Serve the pork over the rice, garnished with the red pepper flakes.

CALORIES: 630   FAT: 22.4G   CARBS: 62.7G   PROTEIN: 45.9G

Bánh Mì–Inspired Bowls

/ RECIPE PAGE 178 /

ABOUT

This pork shoulder series is a real winner and I cannot wait for you to enjoy these colorful, flavorful dinners. The pork is simply prepared and then showcased in the most fun bánh mì–inspired bowls in the first meal. These bowls have it all: cabbage, carrots, Sriracha mayo, rice noodles, and all the fresh herbs of your dreams. For the second dinner in the series, we're having a lot of fun: it's nacho night! Get your hands on some tortilla chips, load them up with refried black beans, cheese, plenty of that delicious shredded pork, and all the fresh fixings, then dig in.

▍ $$

▍ DAIRY-FREE OPTION

▍ EGG-FREE

▍ GLUTEN-FREE OPTION

▍ GRAIN-FREE OPTION

▍ NUT-FREE

MEAL 2

Loaded Nachos

/ RECIPE PAGE 179 /

SUBSTITUTIONS

Make It Dairy-Free:

- **MEAL 1:** Swap olive oil for butter when preparing the pork.

- **MEAL 2:** Substitute vegan cheese for the shredded cheese on the nachos, or omit, and omit the sour cream.

Make It Gluten-Free:

- **MEAL 1:** Substitute gluten-free tamari for the soy sauce in the bánh mì bowls.

Make It Grain-Free:

- **MEAL 1:** Substitute kelp noodles for the vermicelli noodles, or use 4 cups cooked cauliflower rice.

- **MEAL 2:** Use plantain chips or potato chips in place of the tortilla chips.

MEAL 1

BÁNH MÌ-INSPIRED BOWLS

Serves 4

Active time: 50 MINUTES

Total time: 2 HOURS 20 MINUTES TO 8 HOURS 50 MINUTES, DEPENDING ON METHOD

For the Pickled Vegetables

1 cup matchstick-cut carrots

1 seedless cucumber, cut into matchsticks

½ red onion, very thinly sliced

½ teaspoon fine sea salt

¾ cup apple cider vinegar

For the Pork

1 (5-pound) pork shoulder, cut into 4 or 5 pieces

2½ teaspoons fine sea salt

2 tablespoons extra-virgin olive oil

For the Vermicelli Noodles

7 ounces dried rice vermicelli noodles

1 teaspoon toasted sesame oil

½ teaspoon red pepper flakes

For the Sauce

¼ cup coconut aminos

3 tablespoons fish sauce

2 tablespoons honey

2 tablespoons soy sauce

¼ cup fresh cilantro sprigs, for garnish

1. Make the pickled vegetables: Place the carrots, cucumber, onion, and salt in a 32-ounce mason jar, then pour in the vinegar and ½ cup water. Seal the jar and shake vigorously six or seven times to combine. Set aside for at least 15 minutes before using or refrigerate for up to 3 days.

2. Cook the pork: Place the pork in your Instant Pot, sprinkle with 2 teaspoons of the salt, and add ½ cup water. Lock on the lid, making sure the valve is set to "Sealing" rather than "Venting." Press "Manual" and cook on high pressure for 90 minutes. When the pork is done, quick-release the pressure from the Instant Pot by turning the valve to "Venting"; when the pressure has dissipated, remove the lid.

3. To quickly shred the pork, transfer the meat to the bowl of a stand mixer fitted with the paddle attachment. Beat on low speed for 30 seconds, until the meat is evenly shredded into 1-inch pieces. To shred the meat by hand, transfer the pork to a large bowl and use two forks to pull the meat apart into 1-inch pieces. Transfer half the shredded pork (4½ cups) to an airtight container and refrigerate to use for Meal 2. Set the remainder aside.

4. Bring a large pot of water to a boil for the vermicelli noodles. In a large skillet, heat the olive oil over medium-high heat. Add the shredded pork, season with the remaining ½ teaspoon salt, and press the pork into an even layer in the pan. Cook, undisturbed, for 4 to 5 minutes, until the pork starts to crisp on the bottom, then flip and cook for 4 to 5 minutes on the second side.

5. Meanwhile, make the vermicelli noodles: Add the noodles to the boiling water and cook according to the package instructions. Drain the noodles and return them to the pot. Add the sesame oil and toss to coat. Sprinkle with the red pepper flakes and keep warm until ready to serve.

6. Make the sauce: In a small bowl, whisk together the coconut aminos, fish sauce, honey, and soy sauce. Pour the sauce over the pork and toss to combine evenly.

7. Divide the vermicelli noodles among four bowls and top evenly with the pork. Garnish with the pickled vegetables and cilantro and serve.

TIP

- The pickled vegetables can be prepared up to 3 days ahead of time and stored in the fridge until you're ready to serve them.

CALORIES: 621   FAT: 20.8G   CARBS: 62.5G   PROTEIN: 46.7G

VARIATION: SLOW COOKER METHOD

Place the pork in a 6-quart or larger slow cooker and sprinkle the top with 2 teaspoons of the salt. Cover and cook on low for 8 hours, or until the pork shreds easily. Proceed as directed in step 4.

VARIATION: OVEN METHOD

1. Preheat the oven to 325°F.

2. Rub the pork with 2 tablespoons extra-virgin olive oil and place it in a 6-quart Dutch oven with a fitted lid. Sprinkle the top with 2 teaspoons of the salt and cover. Bake for 4 hours, or until the pork shreds easily. Proceed as directed in step 4.

MEAL 2

LOADED NACHOS

Serves 5

Active time: 15 MINUTES   **Total time:** 30 MINUTES

1 (12-ounce) bag corn tortilla chips

1 (15-ounce) can refried black beans

4½ cups cooked shredded pork (reserved from Meal 1; see page 178)

3 tablespoons salted butter, melted

1 teaspoon garlic powder

1 teaspoon chili powder

½ teaspoon fine sea salt

2 cups shredded Mexican-style cheese blend

4 radishes, very thinly sliced

¼ cup sliced green onions

1 avocado, thinly sliced

¼ cup sour cream

1 lime, cut into wedges, for serving

1. Preheat the oven to 400°F.

2. Spread the chips out over one or two rimmed baking sheets. Spoon dollops of the refried beans over the chips.

3. In a large bowl, stir together the shredded pork, melted butter, garlic powder, chili powder, and salt to combine. Spread the seasoned pork over the chips and beans and then spread the cheese evenly over the top. Bake for 15 to 20 minutes, until the cheese has melted completely.

4. Top the nachos with the radishes, green onions, avocado, and sour cream and serve with the lime wedges alongside for squeezing over the top.

TIPS

- For a fun visual twist, grab blue tortilla chips instead of the usual white or yellow corn variety.

- If your refried beans are too thick to spread over the chips, stir in a few tablespoons of chicken broth or water to thin them out.

CALORIES: 879   FAT: 52.8G   CARBS: 52.8G   PROTEIN: 49.8G

Cuban-Inspired Stewed Pork

WITH BLACK BEANS

/ RECIPE PAGE 182 /

ABOUT

In this pork shoulder series, the pork is shredded a bit finer to best suit the dishes you'll make with it. First up is my spin on ropa vieja, a Cuban classic. The name translates to "old clothes," but don't let that scare you off. I recommend plating it with black beans, fresh lime, and cilantro, and don't forget the olives—they make the dish. Second, we're paying tribute to my home state of Texas with a pulled pork King Ranch casserole. My adaptation includes a luscious, indulgent mixture of creamy gravy, Tex-Mex flavors, tortillas, plenty of cheese, and shredded pork. Many suspect the dish, which usually calls for chicken, originated on the large King Ranch.

▨ **$$**
▨ **EGG-FREE**
▨ **GLUTEN-FREE OPTION**
▨ **GRAIN-FREE OPTION**
▨ **NUT-FREE**
▨ **FREEZER-FRIENDLY**

Pork King Ranch Casserole

WITH MIXED BABY GREENS SALAD

/ RECIPE PAGE 183 /

SUBSTITUTIONS

Make It Gluten-Free:

- **MEAL 2:** Substitute cup-for-cup gluten-free flour for the all-purpose flour in the King Ranch casserole.

Make It Grain-Free:

- **MEAL 2:** Use grain-free tortillas instead of corn tortillas and arrowroot starch instead of all-purpose flour for the King Ranch casserole.

Tip

- While these dishes are delicious with the shredded pork, both can also be made with shredded chicken or shredded beef.

MEAL 1

CUBAN-INSPIRED STEWED PORK WITH BLACK BEANS

Serves 4

Active time: 45 MINUTES

Total time: 2 HOURS 10 MINUTES TO 8 HOURS 40 MINUTES, DEPENDING ON METHOD

1 (5-pound) pork shoulder, cut into 4 or 5 pieces

3 teaspoons fine sea salt, plus more if needed

2 tablespoons extra-virgin olive oil

1 small yellow onion, diced

3 garlic cloves, minced

1 red bell pepper, diced

1 tablespoon paprika

1 tablespoon dried oregano

2 teaspoons ground cumin

¼ teaspoon cayenne pepper

1 (28-ounce) can crushed tomatoes

2 tablespoons apple cider vinegar

½ cup pimiento-stuffed green olives, halved

2 (15-ounce) cans black beans, drained and rinsed

1 cup beef broth or chicken broth

2 tablespoons chopped fresh cilantro, for garnish

1 lime, cut into wedges, for serving

1. Place the pork shoulder in your Instant Pot. Sprinkle with 2 teaspoons of the salt and add ½ cup water. Lock on the lid, making sure the valve is set to "Sealing" rather than "Venting." Press "Manual" and cook on high pressure for 90 minutes.

2. When the pork is finished cooking, quick-release the pressure by turning the valve to "Venting"; when the pressure has dissipated, remove the lid.

3. To quickly shred the pork, transfer the meat to the bowl of a stand mixer fitted with the paddle attachment. Beat on low speed for 30 seconds, until the meat is evenly shredded into 1-inch pieces. To shred the meat by hand, transfer the pork to a large bowl and use two forks to pull the meat apart into 1-inch pieces. Transfer half the shredded pork (4½ cups) to an airtight container and refrigerate to use for Meal 2 (it will keep for up to 5 days). Set the remainder aside.

4. In a large pot or skillet, heat the olive oil over medium heat. Add the onion, garlic, and bell pepper and cook, stirring, for 3 to 5 minutes, until fragrant.

5. Add the shredded pork, paprika, oregano, cumin, cayenne, and remaining 1 teaspoon salt and toss to coat. Cook for 2 minutes more, or until the spices darken in color and become more fragrant. Add the tomatoes and vinegar and stir to combine. Bring to a simmer, then cook for 15 minutes, until the veggies are tender and the sauce has reduced slightly, then stir in the olives.

6. Meanwhile, in a saucepan, stir together the beans and the broth and bring to a simmer over medium heat. Cook for 5 minutes, then remove from the heat. Taste and season with salt, if needed.

7. Divide the pork among four bowls, and spoon the beans alongside. Garnish with the cilantro and serve, with the lime wedges alongside for squeezing over the top.

VARIATION: SLOW COOKER METHOD

Place the pork in a 6-quart or larger slow cooker and sprinkle the top with the 2 teaspoons salt. Cover and cook on low for 8 hours, or until the pork shreds easily.

VARIATION: OVEN METHOD

1. Preheat the oven to 325°F.

2. Rub the pork with 2 tablespoons extra-virgin olive oil and place it in a 6-quart Dutch oven with a fitted lid. Sprinkle the top with the 2 teaspoons salt and cover. Bake for 4 hours, or until the pork shreds easily.

CALORIES: 524   FAT: 18.3G   CARBS: 46.6G   PROTEIN: 47.7G

PORK KING RANCH CASSEROLE WITH MIXED BABY GREENS SALAD

Serves 6

Active time: 45 MINUTES

Total time: 1 HOUR 10 MINUTES

2 tablespoons extra-virgin olive oil, plus more for greasing

1 small yellow onion, thinly sliced

2 garlic cloves, minced

2 red bell peppers, thinly sliced

1 jalapeño, seeded and finely diced

1 (14-ounce) can diced tomatoes, drained

¼ cup all-purpose flour

2 cups chicken broth

1 cup heavy cream

2 tablespoons chili powder

1 teaspoon ground cumin

1 teaspoon fine sea salt

½ teaspoon ground black pepper

12 corn tortillas

4½ cups shredded cooked pork (reserved from Meal 1; see page 182)

3 cups shredded Mexican-style cheese blend

For the Baby Greens Salad

6 cups mixed baby greens

2 carrots, thinly sliced into coins

1 bell pepper, thinly sliced

¼ cup red onion, thinly sliced

3 tablespoons extra-virgin olive oil

3 tablespoons red wine vinegar

½ teaspoon fine sea salt

¼ teaspoon ground black pepper

¼ cup chopped green onions, for garnish

1. Preheat the oven to 350°F. Grease a 9 x 13-inch baking dish with olive oil.

2. In a large skillet or pot, heat the olive oil over medium heat. Add the onion, garlic, and bell peppers and toss to combine. Cook, stirring, for 5 minutes, or until fragrant.

3. Add the jalapeño, tomatoes, flour, broth, cream, chili powder, cumin, salt, and pepper and whisk to combine. Bring to a simmer, then cook for 3 to 4 minutes, stirring occasionally, until the tomato gravy starts to thicken.

4. Layer half the tortillas over the bottom of the prepared baking dish. Top with half the shredded pork, then pour half the tomato gravy over the top and sprinkle evenly with half the cheese. Repeat to make a second layer of each ingredient. Cover with aluminum foil and bake for 35 minutes.

5. Meanwhile, make the salad: In a large bowl, combine all the ingredients for the salad and toss until well combined. Set aside or cover and refrigerate until the casserole is ready to serve.

6. Remove the baking dish from the oven and discard the foil. Switch the oven to broil and place the baking dish under the broiler for 3 minutes, or until the cheese starts to crisp and brown just a bit. Remove from the oven and let cool slightly.

7. Serve the casserole warm, garnished with the green onions, with the salad alongside.

CALORIES: 728   FAT: 43.1G   CARBS: 41.4G   PROTEIN: 47.9G

ABOUT

When I designed this dinner series, I had my dad in mind. The man loves chili verde and mac 'n' cheese, which made me think, why not work out an easy way to serve them as back-to-back dinners? With a simply prepared pork shoulder providing the base for this series, anything is possible. The meat is shredded, then used to make a pulled pork chili verde filled with tender kale, green chiles, pinto beans, and just the right amount of lime juice. The rest of the pork is tossed with barbecue sauce, then piled high on a fabulous mac 'n' cheese.

- $$
- EGG-FREE
- GLUTEN-FREE OPTION
- NUT-FREE

MEAL 1

Pulled Pork Chili Verde

/ RECIPE PAGE 186 /

Barbecue Pork Mac 'n' Cheese Bake

/ RECIPE PAGE 187 /

/ RECIPE PAGE 187 /

SUBSTITUTION

Make It Gluten-Free:

- **MEAL 2:** Use gluten-free elbow pasta in the mac 'n' cheese.

Tip

- If you want to make Meal 2 especially easy, opt for a boxed mac 'n' cheese for the base.

MEAL 1

PULLED PORK CHILI VERDE

Serves 4

Active time: 25 MINUTES

Total time: 2 HOURS 10 MINUTES TO 8 HOURS 40 MINUTES, DEPENDING ON METHOD

1 (5-pound) pork shoulder, cut into 4 or 5 pieces

3 teaspoons fine sea salt

2 tablespoons extra-virgin olive oil

½ yellow onion, diced

2 garlic cloves, minced

1 (16-ounce) jar salsa verde

1 (15-ounce) can pinto beans, drained and rinsed

2 cups chicken broth

1 cup sour cream, plus more for serving

2 tablespoons fresh lime juice (from 1 lime)

1 bunch curly kale, leaves stemmed and shredded

¼ cup fresh cilantro sprigs

1 lime, cut into wedges, for serving

1. Place the pork in your Instant Pot. Sprinkle with 2 teaspoons of the salt and add ½ cup water. Lock on the lid, making sure the valve is set to "Sealing" rather than "Venting." Press "Manual" and cook on high pressure for 90 minutes. When the pork is done, quick-release the pressure by turning the valve to "Venting"; when the pressure has dissipated, remove the lid.

2. To quickly shred the pork, transfer the meat to the bowl of a stand mixer fitted with the paddle attachment. Beat on low speed for 30 seconds, until the meat is evenly shredded into 1-inch pieces. To shred the pork by hand, transfer the meat to a large bowl and use two forks to pull the meat apart into 1-inch pieces. Transfer half the shredded pork (4½ cups) to an airtight container and refrigerate to use for Meal 2 (it will keep for up to 5 days). Set the remainder aside.

3. In a large pot, heat the olive oil over medium heat. Add the onion and garlic and cook, stirring, for 3 minutes, or until fragrant. Add the shredded pork, salsa verde, beans, and broth and stir until well combined. Bring to a simmer, then cook for 10 minutes.

4. Add the sour cream, lime juice, kale, and remaining 1 teaspoon salt and stir to combine. Cook for about 3 minutes more, stirring occasionally, until the kale is wilted and bright green. Remove from the heat.

5. Spoon the chili verde into bowls and top with additional sour cream. Garnish with the cilantro and serve, with the lime wedges alongside for squeezing over the top.

VARIATION: SLOW COOKER METHOD

Place the pork in a 6-quart or larger slow cooker and sprinkle the top with 2 teaspoons of the salt. Cover and cook on low for 8 hours, or until the pork shreds easily. Proceed as directed in step 2.

VARIATION: OVEN METHOD

1. Preheat the oven to 325°F.

2. Rub the pork with 2 tablespoons extra-virgin olive oil and place it in a 6-quart Dutch oven with a fitted lid. Sprinkle the top with 2 teaspoons of the salt and cover. Bake for 4 hours, or until the pork shreds easily. Proceed as directed in step 2.

CALORIES: 568   FAT: 29.4G   CARBS: 30.4G   PROTEIN: 53G

BARBECUE PORK MAC 'N' CHEESE BAKE

Serves 4

Active time: 30 MINUTES **Total time:** 50 MINUTES

4 cups milk or water

3 tablespoons salted butter

½ teaspoon fine sea salt

12 ounces dried elbow pasta

2 cups shredded cheddar cheese

4½ cups shredded cooked pork (reserved from Meal 1; see page 186)

1½ cups barbecue sauce

3 tablespoons finely chopped fresh chives, for garnish

1. Preheat the oven to 400°F.

2. In a 3-quart Dutch oven or oven-safe saucepan, combine the milk, butter, and salt. Bring to a boil over medium-high heat, then add the pasta and cook according to the package instructions; do not drain. Add the cheese to the pasta and stir to combine.

3. In a large bowl, stir together the shredded pork and the barbecue sauce. Spread the seasoned pork over the pasta. Bake for 15 minutes, or until the top of the pork has darkened in color. Let cool for about 5 minutes.

4. Serve the mac 'n' cheese garnished with the chives.

TIPS

- While this dish is delicious with the barbecue pork piled high on the mac 'n' cheese, you could also stir it in for a casserolelike spin on this dish.

- Looking for something green to serve alongside this dish? I recommend the baby greens salad on page 183!

CALORIES: 858   FAT: 36.6G   CARBS: 70.4G   PROTEIN: 59G

Chili-Rubbed Pork Tenderloin

WITH CILANTRO CHIMICHURRI AND TOSTONES

/ RECIPE PAGE 190 /

ABOUT

If you're new to using pork tenderloins as a way to make dinnertime more efficient (and more delicious), then I am especially excited for you to try this series. They're so easy to prep. To start, the pork is rubbed with a bold chili mix, seared on the stovetop (for extra flavor), then finished in the oven. For the first dinner, one tenderloin is sliced and served with a fabulous cilantro chimichurri and easy tostones (twice-fried plantains). The second tenderloin is thinly sliced and showcased in the most craveable Asian fusion bowls for Meal 2. These bowls have it all—delicious pork, quinoa, bacon, avocado, and spiced mango—and they're a household favorite of Fed + Fit team member Amber Goulden!

▓ $$
▓ DAIRY-FREE
▓ EGG-FREE
▓ GLUTEN-FREE
▓ GRAIN-FREE OPTION
▓ NUT-FREE

Asian Fusion Bowls

/ RECIPE PAGE 191 /

SUBSTITUTION

Make It Grain-Free

- **MEAL 2:** Substitute 4 cups cooked cauliflower rice for the quinoa in the Asian Fusion bowls.

CHILI-RUBBED PORK TENDERLOIN WITH CILANTRO CHIMICHURRI AND TOSTONES

Serves 4

Active time: 45 MINUTES   **Total time:** 45 MINUTES

For the Chili-Rubbed Pork Tenderloin

2 tablespoons chili powder

2 tablespoons brown sugar or coconut sugar

1 tablespoon dried oregano

1 tablespoon paprika

1 teaspoon ground cinnamon

1 teaspoon garlic powder

1 teaspoon fine sea salt

2 (1-pound) pork tenderloins

1 tablespoon extra-virgin olive oil

For the Tostones

¼ cup extra-virgin olive oil

2 almost-ripe plantains (yellow, not too many brown spots), peeled and cut into ½-inch-thick rounds

½ teaspoon sea salt

For the Cilantro Chimichurri

1 cup packed fresh cilantro

½ cup packed fresh parsley

2 jalapeños, seeded

4 garlic cloves, smashed and peeled

1 shallot, coarsely chopped

⅓ cup extra-virgin olive oil, plus more if needed

2 tablespoons fresh lemon juice (from 1 lemon)

2 tablespoons red wine vinegar

½ teaspoon fine sea salt

1. Cook the pork: Preheat the oven to 425°F.

2. In a small bowl, stir together the chili powder, brown sugar, oregano, paprika, cinnamon, garlic powder, and salt. Rub the spice mixture over both pork tenderloins.

3. In a large oven-safe skillet, heat the olive oil over medium heat until the oil shimmers and runs easily when you tilt the pan. Add the pork, working in batches if the pan is overcrowded by both tenderloins, and sear for 3 to 4 minutes, until a crust starts to form on the bottom, then flip the tenderloins and sear for 3 to 4 minutes on the second side (see Tip on page 191). Turn the pork one last time, then transfer the pan to the oven. Roast for 15 minutes, or until an instant-read thermometer inserted into the pork registers 145°F.

4. Remove from the oven and tent the pork with aluminum foil. Let rest for 5 minutes, then thinly slice one tenderloin and set aside. Transfer the remaining tenderloin to an airtight container and refrigerate to use for Meal 2 (it will keep for up to 5 days).

5. Make the tostones: In a large skillet, heat the olive oil over medium heat. Working in batches, if necessary, add the plantain rounds to the hot oil in an even layer and cook for 3 to 4 minutes, until starting to lightly brown on the bottom. Transfer to a paper towel–lined plate and repeat with the remaining plantain rounds. Using a large spatula or the back of a wooden spoon, flatten each plantain round to about ¼ inch thick. Again working in batches as needed, return the plantains to the hot oil browned-side up and cook for 4 to 5 minutes, until browned all over. Remove from the oil, transfer to a paper towel–lined plate, and sprinkle with the salt.

6. Make the chimichurri: In a food processor, combine the cilantro, parsley, jalapeños, garlic, shallot, olive oil, lemon juice, vinegar, and salt. Pulse until the ingredients are fully combined and the sauce is smooth, adding more olive oil, 1 tablespoon at a time, to thin the sauce, if needed. Set aside or cover and refrigerate until ready to serve.

7. Divide the sliced pork among four plates and drizzle with the chimichurri. Serve with the tostones alongside.

CALORIES: 424   FAT: 21.4G   CARBS: 36.6G   PROTEIN: 25.9G

MEAL 2

ASIAN FUSION BOWLS

Serves 4

Active time: 30 MINUTES   **Total time:** 30 MINUTES

1 cup uncooked tricolor quinoa, rinsed

8 ounces sliced bacon, cut crosswise into 1-inch-wide pieces

1 tablespoon ghee or butter

1 cooked pork tenderloin (reserved from Meal 1; see page 190), thinly sliced, then cut into 1-inch-long strips

½ cup teriyaki sauce

1 large mango, cut into ½-inch chunks

1 avocado, cut into ½-inch chunks

½ teaspoon black sesame seeds, for garnish

¼ cup fresh cilantro sprigs, for garnish

1. Cook the quinoa according to the package instructions.

2. In a large skillet, cook the bacon over medium heat until crispy. Transfer the bacon to a paper towel-lined plate and set aside. Discard the rendered bacon fat from the pan.

3. In the same pan, melt the ghee over medium heat. Add the sliced pork and the teriyaki sauce and toss to combine. Cook, stirring occasionally, for 5 minutes, or until the pork is warmed through.

5. Divide the quinoa among four bowls and top with the pork, mango, avocado, and bacon. Garnish with the sesame seeds and cilantro and serve.

TIP

- Searing the pork adds an extra layer of flavor, but you can skip it if you prefer. Just bake the tenderloins for an additional 5 minutes.

CALORIES: 729   FAT: 38.3G   CARBS: 58.9G   PROTEIN: 38.9G

Honey-Mustard Tenderloin

WITH ROASTED GREEN BEANS

/ RECIPE PAGE 194 /

ABOUT

This pork tenderloin dinner series is a perfect option for those weeks when you want a couple of comforting but easy dinners on the menu. The pork is tossed in a flavorful honey-mustard marinade, seared on the stovetop, then baked. In the first dinner, it's served simply with a side of roasted green beans. The second dinner calls for getting a little creative, as the remaining tenderloin is cut into medallions, lightly breaded, and crisped—my interpretation of schnitzel. The breaded pork medallions are then served with mashed potatoes and a quick mushroom gravy.

‖ $$
‖ DAIRY-FREE OPTION
‖ EGG-FREE
‖ GLUTEN-FREE OPTION
‖ NUT-FREE

MEAL 2
Breaded Pork Medallions

WITH MASHED POTATOES AND GRAVY

/ RECIPE PAGE 195 /

SUBSTITUTIONS

Make It Dairy-Free:

- **MEAL 2:** Substitute full-fat coconut milk for the heavy cream and extra-virgin olive oil for the butter in the mashed potatoes and the gravy for the pork medallions. Also swap coconut milk for the milk in the breading.

Make It Gluten-Free:

- **MEAL 2:** Substitute an equal amount of cup-for-cup gluten-free flour for the all-purpose flour used to bread the pork medallions and make the gravy.

HONEY-MUSTARD TENDERLOIN WITH ROASTED GREEN BEANS

Serves 4

Active time: 40 MINUTES   **Total time:** 40 MINUTES

For the Honey Mustard

2 tablespoons Dijon mustard

2 tablespoons honey

2 tablespoons extra-virgin olive oil

1 teaspoon fine sea salt

¼ teaspoon ground black pepper

2 tablespoons extra-virgin olive oil

2 (1-pound) pork tenderloins

1 pound fresh green beans

½ teaspoon fine sea salt

1. Preheat the oven to 425°F.

2. Make the honey mustard: In a small bowl, stir together the mustard, honey, olive oil, salt, and pepper.

3. In a large skillet, heat 1 tablespoon of the olive oil over medium heat until the oil shimmers and runs easily when you tilt the pan. Spread the honey mustard evenly over both pork tenderloins and place them in the pan. Sear for 3 to 4 minutes, working in batches if the pan is overcrowded by both tenderloins, until a crust starts to form on the bottom, then flip the tenderloins and sear for 3 to 4 minutes on the second side. Turn the pork one last time, then transfer the pan to the oven. Roast for 15 minutes, or until an instant-read thermometer inserted into the pork registers 145°F.

4. Remove from the oven (keep the oven on) and tent the pork with aluminum foil. Let rest for 5 minutes, then thinly slice one tenderloin and set aside. Transfer the remaining tenderloin to an airtight container and refrigerate to use for Meal 2 (it will keep for up to 5 days). Reserve the drippings in the pan for serving.

5. Put the green beans on a rimmed baking sheet, drizzle with the remaining 1 tablespoon olive oil, and toss to coat. Spread the green beans over the pan in an even layer and sprinkle with the salt. Roast for 15 minutes, or until bright green and tender. Remove from the oven.

6. Serve the sliced pork topped with the pan drippings, with the green beans alongside.

TIPS

- You can use ½ cup store-bought honey mustard in place of the homemade honey mustard.

- Searing the pork adds an extra layer of flavor, but you can skip it if you prefer. Just bake the tenderloins for an additional 5 minutes.

CALORIES: 254   FAT: 11.5G   CARBS: 12.3G   PROTEIN: 25.8G

BREADED PORK MEDALLIONS WITH MASHED POTATOES AND GRAVY

Serves 4

Active time: 1 HOUR   **Total time:** 1 HOUR

For the Mashed Potatoes

1 pound Yukon Gold potatoes, skin-on, cut into 2-inch pieces

½ cup heavy cream

4 tablespoons (½ stick) salted butter

½ teaspoon fine sea salt

¼ teaspoon ground black pepper

For the Pork Medallions

¼ cup extra-virgin olive oil

2 eggs, beaten

2 tablespoons milk

¼ cup plus 2 tablespoons all-purpose flour

1 teaspoon fine sea salt, plus more to taste

1 cooked pork tenderloin (reserved from Meal 1; see page 194), cut crosswise into ½-inch-thick rounds

2 tablespoons salted butter

8 ounces sliced baby bella mushrooms

½ cup dry white wine

½ cup chicken broth

¼ cup heavy cream

1 teaspoon chopped fresh thyme

¼ teaspoon ground black pepper

2 tablespoons chopped fresh parsley, for garnish

1 lemon, cut into wedges, for garnish

1. Make the mashed potatoes: Put the potatoes in a medium saucepan and add water to cover. Cover the pot and bring to a boil over medium-high heat, then reduce the heat to maintain a low boil and cook for 10 minutes, or until the potatoes are easily pierced with a fork. Drain the potatoes and return them to the pot.

2. Add the cream, butter, salt, and pepper to the pot with the potatoes. Using a potato masher or a handheld mixer, mash the potatoes until smooth and well combined with the other ingredients. Keep warm until ready to serve.

3. Make the pork medallions: In a large skillet, heat the olive oil over medium heat.

4. In a small bowl, whisk together the eggs and milk. In a separate small bowl, whisk together ¼ cup of the flour and ½ teaspoon of the salt. Working in batches, dip the pork rounds in the egg mixture, letting any excess drip off, then dredge them in the flour mixture to coat. Add the breaded pork to the hot oil and sear for 2 to 3 minutes, until a nice brown crust forms on the bottom, then flip and sear for 2 to 3 minutes on the second side. Transfer the pork medallions to a plate and repeat to bread and fry the remaining pork.

5. Once all the pork is cooked, drain the excess oil from the pan and melt the butter over medium heat. Add the mushrooms, wine, and remaining ½ teaspoon salt. Cook, stirring occasionally, for 10 minutes, or until the mushrooms have reduced in volume by half.

6. In a small bowl, whisk together the remaining 2 tablespoons flour and the broth until smooth. Add the mixture to the pan and stir to combine. Simmer for 5 minutes more, or until the gravy has thickened. Then stir in the cream, thyme, and pepper. Taste and season with additional salt, if needed

7. Divide the mashed potatoes among four plates and top with the pork. Pour over the mushroom gravy, garnish with the parsley and lemon wedges, and serve.

CALORIES: 656   FAT: 41.7G   CARBS: 35.4G   PROTEIN: 31.2G

Island-Style Pork Tenderloin

WITH WILD RICE

/ RECIPE PAGE 198 /

ABOUT

This final pork tenderloin series is not one to miss. The pork is cooked in a barbecue sauce of your choosing, then served with wild rice, Broccolini, and pineapple rounds alongside. It's a delicious dinner your family is sure to love. After the remaining pork is thinly sliced, it gets a complete makeover in pork ramen bowls. These bowls are packed to the brim with perfectly seasoned broth, noodles, crunchy veggies, soft-boiled eggs, green onion, and chili paste—just about everything you'd hope for at your favorite ramen shop!

- $$
- DAIRY-FREE
- EGG-FREE OPTION
- GLUTEN-FREE OPTION
- GRAIN-FREE OPTION
- LOW-CARB OPTION
- NUT-FREE

Pork Ramen Bowl

/ RECIPE PAGE 199 /

SUBSTITUTIONS

Make It Egg-Free:

- **MEAL 2:** Omit the eggs in the ramen bowls.

Make It Gluten-Free:

- **MEAL 2:** Substitute gluten-free tamari for the soy sauce and gluten-free ramen or spaghetti noodles for the ramen in the ramen bowls.

Make It Grain-Free:

- **MEAL 1:** Omit the wild rice or opt for a cauliflower rice instead.

- **MEAL 2:** Substitute grain-free tamari for the soy sauce and 11 ounces zucchini noodles or kelp noodles for the ramen in the ramen bowls.

Make It Low-Carb:

- **MEAL 1:** Use low-carb barbecue sauce for the pork tenderloin and omit the pineapple.

- **MEAL 2:** Substitute 11 ounces zucchini noodles or kelp noodles for the ramen noodles in the ramen bowls.

MEAL 1

ISLAND-STYLE PORK TENDERLOIN WITH WILD RICE

Serves 4

Active time: 30 MINUTES **Total time:** 45 MINUTES

For the Island-Style Pork Tenderloin

1 tablespoon extra-virgin olive oil

½ cup barbecue sauce

2 (1-pound) pork tenderloins

To Serve

1 cup uncooked wild rice, rinsed

1 pound Broccolini

1 tablespoon extra-virgin olive oil

2 tablespoons minced garlic

½ teaspoon fine sea salt

¼ teaspoon ground black pepper

4 pineapple rings (about 6 ounces), canned or fresh

½ cup barbecue sauce

¼ cup fresh cilantro sprigs, for garnish

1. Cook the pork: Preheat the oven to 425°F.

2. In a large oven-safe skillet, heat the olive oil over medium heat until the oil shimmers and runs easily when you tilt the pan. Spread the barbecue sauce evenly over both pork tenderloins and place them in the pan. Sear for 3 to 4 minutes, until a crust starts to form on the bottom, then flip the tenderloins and sear for 3 to 4 minutes on the second side. Turn the pork one last time, then transfer the pan to the oven. Roast for 15 minutes, or until an instant-read thermometer inserted into the pork registers 145°F.

3. Remove from the oven and tent the pork with aluminum foil. Let rest for 5 minutes, then thinly slice one tenderloin and set aside. Transfer the remaining tenderloin to an airtight container and refrigerate to use for Meal 2 (it will keep for up to 5 days).

4. Cook the wild rice according to the package instructions.

5. Set a large skillet over medium heat. In a large bowl, toss the Broccolini with the olive oil and garlic. Add the Broccolini to the skillet and cook, undisturbed, for 4 to 5 minutes, until lightly browned on the bottom, then flip and cook for 4 to 5 minutes on the second side. Season with the salt and pepper.

6. Divide the rice among four plates and top with the sliced pork. Evenly divide the Broccolini and pineapple among the plates. Drizzle the barbecue sauce over the pineapple and pork, garnish with the cilantro, and serve.

TIP

- Searing the pork adds an extra layer of flavor, but you can skip it if you prefer. Just bake the tenderloins for an additional 5 minutes.

CALORIES: 400   FAT: 8.6G   CARBS: 49.1G   PROTEIN: 33.4G

MEAL 2

PORK RAMEN BOWL

Serves 4

Active time: 45 MINUTES   **Total time:** 45 MINUTES

4 eggs

4 cups chicken broth

¼ cup soy sauce

2 tablespoons Thai chili sauce, plus more for serving (optional)

1 tablespoon honey

1 tablespoon extra-virgin olive oil

½ teaspoon toasted sesame oil

1 cooked pork tenderloin (reserved from Meal 1; see page 198), cut into 2-inch-long thin slices

½ teaspoon fine sea salt

10 ounces dried ramen noodles

2 heads baby bok choy, halved lengthwise

8 ounces sliced shiitake mushrooms

1 cup matchstick carrots

1 bunch radishes, thinly sliced

1 tablespoon black sesame seeds

¼ cup finely diced green onions

1 lime, cut into wedges, for serving

1. Bring a medium pot of water to a boil over medium-high heat. Fill a medium bowl with ice and water. Gently lower the eggs into the boiling water using a slotted spoon, then set a timer for exactly 5 minutes. When the timer goes off, use a slotted spoon to transfer the eggs to the ice bath and let cool, about 10 minutes. Drain the eggs, peel, and slice in half lengthwise. Set aside.

2. Meanwhile, in a large pot, stir together the broth, soy sauce, chili sauce, and honey. Bring to a low boil over medium heat.

3. In a large skillet, heat the olive oil and sesame oil over medium heat. Add the pork and toss to coat in the oil. Cook, turning once or twice, until the pork

is browned on most sides. Remove from the heat, season with the salt, and set aside.

4. Cook the ramen noodles in the pot with the broth for a short 5 minutes, or according to the package instructions, then add the pork.

5. Just before serving, submerge the bok choy and mushrooms in the seasoned broth and cook for 5 minutes, or until the bok choy is bright green.

6. Divide the noodles, bok choy, mushrooms, carrots, and pork evenly among four bowls. Ladle the broth into the bowls and top each with 1 egg. Garnish with the radishes, sesame seeds, and green onions. Serve with additional chili sauce, if desired, and the lime wedges alongside for squeezing over the top.

CALORIES: 661   FAT: 16.3G   CARBS: 84.5G   PROTEIN: 45.6G

seafood

Old-Fashioned Crab Bake

/ RECIPE PAGE 206 /

ABOUT

This is the seafood dinner series of my dreams! First we start off with a crab bake that will make you want to kick back for a back-patio dinner as the whole family digs into this festive meal. The bake has it all: crab, shrimp, corn, potatoes, and plenty of lemon to squeeze over it all. Be careful not to polish off all the crab and shrimp, because you'll get to use it in the next dinner: a luscious seafood bisque. This bisque is so satisfying. I recommend enjoying it with a crusty loaf of bread and good company.

▓ $$$

▓ DAIRY-FREE OPTION

▓ EGG-FREE

▓ GLUTEN-FREE OPTION

▓ GRAIN-FREE OPTION

▓ LOW-CARB OPTION

▓ NUT-FREE

MEAL 2

Seafood Bisque

/ RECIPE PAGE 207 /

SUBSTITUTIONS

Make It Dairy-Free:

- **MEAL 1:** Use olive oil in place of the butter in the crab bake.

- **MEAL 2:** Use olive oil in place of the butter and full-fat coconut milk in place of the heavy cream for the seafood bisque.

Make It Gluten-Free:

- **MEAL 2:** Use cup-for-cup gluten-free flour in place of the all-purpose flour for the seafood bisque.

Make It Grain-Free:

- **MEAL 1:** Omit the corn from the crab bake.

- **MEAL 2:** Substitute 2 tablespoons arrowroot starch for the all-purpose flour in the seafood bisque.

Make It Low-Carb:

- **MEAL 1:** Omit the corn and potatoes from the crab bake and serve with a spinach salad (see page 132) instead.

- **MEAL 2:** Substitute 2 tablespoons arrowroot starch for the all-purpose flour in the seafood bisque.

MEAL 1

OLD-FASHIONED CRAB BAKE

Serves 4

Active time: 10 MINUTES   **Total time:** 50 MINUTES

4 tablespoons (½ stick) salted butter, melted

4 garlic cloves, minced

1 pound new potatoes, quartered

3 pounds fresh crab legs or clusters

1 pound large fresh shrimp, shells on

4 ears corn, husked and cut in half crosswise

¼ cup Cajun seasoning

2 tablespoons chopped fresh parsley, for garnish

2 lemons, quartered, for serving

1. Preheat the oven to 375°F.

2. In a large bowl, whisk together the melted butter and the garlic.

3. Divide the potatoes between two rimmed baking sheets. Drizzle about one-third of the butter mixture over the potatoes. Bake for 25 minutes.

4. Add the crab, shrimp, and corn to the bowl with the remaining butter mixture and toss to coat. Remove the baking sheets from the oven and arrange the crab, shrimp, and corn among the potatoes. Sprinkle with the Cajun seasoning. Bake for 20 minutes more, until the crab shells and corn have started to brown.

5. Pick the meat from half the crab legs, coarsely chop it, and transfer to an airtight container. Coarsely chop half the shrimp and add them to the container with the crabmeat (you should have about 2 cups chopped seafood). Refrigerate to use for Meal 2 (it will keep for up to 5 days).

6. Transfer the remaining seafood and the vegetables to a serving dish. Garnish with the parsley and serve warm, with the lemon quarters alongside for squeezing over the top.

TIP

- If you're short on time, skip baking the potatoes and instead wrap them in wet paper towels and microwave them for 5 to 7 minutes, until they feel just tender when squeezed.

CALORIES: 472   FAT: 10.3G   CARBS: 49.9G   PROTEIN: 50.5G

MEAL 2

SEAFOOD BISQUE

Serves 4

Active time: 20 MINUTES   **Total time:** 50 MINUTES

2 tablespoons salted butter

1 medium onion, chopped

2 celery stalks, chopped

3 tablespoons minced garlic

½ teaspoon fine sea salt, plus more if needed

¼ teaspoon ground black pepper, plus more if needed

¼ cup all-purpose flour

2 tablespoons tomato paste

1 cup dry white wine

4 cups seafood broth or chicken broth

1 cup heavy cream

2 bay leaves

About 2 cups coarsely chopped cooked crabmeat and shrimp (reserved from Meal 1; see page 206)

2 tablespoons chopped fresh parsley, for garnish

1. In a large pot, melt the butter over medium heat. Add the onion, celery, and garlic and stir to combine. Cook, stirring, until the celery is soft, 4 to 5 minutes.

2. Add the salt, pepper, flour, tomato paste, and wine. Whisk until smooth and well combined, then bring to a simmer and cook, stirring occasionally, for about 5 minutes, until thickened.

3. If you prefer a smooth bisque, carefully transfer the mixture to a blender and quickly blend until smooth (or blend directly in the pot with an immersion blender).

4. Add the broth, cream, and bay leaves. Bring to a low boil, then reduce the heat to medium-low and simmer for 30 minutes.

5. Remove the bay leaves. Add the crabmeat and shrimp and stir. Taste and season with additional salt and pepper if needed.

6. Serve warm, garnished with the parsley.

CALORIES: 471   FAT: 18.2G   CARBS: 16.5G   PROTEIN: 48.9G

Lemon-Pepper Halibut

WITH BROCCOLI SALAD AND WILD RICE

/ RECIPE PAGE 210 /

ABOUT

Halibut is one of my favorite options for a meaty white-fleshed fish because the flavor is mild enough to take on whatever seasonings or sauces you choose and the flesh is sturdy enough to hold up if you want to get creative and turn it into a second dinner. The first dish here showcases my go-to way to prepare halibut: simply with lemon and pepper. The fish is served with a crunchy broccoli salad and savory wild rice alongside. You won't want to miss out on the second dinner, where the cooked fish is reinvented as a melt with green chiles and a chile-lime tartar sauce. Note that cod, another firm white fish, will also hold up beautifully in these two meals!

▥ **$$$**
▥ **DAIRY-FREE OPTION**
▥ **EGG-FREE OPTION**
▥ **GLUTEN-FREE OPTION**
▥ **NUT-FREE**

DINNER SERIES 44

Chile Verde Halibut Melts

WITH CHILE-LIME TARTAR SAUCE

/ RECIPE PAGE 211 /

SUBSTITUTIONS

Make It Dairy-Free:

- **MEAL 2:** Omit the cheese from the halibut melts.

Make It Egg-Free:

- **MEAL 1:** Use vegan mayo for the broccoli salad and halibut melts, or replace the mayo with plain whole-milk Greek yogurt.

Make It Gluten-Free:

- **MEAL 2:** Use gluten-free bread for the halibut melts.

LEMON-PEPPER HALIBUT WITH BROCCOLI SALAD AND WILD RICE

Serves 4

Active time: 30 MINUTES   **Total time:** 30 MINUTES

1 cup uncooked wild rice, rinsed

For the Lemon-Pepper Halibut

8 (5-ounce) halibut fillets

2 tablespoons extra-virgin olive oil

2 tablespoons fresh lemon juice (from 1 lemon)

1 teaspoon fine sea salt

1 lemon, cut into thin slices

½ teaspoon cracked black pepper

For the Broccoli Salad

¼ cup mayonnaise

3 tablespoons fresh lemon juice (from 1 lemon)

1 teaspoon poppy seeds

½ teaspoon fine sea salt

3 cups chopped broccoli florets

1 red apple, cored and cut into bite-size pieces

¼ red onion, cut into strips

1. Cook the wild rice according to the package instructions.

2. Make the halibut: Preheat the oven to 375°F.

3. Rub the halibut fillets with the olive oil and then drizzle with the lemon juice. Place in a baking dish large enough to hold the fillets in a single layer and season with the salt. Cover with the lemon slices, then sprinkle with the pepper. Bake for 15 minutes, or until the thickest fillet flakes easily with a fork.

4. Meanwhile, make the broccoli salad: In a small bowl, whisk together the mayonnaise, lemon juice, poppy seeds, and salt.

5. In a large bowl, combine the broccoli, apple, and onion. Pour the dressing over and toss to coat.

6. Transfer four of the halibut fillets to an airtight container and refrigerate to use for Meal 2 (it will keep for up to 5 days). Serve the remaining halibut warm, with the wild rice and broccoli salad.

CALORIES: 595   FAT: 34.6G   CARBS: 45.3G   PROTEIN: 28.9G

CHILE VERDE HALIBUT MELTS WITH CHILE-LIME TARTAR SAUCE

Serves 4

Active time: 15 MINUTES   **Total time:** 15 MINUTES

4 cooked halibut fillets (reserved from Meal 1; see page 210)

4 slices Muenster cheese

½ cup mayonnaise

½ cup diced green chiles

2 tablespoons fresh lime juice (from 1 lime)

½ teaspoon fine sea salt

8 slices sandwich bread

4 lettuce leaves

Potato chips, for serving

1. Preheat the oven to 375°F.

2. Place the cooked halibut fillets on a rimmed baking sheet and place a piece of the cheese over each. Bake for 10 minutes, or until the fish is warmed through and the cheese has melted.

3. Meanwhile, in a small bowl, whisk together the mayonnaise, green chiles, lime juice, and salt.

4. To assemble the melts, spread the chile-lime tartar sauce over one side of each slice of bread. Place a warmed halibut fillet on 4 slices of the bread, top each with a leaf of lettuce, and finish with a second slice of bread.

5. Enjoy warm, with potato chips on the side.

CALORIES: 510   FAT: 24.9G   CARBS: 31.6G   PROTEIN: 38.5G

Dill Aioli Salmon Bake

WITH FINGERLING POTATOES

/ RECIPE PAGE 214 /

ABOUT

A whole salmon fillet (also called a side of salmon) is my favorite cut of this incredibly nutritious seafood to cook. It's more affordable and versatile, and will yield more consistent results than smaller-portioned salmon fillets. And if you're creative enough, a whole fillet provides enough salmon for two nights' worth of dinners. In this series, I'm showing you my all-time favorite way to prepare a whole salmon fillet: as a sheet pan dinner, doused in a dill aioli and baked alongside fingerling potatoes. Half of the salmon is then repurposed into the most delicious salmon cakes that have the loveliest crust, served alongside pan-seared green beans.

☐ $$
☐ DAIRY-FREE
☐ GLUTEN-FREE OPTION
☐ NUT-FREE

MEAL 2

Salmon Cakes

WITH PAN-SEARED GREEN BEANS

/ RECIPE PAGE 215 /

SUBSTITUTION

Make It Gluten-Free:

- **MEAL 2:** Use gluten-free bread crumbs and a 1:1 gluten-free all-purpose flour for the salmon cakes.

Tip

- If you can't find a full salmon fillet, you can use 8 smaller fillets (about 5 ounces each) instead—just bake them for 8 to 10 minutes, until the thickest fillet flakes easily with a fork.

MEAL 1

DILL AIOLI SALMON BAKE WITH FINGERLING POTATOES

Serves 4

Active time: 10 MINUTES   **Total time:** 1 HOUR

2 pounds fingerling or baby potatoes, cut into bite-size pieces

2 tablespoons extra-virgin olive oil

1½ teaspoons fine sea salt

½ cup mayonnaise

2 tablespoons fresh lemon juice (from 1 lemon)

2 tablespoons dried dill

2 (1¼-pound) salmon fillets

1 lemon, cut into wedges, for serving

1. Preheat the oven to 375°F.

2. On a rimmed baking sheet, toss the potatoes with 1 tablespoon of the olive oil and sprinkle with ½ teaspoon of the salt. Bake for 40 minutes, or until the potatoes are soft to the touch and starting to brown on top.

3. Meanwhile, in a small bowl, whisk together the mayonnaise, lemon juice, dill, and ½ teaspoon of the salt.

4. Remove the potatoes from the oven and push them to the sides of the pan, making a space in the middle large enough for the salmon. Place 1 salmon fillet on the baking sheet and spread the mayonnaise mixture over the top. Place the second salmon fillet on a separate baking sheet, rub with the remaining 1 tablespoon olive oil, and season with the remaining ½ teaspoon salt. Bake both fillets for 12 to 15 minutes, until the salmon flakes easily with a fork at its thickest point. Remove from the oven.

5. Transfer the salmon without the mayonnaise topping to an airtight container and refrigerate to use for Meal 2 (it will keep for up to 5 days).

6. Serve the remaining salmon warm, with the potatoes alongside and lemon wedges for squeezing over the top.

CALORIES: 583   FAT: 31G   CARBS: 41.2G   PROTEIN: 36.8G

SALMON CAKES WITH PAN-SEARED GREEN BEANS

Serves 4

Active time: 20 MINUTES   **Total time:** 20 MINUTES

For the Salmon Cakes

1 cooked salmon fillet (reserved from Meal 1; see page 214)

½ cup mayonnaise

2 large eggs

2 green onions, thinly sliced

¾ cup dried bread crumbs

⅓ cup all-purpose flour

2 tablespoons Dijon mustard

¼ teaspoon ground black pepper

3 tablespoons extra-virgin olive oil

½ teaspoon fine sea salt

For the Pan-Seared Green Beans

1 pound green beans

1 tablespoon extra-virgin olive oil

½ teaspoon fine sea salt

1 lemon, cut into wedges, for serving

1. Make the salmon cakes: In a large bowl, combine the salmon, mayonnaise, eggs, green onions, bread crumbs, flour, mustard, and pepper and mash with a fork until smooth. Form the mixture into 4 to 6 equal-size patties.

2. In the skillet, heat the olive oil over medium heat until it shimmers and runs easily when you tilt the pan. Add the salmon cakes and cook for 3 to 4 minutes, until darkened in color on the bottom and starting to crisp, then flip and cook for 3 to 4 minutes on the second side. Remove the salmon cakes from the pan and sprinkle with the salt.

3. Make the green beans: In the same skillet, toss the green beans with the olive oil to coat and season with the salt. Cook over medium heat, without stirring, for 4 to 5 minutes, then stir and cook, stirring occasionally, for 4 to 5 minutes more, until the beans are starting to wilt and brown slightly. Remove from the heat.

4. Serve the salmon cakes with the green beans alongside and lemon wedges for squeezing over the top.

CALORIES: 635   FAT: 41.2G   CARBS: 26.3G   PROTEIN: 40G

Teriyaki Salmon Bake

WITH WHITE RICE AND ASPARAGUS

/ RECIPE PAGE 218 /

ABOUT

Because I love whole salmon fillets (aka sides of salmon) so much, I've featured them in two series for you to enjoy. In this series, a whole fillet is flavored with teriyaki sauce, baked, and then served alongside white rice and perfectly cooked asparagus. The second portion of salmon is then formed into burgers. These delicious salmon burgers are flavored with feta, cranberries, and parsley and served alongside shoestring sweet potato fries.

▥ $$$
▥ DAIRY-FREE OPTION
▥ EGG-FREE OPTION
▥ GLUTEN-FREE OPTION
▥ GRAIN-FREE OPTION
▥ NUT-FREE

Salmon Burgers

WITH SWEET POTATO FRIES

/ RECIPE PAGE 219 /

SUBSTITUTIONS

Make It Dairy-Free:

- **MEAL 2:** Omit the feta cheese from the salmon burgers.

Make It Egg-Free:

- **MEAL 2:** Substitute vegan mayonnaise.

Make It Gluten-Free:

- **MEAL 2:** Use gluten-free buns and gluten-free bread crumbs for the salmon burgers.

Make It Grain-Free:

- **MEAL 1:** Use 4 cups cooked cauliflower rice in place of the white rice served with the salmon bake.

- **MEAL 2:** Omit the buns and use almond flour in place of the bread crumbs.

TERIYAKI SALMON BAKE WITH WHITE RICE AND ASPARAGUS

Serves 4

Active time: 10 MINUTES   **Total time:** 40 MINUTES

1 bunch asparagus, trimmed

1 tablespoon plus 2 teaspoons extra-virgin olive oil

1 teaspoon fine sea salt

¼ teaspoon ground black pepper

2 (1¼-pound) salmon fillets

½ cup teriyaki sauce

1 cup uncooked white rice, rinsed

2 tablespoons chopped fresh cilantro, for garnish

1 tablespoon white sesame seeds, for garnish

1. Preheat the oven to 375°F.

2. On a rimmed baking sheet, toss the asparagus with 2 teaspoons of the olive oil and sprinkle with ½ teaspoon of the salt. Bake for 15 minutes, or until bright green and wilted.

3. Remove the asparagus from the oven and push it to the sides of the pan, making a space in the middle large enough for the salmon. Place 1 salmon fillet on the baking sheet and spread the teriyaki sauce over the top. Place the second salmon fillet on a separate baking sheet, rub with the remaining 1 tablespoon olive oil, and season with the remaining ½ teaspoon salt. Bake both fillets for 12 to 15 minutes, until the salmon flakes easily with a fork at its thickest point.

4. Meanwhile, cook the rice according to the package instructions.

5. Remove the salmon and asparagus from the oven. Transfer the salmon without the teriyaki sauce to an airtight container, let cool, and refrigerate to use for Meal 2 (it will keep for up to 5 days).

6. Serve the remaining salmon with the asparagus and rice, garnished with the cilantro and sesame seeds.

CALORIES: 440   FAT: 10.5G   CARBS: 49.9G   PROTEIN: 36.6G

MEAL 2

SALMON BURGERS WITH SWEET POTATO FRIES

Serves 4

Active time: 35 MINUTES	**Total time:** 1 HOUR 10 MINUTES

1 pound sweet potatoes, cut into ½-inch-thick sticks

3 tablespoons extra-virgin olive oil

½ teaspoon fine sea salt

1 cooked salmon fillet (reserved from Meal 1; see page 218)

2 large eggs

½ cup bread crumbs

½ cup unsweetened dried cranberries

½ cup crumbled feta cheese

¼ cup chopped fresh parsley

2 tablespoons salted butter (or olive oil spray, if grilling the burgers)

4 tablespoons mayonnaise

4 hamburger buns, toasted

4 lettuce leaves

4 teaspoons capers, drained

1. Preheat the oven to 400°F. Line a baking sheet with parchment paper.

2. Toss the sweet potatoes with the olive oil, spread them out over the prepared baking sheet, and sprinkle with the salt. Bake for 15 minutes, then flip the fries and bake for 10 to 15 minutes more, until they look crispy.

3. Meanwhile, if you plan to grill your salmon burgers, heat a grill to high.

4. Put the salmon in a large bowl and use a fork to break it up into small pieces. Add the eggs, bread crumbs, cranberries, feta, and parsley and stir to combine. Form the salmon mixture into 4 equal-size patties.

5. *To cook the salmon burgers on the stovetop*, melt the butter in a medium skillet over medium heat. Add the patties and cook for 3 to 4 minutes on each side, until darkened in color.

6. *To grill the burgers*, clean the grill grates, spray them with oil, and grill the patties for about 3 minutes on each side, until browned.

7. To assemble the burgers, spread 1 tablespoon of mayonnaise on the bottom half of each bun, then top each with a burger patty, 1 lettuce leaf, and 1 teaspoon of the capers. Serve warm, with the sweet potato fries alongside.

CALORIES: 803   FAT: 39.7G   CARBS: 68.1G   PROTEIN: 39.8G

Blackened Shrimp Taco Bowls

WITH WHITE RICE AND ZESTY SLAW

/ RECIPE PAGE 222 /

ABOUT

If you plan well, shrimp can actually be a prep-ahead-friendly protein. In this meal series, you'll cook plenty of shrimp and then divide them between two fabulous dinners. The first is a blackened shrimp taco bowl served over white rice and topped with a craveable zesty slaw. The second dinner is a hearty seafood jambalaya, complete with chorizo, chicken (I prefer thighs for added flavor), and all the spices you'd expect in a good jambalaya. Serve it with a generous portion of crusty bread alongside, and enjoy!

▥ $$$
▥ DAIRY-FREE OPTION
▥ EGG-FREE
▥ GLUTEN-FREE OPTION
▥ GRAIN-FREE OPTION
▥ LOW-CARB OPTION
▥ NUT-FREE

Seafood Jambalaya

/ RECIPE PAGE 223 /

SUBSTITUTIONS

Make It Gluten-Free:

- **MEAL 2:** Substitute gluten-free tamari for the soy sauce in the jambalaya. Use a gluten-free bread for serving.

Make It Grain-Free:

- **MEAL 1:** Substitute 4 cups cooked cauliflower rice for the white rice in the shrimp taco bowls.

- **MEAL 2:** Substitute 3 cups uncooked cauliflower rice for the white rice in the seafood jambalaya. Stir the cauliflower rice into the jambalaya at the same time you add the shrimp in step 3.

Make It Low-Carb:

- **MEAL 1:** Substitute 4 cups cooked cauliflower rice for the white rice in the shrimp taco bowls and omit the mango from the slaw.

- **MEAL 2:** Substitute 3 cups uncooked cauliflower rice for the white rice in the seafood jambalaya. Stir the cauliflower rice into the jambalaya at the same time you add the shrimp in step 3.

BLACKENED SHRIMP TACO BOWLS WITH WHITE RICE AND ZESTY SLAW

Serves 4

Active time: 35 MINUTES   **Total time:** 35 MINUTES

For the Blackened Shrimp

3 pounds raw shrimp, peeled and deveined

¼ cup extra-virgin olive oil

2 tablespoons fresh lime juice (from 1 lime)

3 tablespoons chili powder

1 tablespoon paprika

1 teaspoon garlic powder

½ teaspoon ground cumin

½ teaspoon fine sea salt

¼ teaspoon ground black pepper

For the Zesty Slaw

½ head purple cabbage, shredded

1 mango, peeled and cut into thin strips

2 carrots, shredded

½ cup packed fresh cilantro, coarsely chopped

1 jalapeño, seeded and finely diced

¼ cup fresh lime juice (from about 2 limes)

2 tablespoons extra-virgin olive oil

½ teaspoon fine sea salt

To Serve

1 cup uncooked white rice, rinsed

2 tablespoons salted butter (or olive oil spray, if using a grill)

1 jalapeño, sliced

1 avocado, cut into wedges

1 lime, cut into wedges

1. Marinate the shrimp: In a large bowl, toss the shrimp with the olive oil and lime juice and set aside to marinate for up to 20 minutes (no longer) while you make the slaw and dry rub. If you will be grilling the shrimp, heat a grill to high.

2. In a large bowl, stir together the chili powder, paprika, garlic powder, cumin, salt, and pepper; set the dry rub aside.

3. Make the slaw: In a large bowl, toss all the slaw ingredients together and set aside. If desired, cook the rice according to the package directions.

4. Cook the shrimp: Drain the shrimp, add them to the bowl with the dry rub, and toss until evenly coated on all sides.

5. *To cook the shrimp on the stovetop*, in a large skillet, melt the butter over high heat. Add half the shrimp, spreading them in an even layer in the pan so that no two shrimp touch each other. Cook until darkened in color and curled in on themselves, 2 to 3 minutes on each side. Transfer to a plate and repeat with the remaining shrimp.

6. *To grill the shrimp*, skewer 5 or 6 shrimp on a metal or wooden skewer. Clean the grill grates and spray them with oil, then grill the shrimp for 2 to 3 minutes on each side, until the shrimp have turned white and opaque and started to curl in on themselves.

7. Transfer half the shrimp (about 2 cups) to an airtight container and refrigerate to use for Meal 2 (it will keep for up to 5 days).

8. Plate the remaining warm shrimp over the slaw and rice (if using). Garnish with the jalapeño and avocado and serve, with the lime wedges alongside for squeezing over the top.

TIPS

- Use 6 cups coleslaw mix for the slaw instead of shredding your own cabbage and carrots.

- If using wooden skewers for the shrimp, soak them for 20 minutes while the shrimp marinates to keep them from burning.

CALORIES: 587   FAT: 18G   CARBS: 70.8G   PROTEIN: 41.9G

MEAL 2

SEAFOOD JAMBALAYA

Serves 6

Active time: 30 MINUTES   **Total time:** 45 MINUTES

1 pound Mexican (uncured) chorizo, bulk or link style

1 pound boneless, skinless chicken breast or thighs, cut into ½-inch pieces

2 tablespoons salted butter or olive oil

2 cups chopped celery (about 6 stalks)

1 small onion, chopped

1 red bell pepper, chopped

5 garlic cloves, minced

1 (28-ounce) can diced tomatoes, with their juice

3 cups chicken broth

1 cup uncooked white rice, rinsed

½ cup Frank's RedHot sauce

¼ cup soy sauce

2 tablespoons dried oregano

½ teaspoon ground black pepper

½ teaspoon cayenne pepper

About 2 cups cooked shrimp (reserved from Meal 1; see page 222)

2 tablespoons fresh lemon juice (from 1 lemon)

¼ cup chopped fresh parsley, for garnish

Crusty bread, for serving

1. In a large pot, brown the chorizo until crispy. Add the chicken and cook, stirring occasionally, for 7 to 9 minutes, until cooked through. Spoon the cooked sausage and chicken into a large bowl.

2. In the same pot, melt the butter over medium heat. Add the celery, onion, bell pepper, and garlic. Toss to combine and cook, stirring, for 10 minutes, or until the vegetables are soft.

3. Add the chorizo and chicken back to the pot, along with the tomatoes with their juice, the broth, rice, hot sauce, soy sauce, oregano, black pepper, and cayenne and stir to combine. Cook, stirring occasionally, for 10 minutes, then add the shrimp and lemon juice. Simmer for a few minutes more, stirring occasionally, until the shrimp are warmed through, then remove from the heat.

4. Serve the jambalaya garnished with the parsley, with crusty bread alongside.

TIPS

- If using link-style chorizo, remove the casings and break up the meat while cooking.

- You can use 2 cups shredded cooked chicken (leftover or cooked from scratch; see page 30) in place of the chicken breast or thighs for the jambalaya.

CALORIES: 769   FAT: 39G   CARBS: 39.8G   PROTEIN: 64.2G

Chili-Lime Tuna Steak

WITH TRICOLOR QUINOA

/ RECIPE PAGE 226 /

ABOUT

This seafood dinner series is a perfect balance of both lightness and comfort. If you're unfamiliar with cooking tuna, don't sweat it—I'll walk you through exactly how to cook these steaks so you can feel confident and at ease in your kitchen. The tuna first marinates in a zesty chili-lime marinade that's my absolute favorite for fish (the flavor combination will knock your socks off!). The steaks then get cooked in butter and paired with fluffy tricolor quinoa for the first dinner. For the second dinner, we get creative by taking the remaining cooked tuna steaks, breaking them up, and using them as the protein anchor for my famous tuna-noodle casserole.

- $$
- DAIRY-FREE OPTION
- EGG-FREE
- GLUTEN-FREE OPTION
- NUT-FREE

Tuna-Noodle Casserole

/ RECIPE PAGE 227 /

SUBSTITUTIONS

Make It Dairy-Free:

- **MEAL 2:** Substitute olive oil for the butter in the tuna casserole and replace the whole milk with an additional 1 cup chicken broth plus ⅔ cup full-fat coconut milk. Either omit the mozzarella cheese topping or substitute vegan cheese.

Make It Gluten-Free:

- **MEAL 2:** Use gluten-free pasta and substitute cup-for-cup gluten-free flour for the all-purpose flour in the tuna casserole.

CHILI-LIME TUNA STEAK WITH TRICOLOR QUINOA

Serves 4

Active time: 25 MINUTES   **Total time:** 35 MINUTES

1 cup uncooked tricolor quinoa, rinsed

2 tablespoons Thai chili sauce

2 tablespoons soy sauce or tamari

2 tablespoons fresh lime juice (from 1 lime)

4 tablespoons extra-virgin olive oil

3 pounds (1-inch-thick) tuna steaks

2 tablespoons salted butter or olive oil spray

½ teaspoon fine sea salt

2 tablespoons chopped fresh cilantro, for garnish

1 tablespoon white sesame seeds, for garnish

1 lime, cut into wedges, for garnish

1. Cook the quinoa according to the package instructions.

2. In a small bowl, whisk together the chili sauce, soy sauce, lime juice, and 2 tablespoons of the olive oil. Put half the tuna steaks in a large zip-top bag, pour in the chili sauce mixture, and marinate for at least 10 minutes or in the refrigerator for up to 2 hours.

3. Coat the unmarinated tuna steaks with the remaining 2 tablespoons olive oil and season with the salt. Add the steaks to the skillet and cook for 3 to 4 minutes, until a slight crust forms on the bottom, then flip and cook for 3 to 4 minutes on the second side. Transfer to an airtight container and refrigerate to use for Meal 2 (it will keep for up to 5 days). Working in the same skillet, melt the butter over medium heat. Discard the marinade and add marinated steaks to the skillet and cook for 3 to 4 minutes, until a slight crust forms on the bottom. Flip and cook for 3 to 4 minutes on the second side.

4. Divide the tuna among four plates and spoon the quinoa alongside. Garnish with the cilantro and sesame seeds and serve, with lime wedges alongside for squeezing over the top.

CALORIES: 470   FAT: 17.3G   CARBS: 28.5G   PROTEIN: 48.4G

MEAL 2

TUNA-NOODLE CASSEROLE

Serves 5

Active time: 20 MINUTES   **Total time:** 40 MINUTES

9 ounces dried tagliatelle or linguine

2 tablespoons salted butter

½ yellow onion, diced

2 garlic cloves, minced

4 ounces button or baby bella mushrooms, sliced

2 tablespoons all-purpose flour

1⅔ cups whole milk

½ cup chicken broth

Cooked tuna steaks (reserved from Meal 1; see page 226), coarsely chopped into ½-inch pieces

1 cup frozen peas

1 teaspoon fine sea salt

½ teaspoon ground black pepper

1 cup shredded mozzarella cheese, for topping

1 tablespoon chopped fresh parsley, for garnish

1. Preheat the oven to 350°F.

2. Bring a large pot of water to a boil. Cook the noodles according to the package instructions.

3. While the noodles are cooking, in a large Dutch oven or other oven-safe pot, melt the butter over medium heat. Add the onion, garlic, and mushrooms and cook, stirring, for 4 to 5 minutes, until the onion and mushrooms have reduced in size. Add the flour and stir to combine. Slowly whisk in the milk and broth until smooth.

4. Add the tuna, peas, salt, and pepper and bring to a low boil.

5. When the pasta is done cooking, drain it and add it to the pot. Stir gently to combine.

6. Top with the cheese and transfer the pot to the oven. Bake for 20 minutes, or until hot and bubbling. Remove from the oven, garnish with the parsley, and serve.

CALORIES: 554   FAT: 14.5G   CARBS: 51.5G   PROTEIN: 52.4G

vegetarian

Plantain Black Bean Bowls

/ RECIPE PAGE 232 /

ABOUT

If you whip up a big batch of black beans and white rice, most of your work for this dinner series is done! We creatively transform these humble ingredients into two distinct bold, nourishing dinners. The Peruvian-inspired plantain black bean bowls are the perfect way to enjoy plantains and a spicy cilantro crema. I have a hard time moving on to the second dinner in this series because the plantain bowls are just so good. That said, the barbecue bean casserole is fawn-worthy on its own. White rice, perfectly seasoned kale, black beans, and plenty of tangy, sweet barbecue sauce come together in a vegetarian casserole that will be a hit with the whole family.

▌ $
▌ DAIRY-FREE
▌ EGG-FREE OPTION
▌ GLUTEN-FREE
▌ GRAIN-FREE OPTION
▌ NUT-FREE
▌ FREEZER-FRIENDLY

Barbecue Bean Casserole

/ RECIPE PAGE 233 /

SUBSTITUTIONS

Make It Egg-Free:

- **MEAL 1:** Use your favorite vegan mayo or whole-milk Greek yogurt in the sauce for the plantain bowls.

Make It Grain-Free:

- **MEALS 1 AND 2:** Use 4 cups cooked cauliflower rice in place of the white rice in both meals.

Tip

- Use canned black beans instead of cooking them from scratch. You'll need four 15-ounce cans to cover both meals. Drain and rinse the beans, then use 2 cups for Meal 1 and reserve 4 cups in an airtight container in the fridge to use for Meal 2.

PLANTAIN BLACK BEAN BOWLS

Serves 4

Active time: 40 MINUTES

Total time: 1 HOUR, 30 MINUTES, PLUS 8 HOURS FOR SOAKING THE BEANS

For the Black Beans

1 pound dried black beans, rinsed

1 small yellow onion, quartered

3 garlic cloves, smashed and peeled

1 bay leaf

1 tablespoon fine sea salt

2 cups uncooked white rice, rinsed

For the Plantains

3 tablespoons extra-virgin olive oil

2 large ripe plantains (dark yellow or brown, not green), peeled and cut on an angle into 1-inch-thick pieces

½ teaspoon fine sea salt

¼ teaspoon paprika

For the Sauce

1 cup packed fresh cilantro

1 medium jalapeño, seeded

1 garlic clove

⅓ cup mayonnaise

2 tablespoons fresh lime juice (from 1 lime)

¼ teaspoon fine sea salt

Chopped fresh cilantro, for garnish

1 lime, cut into wedges, for serving

1. Cook the black beans: Place the beans in a large pot and add water to cover. Set aside to soak for at least 8 hours or up to overnight.

2. Drain and rinse the beans, return them to the pot, and add fresh water to cover. Add the onion, garlic, bay leaf, and salt. Bring to a low boil over medium heat, then cover and cook, stirring occasionally, for 1 to 1½ hours, until the beans are tender. Remove

from the heat and discard the onion, garlic, and bay leaf.

3. Cook the rice according to the package instructions.

4. Make the plantains: In a large skillet, heat the olive oil over medium heat until the oil shimmers and runs easily when you tilt the pan. Add the plantains in an even layer and fry for 3 to 4 minutes, until golden brown on the bottom, then flip and cook for 3 to 4 minutes more, until golden brown on the second side. Transfer the plantains to a paper towel to drain and sprinkle with the salt and paprika.

5. Make the sauce: In a blender, combine the cilantro, jalapeño, garlic, mayonnaise, lime juice, and salt and blend until smooth.

6. Transfer 4 cups of the cooked black beans to an airtight container and 4 cups of the cooked rice to a separate airtight container; refrigerate both to use for Meal 2 (it will keep for up to 5 days).

7. Warm the remaining black beans and rice, if needed, then use a slotted spoon to scoop the beans onto four plates. Divide the rice, plantains, and green sauce among the plates. Garnish with cilantro and serve, with the lime wedges alongside for squeezing over the top.

TIP

- If using canned black beans, proceed to step 2 and cook over medium heat for 15 to 20 minutes, until the onion is softened.

CALORIES: 517   FAT: 21.8G   CARBS: 73.4G   PROTEIN: 11.3G

MEAL 2

BARBECUE BEAN CASSEROLE

Serves 5

Active time: 20 MINUTES   **Total time:** 50 MINUTES

1 tablespoon extra-virgin olive oil

2 bunches Italian kale, leaves stemmed and coarsely chopped

1 tablespoon fresh lemon juice (from about ½ lemon)

¼ teaspoon fine sea salt

4 cups cooked white rice (reserved from Meal 1; see page 232)

4 cups cooked black beans (reserved from Meal 1; see page 232)

1 cup barbecue sauce, plus more for serving

⅓ cup finely chopped red onion, for granish

¼ cup chopped fresh cilantro, for granish

TIPS

- Other delicious topping ideas can include fresh or pickled jalapeños, green onion, or even pickled onions.

- If barbecue sauce isn't your favorite, season the beans however you like! Pull out your favorite seasoning blend, dressing, or marinade to mix up the flavor profile.

1. Preheat the oven to 350°F.

2. In a large skillet, heat the olive oil over medium heat. Add the kale and toss to coat with the oil. Cook, stirring occasionally, for about 5 minutes, until the kale has wilted. Add the lemon juice and salt, stir to combine, and remove from the heat.

3. Spread the rice over the bottom of a 2-quart casserole or baking dish. Spread the cooked kale over the rice.

4. In a large bowl, stir together the beans and the barbecue sauce, then spread the mixture over the kale.

5. Bake, uncovered, for 30 minutes, until warmed through.

6. Garnish with the red onion and cilantro and serve with additional barbecue sauce.

CALORIES: 541   FAT: 4.8G   CARBS: 103.2G   PROTEIN: 20.2G

Enchilada-Stuffed Zucchini Boats

/ RECIPE PAGE 236 /

ABOUT

Black beans, one of my top-two favorite legumes, are center stage in this creative dinner series. First they're put to excellent use in some festive enchilada-stuffed zucchini boats. If you've ever attempted zucchini boats before, you know that there's a bit of a trick to perfecting the method. In my opinion, not overcooking them is key. These boats are light, fresh, and gorgeous. The second dinner in this series is actually one of my favorites in the whole book: a smoky vegetarian chili that I like to serve with vegan corn bread alongside. The chili is a comforting, satisfying option when you want a meatless meal that won't leave you missing the meat. I top mine with plenty of avocado and a large slice of the fluffy one-bowl corn bread.

▥ **$**

▥ **DAIRY-FREE OPTION**

▥ **EGG-FREE**

▥ **GLUTEN-FREE OPTION**

▥ **GRAIN-FREE OPTION**

▥ **NUT-FREE**

▥ **FREEZER-FRIENDLY**

Vegetarian Chili

WITH VEGAN CORN BREAD

/ RECIPE PAGE 237 /

SUBSTITUTIONS

Make It Dairy-Free:

- **MEAL 1:** Omit the cheese from the zucchini boats, or substitute your favorite vegan cheese. Substitute ½ cup coconut cream from full-fat coconut milk for the sour cream.

Make It Gluten-Free:

- **MEAL 2:** Use gluten-free all-purpose flour in the corn bread.

Make It Grain-Free:

- **MEAL 2:** Skip the vegan corn bread. If you like, make a side salad like the one on page 154 to serve alongside the chili instead.

ENCHILADA-STUFFED ZUCCHINI BOATS

Serves 4

Active time: 30 MINUTES

Total time: 2 HOURS 15 MINUTES, PLUS 8 HOURS FOR SOAKING THE BEANS

For the Black Beans

1½ cups dried black beans, rinsed

1 small yellow onion, quartered

2 garlic cloves, smashed and peeled

1 bay leaf

2 teaspoons fine sea salt

For the Zucchini Boats

1 cup prepared red enchilada sauce

4 medium zucchini, halved lengthwise and soft seedy cores scraped out with a spoon

1 cup shredded Monterey Jack cheese

To Serve

½ cup sour cream

1 teaspoon ground cumin

2 tablespoons fresh lime juice (from 1 lime)

1 avocado, sliced

¼ cup chopped fresh cilantro, for garnish

1. Cook the black beans: Place the beans in a large pot and add water to cover. Set aside to soak for at least 8 hours or up to overnight.

2. Drain and rinse the beans, return them to the pot, and add fresh water to cover. Add the onion, garlic, bay leaf, and salt. Bring to a low boil over medium heat, then cover and cook, stirring occasionally, for 1 to 1½ hours, until the beans are tender. Remove from the heat and discard the onion, garlic, and bay leaf. Transfer 2½ cups of the beans to an airtight container and refrigerate to use for Meal 2 (it will keep for up to 5 days).

3. Make the zucchini boats: Preheat the oven to 375°F.

4. In a large bowl, stir together the remaining 2 cups beans and the enchilada sauce. Place the zucchini boats cut side up in a large baking dish. Spoon the beans into the zucchini boats. Sprinkle the tops with the cheese. Bake for 30 minutes, or until the tops are bubbling and starting to brown and the zucchini is cooked through (when easily pierced with a fork).

5. Meanwhile, in a small bowl, whisk together the sour cream, cumin, and lime juice.

6. Serve the zucchini boats drizzled with the cumin sour cream and garnished with the avocado and cilantro.

TIP

- If you'd like to substitute canned black beans, there's no need to cook them beforehand. Simply drain and rinse four 15-ounce cans of beans, then store 2½ cups in an airtight container in the refrigerator for Meal 2 and use 2 cups for tonight's meal. Proceed to step 2 and cook over medium heat for 15 to 20 minutes, until the onion is softened.

CALORIES: 387   FAT: 20.2G   CARBS: 34.4G   PROTEIN: 20.5G

MEAL 2

VEGETARIAN CHILI WITH VEGAN CORN BREAD

Serves 4

Active time: 45 MINUTES **Total time:** 30 MINUTES

For the Vegan Corn Bread

½ cup coconut oil, melted, plus more for greasing

1½ cups cornmeal

1 cup all-purpose flour

¼ cup sugar

1 tablespoon baking powder

1 tablespoon ground flaxseed

1 teaspoon fine sea salt

1½ cups coconut milk or other unsweetened nondairy milk

For the Vegetarian Chili

2 tablespoons extra-virgin olive oil

½ yellow onion, finely chopped

4 garlic cloves, minced

½ cup dried red lentils

2½ cups cooked black beans (reserved from Meal 1; see page 236)

1 (28-ounce) can crushed tomatoes

¼ cup mild chili powder

3 tablespoons ground cumin

1 teaspoon fine sea salt

½ teaspoon ground black pepper

1 ripe avocado, cut into 1-inch cubes, for serving

¼ cup chopped fresh cilantro, for garnish

1. Make the corn bread: Preheat the oven to 350°F. Grease an 8- or 9-inch cast-iron skillet or round cake pan with coconut oil or line with parchment paper.

2. In a large bowl, whisk together the cornmeal, flour, sugar, baking powder, flaxseed, and salt. Add the coconut milk and melted coconut oil to the bowl and mix until the batter is smooth.

3. Pour the batter into the prepared pan. Bake for 25 to 30 minutes, until a toothpick inserted into the center of the cornbread comes out clean. Remove from the oven and let cool in the pan.

4. While the corn bread is baking, make the chili: In a large pot, heat the olive oil over medium heat. Add the onion and garlic, stir to combine, and cook, stirring occasionally, for 3 to 5 minutes, until fragrant and starting to brown.

5. Add the lentils, black beans, tomatoes, chili powder, cumin, salt, and pepper. Fill the empty tomato can with water and pour it into the pot (or just add 3½ cups water), then stir to combine. Bring to a simmer, then cook, stirring occasionally, for 20 minutes, or until the lentils have swollen and started to pop.

6. Serve the chili topped with the avocado and garnished with the cilantro, with slices of the corn bread alongside.

TIP

- This recipe makes enough corn bread to serve six, so you'll have some left over. Store the extra corn bread in an airtight container in the refrigerator for up to 4 days.

CALORIES: 702   FAT: 31.2G   CARBS: 93.6G   PROTEIN: 19.3G

Baked Falafel Bowls

/ RECIPE PAGE 240 /

ABOUT

This vegetarian meal series is such a creative and delicious way to get more mileage out of a prepared falafel dough. Half the dough will be used in the flavorful baked falafel bowls, while the other half is creatively used as a crust for the goat cheese and mushroom quiche. Falafels are traditionally fried, but we bake them in the oven for a healthier spin. The nutrition of the bowls gets even more robust with the addition of the lemony kale salad.

- $$
- DAIRY-FREE OPTION
- GLUTEN-FREE OPTION
- NUT-FREE

Goat Cheese and Mushroom Quiche

/ RECIPE PAGE 241 /

SUBSTITUTIONS

Make It Dairy-Free:

- **MEAL 1:** Omit the feta cheese from the falafel bowls.

- **MEAL 2:** Omit the goat cheese from the quiche, and substitute an equal amount of full-fat coconut milk for the heavy cream.

Make It Gluten-Free:

- **MEALS 1 AND 2:** Use cup-for-cup gluten-free flour in place of the all-purpose flour in the falafel dough.

Tips

- The falafel dough can be prepared in advance and stored in an airtight container in the refrigerator for up to 24 hours. Note that falafel made with chilled dough may need about 5 minutes more in the oven.

- To save some time, make the falafel dough, then bake the falafel for Meal 1 and the falafel crust for the quiche at the same time. Let the crust cool, then wrap it in plastic wrap and store it in the refrigerator for up to 2 days; fill it on the day you plan to serve the quiche.

MEAL 1

BAKED FALAFEL BOWLS

Serves 4

Active time: 30 MINUTES   **Total time:** 50 MINUTES

For the Falafel

2 (16-ounce) cans chickpeas, drained and rinsed

½ red onion

3 garlic cloves

1 cup packed fresh cilantro

1 cup packed fresh parsley

¼ cup all-purpose flour

¼ cup plus 2 tablespoons extra-virgin olive oil

1¾ teaspoons fine sea salt

1 teaspoon baking powder

1 teaspoon ground cumin

½ teaspoon ground black pepper

For the Bowls

1 bunch curly kale, leaves stemmed and finely chopped

1 bunch parsley, finely chopped

2 tablespoons extra-virgin olive oil

2 tablespoons fresh lemon juice (from 1 lemon)

¼ teaspoon fine sea salt

¼ teaspoon ground black pepper

1 cup prepared hummus

12 ounces jarred roasted red peppers, drained and sliced into long strips

1 cucumber, cut into ¼-inch-thick rounds

¼ cup pitted kalamata olives

¼ cup crumbled feta cheese

1 lemon, cut into wedges, for serving

Pita bread, for serving (optional)

1. Make the falafel: Preheat the oven to 350°F.

2. In a food processor, combine the chickpeas, onion, garlic, cilantro, parsley, flour, ¼ cup of the olive oil, 1½ teaspoons of the salt, the baking powder, cumin, and pepper. Pulse until well combined. Transfer 1½ cups of the falafel dough to an airtight container and refrigerate to use for Meal 2; it will keep for up to 24 hours.

3. Form the remaining dough into roughly twelve 2-tablespoon balls and place them on a rimmed baking sheet. Flatten the balls to about ½ inch thick and drizzle with the remaining 2 tablespoons olive oil. Bake for 30 to 35 minutes, until the tops start to turn light golden brown. Sprinkle the tops with the remaining ¼ teaspoon salt.

4. Assemble the bowls: In a large bowl, combine the kale and parsley, reserving some of the parsley for garnish. Add the olive oil, lemon juice, salt, and pepper and massage them into the kale leaves until the kale has softened slightly, about 2 minutes.

5. Divide the kale mixture evenly among four bowls. Top each with three falafel and ¼ cup of the hummus. Divide the roasted red peppers, cucumber, olives, and feta evenly among the bowls. Serve each with a lemon wedge and a piece of pita, if desired.

CALORIES: 562   FAT: 35.2G   CARBS: 53.4G   PROTEIN: 15.1G

MEAL 2

GOAT CHEESE AND MUSHROOM QUICHE

Serves 4

Active time: 15 MINUTES

Total time: 1 HOUR 15 MINUTES

2 tablespoons extra-virgin olive oil

1½ cups falafel dough (reserved from Meal 1; see page 240)

1 shallot, minced

5 ounces sliced shiitake mushrooms

8 large eggs

½ cup heavy cream or full-fat coconut milk

½ teaspoon fine sea salt

¼ teaspoon ground black pepper

4 ounces goat cheese, crumbled

1 tablespoon chopped fresh parsley, for garnish

1. Preheat the oven to 350°F. Grease a 9-inch springform pan or pie dish with 1 tablespoon of the olive oil.

2. Press the falafel dough over the bottom of the prepared pan. Bake the crust for 25 to 30 minutes, until lightly browned.

3. Meanwhile, in a medium skillet, heat the remaining 1 tablespoon olive oil over medium heat. Add the shallot and cook, stirring, for 3 to 4 minutes, until it starts to become translucent. Add the mushrooms and cook, stirring occasionally, for 5 minutes more, or until the mushrooms have reduced in size. Remove from the heat.

4. In a medium bowl, whisk together the eggs, cream, salt, and pepper.

5. When the crust is ready, spread the mushroom mixture evenly over the bottom, then pour in the egg mixture. Sprinkle the goat cheese evenly over the top and bake for 30 to 35 minutes, until the filling no longer jiggles when the pan is gently shaken. Remove from the oven and let cool for 10 minutes.

6. Remove the quiche from the springform pan. Slice the quiche into wedges, garnish with the parsley, and serve.

CALORIES: 474   FAT: 32G   CARBS: 23.9G   PROTEIN: 24.9G

General Tso's Cauliflower

/ RECIPE PAGE 244 /

ABOUT

This dinner series will leave you with a love-of-cauliflower vow renewal. Simply roasted cauliflower florets are transformed into a craveable, nourishing General Tso's take on cauliflower and then into the most satisfying tacos inspired by tinga, a Mexican stew. The bold flavors of the sauces and the way we quickly recrisp the cauliflower creates the magic. You will not be bored by these dishes, and I bet you'll find yourself craving them often.

▨ $

▨ DAIRY-FREE

▨ EGG-FREE

▨ GLUTEN-FREE OPTION

▨ NUT-FREE

Cauliflower Tinga Tacos

/ RECIPE PAGE 245 /

GENERAL TSO'S CAULIFLOWER

Serves 4

Active time: 30 MINUTES   **Total time:** 55 MINUTES

4 medium heads cauliflower (2½ pounds total), cut into florets

¼ cup plus 2 tablespoons extra-virgin olive oil

½ teaspoon fine sea salt

1½ cups uncooked white rice, rinsed

2 garlic cloves, minced

2 teaspoons grated fresh ginger

⅓ cup honey

¼ cup rice vinegar

2 tablespoons soy sauce

2 tablespoons chili garlic sauce (see Tip)

2 teaspoons toasted sesame oil

½ teaspoon fish sauce

1 tablespoon cornstarch

1 cup vegetable broth or water

¼ cup thinly sliced green onions (sliced on an angle), for garnish

1 tablespoon white sesame seeds, for garnish

1. Preheat the oven to 400°F.

2. Toss the cauliflower florets with ¼ cup of the olive oil, then divide them between two rimmed baking sheets, arranging them in an even layer, and sprinkle with the salt. Roast for 35 to 40 minutes, until the tops of the florets start to brown.

3. Meanwhile, cook the rice according to the package instructions.

4. In a large skillet or wok, heat the remaining 2 tablespoons olive oil over medium heat. Add the garlic and ginger and cook, stirring, for 2 to 3 minutes, until fragrant.

5. Add the honey, vinegar, soy sauce, chili garlic sauce, sesame oil, fish sauce, cornstarch, and broth

and whisk until well combined and smooth. Simmer for about 5 minutes, until the sauce thickens.

6. Transfer half the cooked cauliflower (about 6 cups) to an airtight container and refrigerate to use for Meal 2 (it will keep for up to 5 days). Add the remaining cauliflower to the pan with the sauce. Toss to combine, then remove from the heat.

7. Serve the cauliflower over the rice, garnished with the green onions and sesame seeds.

TIPS

- Look for chili garlic sauce, a bright red Vietnamese condiment, in the international foods aisle. I use the Huy Fong brand with the rooster on it. This is the same brand as our beloved Sriracha.

- If you like less heat, use just 1 teaspoon chili garlic sauce to make the dish milder.

- If you follow a vegan or vegetarian diet, use a vegan fish sauce.

CALORIES: 580   FAT: 18.7G   CARBS: 96.7G   PROTEIN: 11.9G

MEAL 2

CAULIFLOWER TINGA TACOS

Serves 4

Active time: 15 MINUTES   **Total time:** 30 MINUTES

3 canned chipotle chiles in adobo sauce, finely chopped

½ cup tomato paste

⅓ cup fresh lime juice

2 teaspoons dried oregano

1 teaspoon ground cumin

1 teaspoon fine sea salt

½ teaspoon ground black pepper

About 6 cups roasted cauliflower (reserved from Meal 1; see page 244)

8 corn tortillas, warmed

1 avocado, thinly sliced, for garnish

¼ cup chopped fresh cilantro, for garnish

¼ cup finely chopped red onion, for garnish

1 lime, cut into wedges, for serving

1. Preheat the oven to 375°F.

2. In a large bowl, whisk together the chipotles, tomato paste, lime juice, oregano, cumin, salt, pepper, and 6 tablespoons water. Add the cauliflower and toss to coat evenly.

3. Spread the cauliflower evenly over a rimmed baking sheet. Bake for 15 minutes, or until the tops of the cauliflower florets start to darken.

4. Divide the roasted cauliflower among the tortillas. Top with the avocado, cilantro, and onion and serve, with the lime wedges alongside for squeezing over the top.

CALORIES: 347   FAT: 14.7G   CARBS: 48.2G   PROTEIN: 10.8G

Vegetarian Taco Casserole

/ RECIPE PAGE 248 /

ABOUT

In this meatless dinner series, we turn our eyes to playing with white rice. Sound basic? These dinners are anything but. The first meal, a colorful vegetarian taco casserole, is so satisfying. The Mexican rice, bubbling cheese, beans, kale, and toppings make for a dinner that's as much fun to make as it is to eat. For the second dinner, the rice takes center stage, with a peanut-focused, satay-inspired tofu skewer playing a supporting role. The sauce is notable in its own right, but the whole dish is an easy dinner triumph.

▓ $
▓ DAIRY-FREE OPTION
▓ EGG-FREE
▓ GLUTEN-FREE OPTION
▓ NUT-FREE OPTION

Tofu Satay Bowls

/ RECIPE PAGE 249 /

SUBSTITUTIONS

Make It Dairy-Free:

- **MEAL 1:** Either omit the cheese from the taco casserole or use your favorite vegan cheese instead.

Make It Gluten-Free:

- **MEAL 2:** Substitute gluten-free tamari for the soy sauce in the satay bowls.

Make It Nut-Free:

- **MEAL 2:** Substitute sunflower seed butter in place of the peanut butter in the peanut sauce for the satay bowls and omit the peanut garnish.

VEGETARIAN TACO CASSEROLE

Serves 4

Active time: 25 MINUTES   **Total time:** 55 MINUTES

- 2 cups uncooked white rice, rinsed
- 1 tablespoon extra-virgin olive oil
- 1 bunch curly kale, leaves stemmed and shredded
- 2 tablespoons fresh lime juice (from 1 lime)
- ½ teaspoon fine sea salt
- 1 (16-ounce) can pinto beans, drained and rinsed
- 1 tablespoon mild chili powder
- ½ teaspoon ground cumin
- ½ teaspoon dried oregano
- ½ cup canned diced tomatoes and green chiles (such as Ro-Tel)
- ¼ teaspoon ground black pepper
- 2 cups shredded Mexican-style cheese blend
- 1 (2.25-ounce) can sliced black olives, drained, for serving
- 1 avocado, cut into ½-inch cubes, for serving

1. Preheat the oven to 350°F.

2. Cook the rice according to the package instructions.

3. Meanwhile, in a large skillet, heat the olive oil over medium heat. Add the kale, toss to coat with the oil, and cook, stirring occasionally, for 3 to 4 minutes, until wilted. Add 1 tablespoon of the lime juice and ½ teaspoon of the salt and toss to combine. Remove from the heat.

4. Spread the beans evenly over the bottom of a 2-quart baking dish, then stir in the chili powder, cumin, and oregano. Spread the kale in an even layer over the beans.

5. Transfer half the cooked rice (3 cups) to an airtight container and refrigerate to use for Meal 2 (it will keep for up to 5 days). Put the remaining rice in a large bowl and stir in the diced tomatoes and green chiles, remaining 1 tablespoon lime juice, remaining ½ teaspoon salt, and the pepper. Spread the seasoned rice over the kale.

6. Top evenly with the cheese and bake for 30 minutes, or until the cheese is bubbling.

7. Top with the olives and avocado and serve.

CALORIES: 570   FAT: 27.9G   CARBS: 59.3G   PROTEIN: 22.9G

TOFU SATAY BOWLS

Serves 4

Active time: 25 MINUTES

Total time: 25 MINUTES, PLUS 2 TO 12 HOURS MARINATING TIME

For the Tofu Kabobs

1 (14-ounce) block extra-firm tofu

½ cup full-fat coconut milk

2 tablespoons fresh lime juice (from 1 lime)

2 tablespoons soy sauce

1 tablespoon fish sauce

2 garlic cloves, grated

1 teaspoon grated fresh ginger

1 teaspoon sambal oelek (Indonesian chile paste) (see Tip)

2 tablespoons brown sugar

1 teaspoon ground turmeric

For the Peanut Sauce

¼ cup creamy natural peanut butter

2 tablespoons coconut aminos

1 tablespoon fresh lime juice

2 teaspoons brown sugar

1 teaspoon toasted sesame oil

Pinch of red pepper flakes

To Serve

2 tablespoons extra-virgin olive oil, for cooking the kabobs

3 cups cooked white rice (reserved from Meal 1; see page 248)

1 cucumber, thinly sliced

¼ cup fresh cilantro, for garnish

2 tablespoons crushed salted peanuts, for garnish

1 teaspoon red pepper flakes, for garnish

1 lime, cut into wedges, for serving

1. If you have a tofu press, press the tofu for at least 10 minutes. Otherwise, wrap the tofu in a clean kitchen towel, set it on a plate, and top it with a heavy pan (or with another plate weighted down with a few cans); let stand for 10 minutes to press the tofu. Cut the tofu into 1-inch cubes.

2. Marinate the tofu: In a large bowl, whisk together the coconut milk, lime juice, soy sauce, fish sauce, garlic, ginger, sambal oelek, brown sugar, and turmeric until smooth. Add the tofu and toss to combine. Cover and refrigerate for at least 2 hours or up to 12 hours.

3. Meanwhile, make the peanut sauce: In a blender, combine the peanut butter, coconut aminos, lime juice, brown sugar, sesame oil, and red pepper flakes. Add 2 tablespoons water and blend until smooth. (If you won't be serving the sauce right away, it will keep in an airtight container in the refrigerator for up to 5 days.)

4. Cook the tofu: Thread 5 or 6 pieces of tofu onto metal or wooden skewers.

5. In a large skillet or grill pan, heat the olive oil over medium heat. Working in batches, add the tofu kabobs and sear for 1 to 2 minutes on each side, until they darken in color; do not let them burn. Transfer to a large plate and repeat with the remaining kabobs.

6. Divide the rice among four bowls. Top with the tofu kabobs, then drizzle with the peanut sauce. Garnish with the cucumber, cilantro, peanuts, and red pepper flakes and serve, with the lime wedges alongside for squeezing over the top.

TIPS

- If using wooden skewers, soak them in water for 20 minutes.

- The best way to get crispy tofu is to make sure it is fully drained of water. Follow the instructions in step 1 to press the tofu, then wrap it in a fresh kitchen towel, set it on a plate, and store in the refrigerator until ready to use.

- If you follow a vegan or vegetarian diet, use a vegan fish sauce in the tofu satay.

- Look for sambal oelek, a bright red Indonesian chile paste, in the international foods aisle.

- You can often find prepared peanut sauce in the Asian foods section at the grocery store, if you don't want to make your own.

CALORIES: 505   FAT: 22.2G   CARBS: 59.6G   PROTEIN: 19.6G

Pesto Potato and Mushroom Pizzas

/ RECIPE PAGE 252 /

DINNER SERIES 54

ABOUT

Baby Yukon Gold potatoes are the focus of this winning dinner series. Roasting the potatoes is most of the work for two whole dinners. They're first used to make delicious vegetarian pizza with pesto and mushrooms. To keep things easy, I like to make these pizzas on store-bought pizza crusts. The potatoes are then smashed and crisped for their debut in the second dinner, cauliflower tabbouleh bowls. These bright, flavorful bowls include a generous dollop of simple tzatziki.

- $$
- EGG-FREE
- GLUTEN-FREE OPTION
- GRAIN-FREE OPTION
- NUT-FREE

Smashed Potato Bowls

WITH CAULIFLOWER TABBOULEH

/ RECIPE PAGE 253 /

SUBSTITUTIONS

Make It Gluten-Free:

- **MEAL 1:** Buy gluten-free crusts for the pizzas.

Make It Grain-Free:

- **MEAL 1:** Buy grain-free crusts for the pizzas.

Tip

- Need your potatoes done in a hurry? Instead of roasting them, wrap them in wet paper towels and microwave for 6 to 7 minutes, until easily pierced with a fork.

PESTO POTATO AND MUSHROOM PIZZAS

Makes 2 PIZZAS, TO SERVE 4

Active time: 15 MINUTES   **Total time:** 1 HOUR 15 MINUTES

For the Roasted Potatoes

3 pounds baby Yukon Gold potatoes

1 tablespoon extra-virgin olive oil

½ teaspoon fine sea salt

For the Pizzas

2 (10-inch) store-bought plain pizza crusts

1 cup prepared basil pesto

1 cup shredded mozzarella cheese

5 ounces sliced shiitake mushrooms

2 tablespoons extra-virgin olive oil

½ teaspoon fine sea salt

¼ teaspoon ground black pepper

¼ cup grated Parmesan cheese, for serving

¼ cup fresh basil leaves, for garnish

1. Roast the potatoes: Preheat the oven to 375°F.

2. Toss the potatoes with the olive oil and spread them over a rimmed baking sheet. Sprinkle with the salt. Bake the potatoes for 40 minutes, or until soft to the touch. Remove from the oven; keep the oven on.

3. Transfer two-thirds of the roasted potatoes to an airtight container and refrigerate to use for Meal 2 (it will keep for up to 5 days). Cut the remaining potatoes into ½-inch cubes and set aside.

4. Make the pizzas: Place the pizza crusts on two baking sheets or pizza stones.

5. Divide the pesto between the crusts and spread it into an even layer over each, leaving a ½-inch border. Top evenly with the mozzarella, potatoes, and mushrooms. Drizzle with the olive oil and sprinkle with the salt and pepper.

6. Bake for 15 to 20 minutes, until the tops are golden brown and the cheese is bubbling.

7. Sprinkle the pizzas evenly with the Parmesan, garnish with the basil, and serve.

CALORIES: 870   FAT: 49.7G   CARBS: 85.3G   PROTEIN: 21.1G

SMASHED POTATO BOWLS WITH CAULIFLOWER TABBOULEH

Serves 4

Active time: 35 MINUTES **Total time:** 25 MINUTES

For the Smashed Potatoes

2 pounds cooked potatoes (reserved from Meal 1; see page 252)

2 tablespoons extra-virgin olive oil

½ teaspoon fine sea salt

½ teaspoon ground black pepper

½ teaspoon garlic powder

For the Easy Tzatziki

¾ cup plain full-fat Greek yogurt

3 tablespoons grated and drained fresh cucumber (water squeezed out)

1 garlic clove, finely grated

Pinch of fine sea salt

For the Cauliflower Tabbouleh

1 tablespoon extra-virgin olive oil

12 ounces cauliflower rice

1 large cucumber, diced

2 medium tomatoes, diced

1 cup packed fresh parsley leaves, finely chopped

¼ cup fresh mint leaves, chopped

2 garlic cloves, grated

2 tablespoons fresh lemon juice (from 1 lemon)

½ teaspoon fine sea salt

1. Preheat the oven to 425°F.

2. Place the potatoes on a rimmed baking sheet and smash them with a spatula. Brush with the olive oil, then season with the salt, pepper, and garlic powder. Bake for 20 to 25 minutes, flipping the potatoes halfway through, until crisp and golden brown.

3. Make the tzatziki: In a small bowl, whisk together the yogurt, cucumber, garlic, and salt. Use immediately, or cover and refrigerate for up to 5 days.

4. Make the cauliflower tabbouleh: In a medium skillet, heat the olive oil over medium heat. Add the cauliflower rice and cook, stirring occasionally, for 4 to 5 minutes, until the rice is softened and cooked through. Remove from the heat and add the cucumber, tomatoes, parsley, mint, garlic, lemon juice, and salt. Toss to combine.

5. Spoon the cauliflower tabbouleh into four bowls. Top with the tzatziki and smashed potatoes and serve.

CALORIES: 355 FAT: 14G CARBS: 50G PROTEIN: 12G

Harvest Stuffed Squash

/ RECIPE PAGE 256 /

ABOUT

I revisit acorn squash time and again when cooking and dreaming up new recipes. Squash is especially wonderful when approaching mealtime in the cook-once style because you can roast several at a time and use them however and whenever you like. In this dinner series, I'm giving it two different flavor treatments I know you're going to love: a rustic, harvest-flavor-inspired stuffed squash, and then in a bold yellow curry with crispy spiced tofu. For added depth and nutrition, quinoa, another component you can easily prep for two meals at once, finds its way into both dishes.

/// **$**
/// **DAIRY-FREE OPTION**
/// **EGG-FREE**
/// **GLUTEN-FREE OPTION**
/// **GRAIN-FREE OPTION**
/// **NUT-FREE**
/// **FREEZER-FRIENDLY**

Yellow Curry

WITH SQUASH AND CRISPY SPICED TOFU

/ RECIPE PAGE 257 /

SUBSTITUTIONS

Make It Dairy-Free:

- **MEAL 1:** Substitute an equal amount of plain dairy-free yogurt or mayonnaise for the yogurt in the stuffed squash.

Make It Gluten-Free:

- **MEAL 2:** Use gluten-free tamari in place of the soy sauce in the curry.

Make It Grain-Free:

- **MEALS 1 AND 2:** Substitute 3 cups cooked cauliflower rice for the quinoa in either recipe.

- **MEAL 2:** Substitute tamari for the soy sauce.

HARVEST STUFFED SQUASH

Serves 4

Active time: 30 MINUTES

Total time: 1 HOUR 30 MINUTES

2 cups dried tricolor quinoa, rinsed

3 medium acorn squash, halved and seeded

8 ounces Brussels sprouts, shredded

2 tablespoons extra-virgin olive oil

½ cup fresh or frozen cranberries

1 teaspoon fine sea salt

2 tablespoons fresh lemon juice (from 1 lemon)

½ cup plain whole-milk yogurt

2 tablespoons orange zest

2 tablespoons fresh orange juice

2 tablespoons chopped fresh parsley, for garnish

1. Preheat the oven to 375°F.

2. Cook the quinoa according to the package instructions.

3. Meanwhile, place the squash cut side up on a rimmed baking sheet, along with the shredded Brussels sprouts. Cover everything with the olive oil. Bake for 40 to 50 minutes, or until the squash is fork-tender.

4. Transfer half the cooked quinoa (about 3 cups) to an airtight container and refrigerate to use for Meal 2 (it will keep for up to 5 days). Put the remaining quinoa in a medium bowl and add the cranberries, salt, and lemon juice. Stir to combine.

5. Remove the squash and Brussels sprouts from the oven and set aside 2 of the squash halves. Stir the Brussels sprouts into the quinoa mixture, then spoon the quinoa mixture into the 4 remaining

squash halves, return the stuffed squash to the oven, and bake for 20 minutes, or until the cranberries are tender and starting to burst.

6. Meanwhile, scoop the flesh from the reserved squash halves into an airtight container (you should have about 1½ cups), discarding the skins; refrigerate to use for Meal 2 (it will keep for up to 5 days).

7. In a small bowl, whisk together the yogurt, orange zest, and orange juice.

8. Serve the stuffed squash warm, topped with the orange-yogurt sauce and garnished with the parsley.

TIPS

- To make quick work of shredded the Brussels sprouts, use the slicing blade on your food processor.

- To save even more time, you can buy preshredded Brussels sprouts.

CALORIES: 361   FAT: 11G   CARBS: 60.1G   PROTEIN: 10.9G

YELLOW CURRY WITH SQUASH AND CRISPY SPICED TOFU

Serves 4

Active time: 20 MINUTES   **Total time:** 45 MINUTES

1 (14-ounce) block extra-firm tofu, drained

2 tablespoons extra-virgin olive oil

2 tablespoons soy sauce

2 teaspoons red curry paste

1 (13.5-ounce) can full-fat coconut milk

About 1½ cups cooked acorn squash (reserved from Meal 1; see page 256)

2 tablespoons fresh lime juice (from 1 lime)

1 teaspoon fish sauce

About 3 cups cooked quinoa (reserved from Meal 1; see page 256), for serving

½ cup fresh cilantro, for garnish

1 teaspoon red pepper flakes, for garnish

1 lime, cut into wedges, for serving

1. Preheat the oven to 400°F.

2. If you have a tofu press, press the tofu for at least 10 minutes. Otherwise, wrap the tofu in a clean kitchen towel, set it on a plate, and top it with a heavy pan (or with another plate weighted down with a few cans); let stand for 10 minutes to press the tofu. Cut the tofu into 1-inch cubes.

3. In a large bowl, whisk together the olive oil, soy sauce, and curry paste. Toss the tofu in the mixture to coat, then spread it out on a baking sheet. Bake for 20 to 30 minutes, until the tofu is crispy, flipping it once halfway through the baking time.

4. Meanwhile, in a blender, combine the coconut milk and acorn squash and blend until smooth. Pour the mixture into a large skillet and whisk in the lime juice and fish sauce to combine. Bring to a simmer over medium heat, then simmer for 3 minutes. Remove from the heat.

5. Divide the quinoa among four plates and spoon the squash purée over the top. Top with the crispy tofu, garnish with the cilantro and red pepper flakes, and serve, with the lime wedges alongside for squeezing over the top.

TIPS

- Tofu is best when it is fully drained of water. Follow the instructions in step 2 to press the tofu, then wrap it in a fresh kitchen towel, set it on a plate, and store in the refrigerator until ready to use.

- Use a vegan fish sauce to make this meal vegetarian.

CALORIES: 561   FAT: 35.2G   CARBS: 47.3G   PROTEIN: 19.8G

Black Rice Salad

/ RECIPE PAGE 260 /

ABOUT

This dinner series takes a special peek at an unassuming vegetable that is fabulous for the efficient cook-once kitchen: tomatoes, specifically roasted tomatoes. Roasted tomatoes are incredibly easy to prepare (you just toss them with olive oil, salt, and pepper, then let the oven do its magic) and are incredibly versatile once cooked. They're featured in the first dinner by way of a Moroccan-inspired rice salad. If I could just be a fly on the wall the first time you take a bite of this salad, I would! The combination of mint, lemon, garlic, and pomegranate is truly special. The roasted tomatoes then get an entirely different treatment in a rustic lasagna soup. With long lasagna noodles, a roasted-tomato base, and plenty of cheese, this soup is certain to become a household favorite.

▥ $$$
▥ EGG-FREE
▥ GLUTEN-FREE OPTION
▥ NUT-FREE

Rustic Lasagna Soup

/ RECIPE PAGE 261 /

SUBSTITUTION

Make It Gluten-Free:

- **MEAL 2:** Use gluten-free lasagna noodles in the lasagna soup.

Tip

- Don't want to roast the tomatoes yourself? You can use canned whole peeled tomatoes in their place in both of these meals. You'll need one 28-ounce can for each meal.

MEAL 1

BLACK RICE SALAD

Serves 4

Active time: 35 MINUTES   **Total time:** 1 HOUR

For the Roasted Tomatoes

4 pounds cherry tomatoes

2 tablespoons extra-virgin olive oil

½ teaspoon fine sea salt

For the Black Rice Salad

1 cup uncooked black rice, rinsed

1 tablespoon extra-virgin olive oil

3 garlic cloves, grated

2 cups shredded carrots

1 cup sun-dried black olives, pitted and coarsely chopped

½ cup coarsely chopped fresh parsley

¼ cup coarsely chopped fresh mint

2 tablespoons fresh lemon juice (from 1 lemon)

1 teaspoon fine sea salt

¼ teaspoon ground black pepper

½ cup pomegranate seeds, for garnish (optional)

1. Roast the tomatoes: Preheat the oven to 375°F.

2. Toss the tomatoes with the olive oil, then spread them out over two rimmed baking sheets and sprinkle with the sea salt. Roast the tomatoes for 45 minutes, or until the skins have started to burst and the juices begin to caramelize.

3. Meanwhile, make the rice salad: Cook the rice according to the package instructions.

4. In a large pot, heat the olive oil over medium heat. Add the garlic and sauté for about 3 minutes, until fragrant. Add the carrots and toss to combine. Reduce the heat to low and cook, stirring occasionally, for about 10 minutes, until the carrots have softened.

5. When the tomatoes are done cooking, transfer all but 1 cup (about 3 cups) to an airtight container and refrigerate to use for Meal 2 (it will keep for up to 5 days).

6. Add the remaining 1 cup tomatoes to the pot with the carrot mixture, then add the rice, olives, parsley, mint, lemon juice, salt, and pepper. Stir to combine.

7. Serve the rice salad warm, garnished with the pomegranate seeds, if desired.

TIPS

- If you're using canned whole peeled tomatoes instead of roasting them from scratch, omit the olive oil and salt used for roasting, and add 1 cup tomatoes (from step 6), sliced into 1-inch pieces.

- Black rice is sometimes called forbidden rice (but don't worry, that doesn't mean you shouldn't buy it!). Centuries ago in China, black rice was forbidden to everyone but Chinese royalty, hence the seemingly ominous name.

CALORIES: 361   **FAT:** 16G   **CARBS:** 51.6G   **PROTEIN:** 6.3G

MEAL 2

RUSTIC LASAGNA SOUP

Serves 4

Active time: 30 MINUTES   **Total time:** 40 MINUTES

9 ounces dried lasagna noodles

2 tablespoons extra-virgin olive oil

1 small onion, diced

4 garlic cloves, minced

About 3 cups roasted tomatoes (reserved from Meal 1; see page 260)

½ cup red wine, or 2 tablespoons balsamic vinegar

4 cups vegetable broth

6 ounces tomato paste

1 teaspoon fine sea salt

2 tablespoons Italian seasoning

½ teaspoon ground black pepper

8 ounces ricotta cheese

1 cup shredded mozzarella cheese

½ cup grated Parmesan cheese

2 tablespoons chopped fresh parsley, for garnish

1. Bring a large pot of water to boil and cook the lasagna noodles according to the package instructions. Once cooked, drain, then set aside.

2. Meanwhile, in a large pot, heat the olive oil over medium heat. Add the onion and garlic and cook, stirring, for 5 to 10 minutes, until the mixture is fragrant and the onion is starting to brown. Add the tomatoes and wine and simmer for 5 minutes more.

3. Add the broth, tomato paste, and salt and stir to combine. Using an immersion blender, blend the soup directly in the pot until smooth. (Alternatively, carefully transfer to a standing blender, working in batches, if needed, and blend until smooth, then return to the pot.) Stir in the Italian seasoning and pepper, then add the lasagna noodles.

4. In a small bowl, mix together the ricotta and mozzarella until fully combined, then drop the ricotta mixture into the soup by the heaping tablespoonful and remove the soup from heat.

5. Top the soup with the Parmesan and garnish with the parsley just before serving.

TIP

- You can break the lasagna noodles to fit them into the pot; if you prefer to leave the noodles long, do your best to slowly submerge them in the water until they soften and fit the pot.

CALORIES: 599   FAT: 22.1G   CARBS: 73.7G   PROTEIN: 25.9G

Ricotta-Stuffed Eggplant

/ RECIPE PAGE 264 /

ABOUT

In this dinner series, we're taking a trip to the Mediterranean and focusing on eggplant. I cannot wait for you to make these vegetarian meals! The first features eggplant that is stuffed with the fluffiest ricotta cheese filling and then baked. The second is an eggplant-focused tomato and pepper skillet. The flavorful tomato sauce, a variation of the traditional shakshuka dish, is cooked with a few extra veggies and then eggs are dropped in and lightly poached until perfectly cooked. Shakshuka originated in North Africa and is popular in the Middle East as well. I have a feeling you're going to love it.

- $
- GLUTEN-FREE
- GRAIN-FREE
- NUT-FREE

Eggplant Pepper Skillet

/ RECIPE PAGE 265 /

Tip

- Don't like eggplant? Try this dinner series with portobello mushrooms instead.

RICOTTA-STUFFED EGGPLANT

Serves 4

Active time: 30 MINUTES

Total time: 1 HOUR 15 MINUTES

For the Roasted Eggplant

2 medium eggplants

2 tablespoons extra-virgin olive oil

½ teaspoon fine sea salt

For the Filling

1 (15-ounce) container whole-milk ricotta cheese

10 ounces frozen spinach, thawed and drained

1 large egg

½ teaspoon fine sea salt

1 (28-ounce) can tomato sauce

2 cups shredded mozzarella cheese

2 tablespoons thinly sliced fresh basil, for garnish

1. Roast the eggplant: Preheat the oven to 375°F.

2. Halve the eggplants lengthwise, then scoop out the flesh, leaving at least a ½-inch-thick layer of flesh attached to the skin on all sides. Coarsely chop the scooped-out flesh (you should have about 4 cups), transfer it to an airtight container, and refrigerate to use for Meal 2 (it will keep for up to 5 days).

3. Rub both the insides and the outsides of the eggplant halves evenly with the olive oil, then place them cut side up on a rimmed baking sheet, and sprinkle with the salt. Roast for 25 to 30 minutes, until easily pierced with a fork.

4. Meanwhile, make the filling: In a large bowl, mix the ricotta, spinach, egg, and salt until well combined. Set aside until the eggplant boats have finished roasting.

5. Remove the eggplant boats from the oven (keep the oven on) and divide the filling evenly among them. Pour the tomato sauce over the top of each boat, dividing it evenly, then top each with ¼ cup of the mozzarella.

6. Cover loosely with aluminum foil and roast for 20 minutes, then remove the foil and roast for 5 minutes more, or until the cheese is bubbling.

7. Garnish the eggplant boats with the fresh basil and serve.

TIP

• Use a grapefruit spoon to scoop out the eggplant flesh. It makes quick work of this task.

CALORIES: 484   FAT: 22.3G   CARBS: 36.3G   PROTEIN: 41.3G

DINNER SERIES 57

MEAL 2

EGGPLANT PEPPER SKILLET

Serves 4

Active time: 45 MINUTES   **Total time:** 45 MINUTES

2 tablespoons extra-virgin olive oil

½ yellow onion, finely chopped

1 red bell pepper, cut into thin strips

About 4 cups eggplant flesh (reserved from Meal 1; see page 264)

3 garlic cloves, minced

1 (28-ounce) can crushed tomatoes

2 tablespoons fresh lemon juice (from 1 lemon)

2 teaspoons paprika

1 teaspoon mild chili powder

1 teaspoon ground cumin

½ teaspoon fine sea salt

½ teaspoon ground black pepper

6 large eggs

¼ cup chopped fresh cilantro, for garnish

¼ cup chopped fresh parsley, for garnish

1. In a large skillet, heat the olive oil over medium heat. Add the onion, bell pepper, eggplant flesh, and garlic and cook, stirring occasionally, for 10 to 15 minutes, until the vegetables are wilted and starting to caramelize. Stir in the tomatoes, lemon juice, paprika, chili powder, cumin, salt, and pepper and simmer for 5 minutes more.

2. Using the back of a spoon, create 6 wells in the tomato mixture and crack an egg into each one. Reduce the heat to medium-low, cover the pan with a loose-fitting lid, and cook for about 8 minutes, until the egg whites are set and completely opaque. Remove from the heat.

3. Combine the cilantro and parsley and sprinkle them over the skillet, then serve.

CALORIES: 285   FAT: 15.4G   CARBS: 26.8G   PROTEIN: 14.8G

Caramelized Onion Lentils

WITH TOMATO SALAD

/ RECIPE PAGE 268 /

ABOUT

Though it's not difficult, preparing lentils can be a bit of a process, which is why I'm a big fan of using the work for two different dinners. In this series, I'm combining lentils with wild rice in two fabulous meals. In the first dinner, we get to explore flavors inspired by mujadara, a Lebanese dish. This is such an exciting meal that combines bold flavors like cinnamon and cumin with a heaping helping of caramelized onions, lemon, Greek yogurt, and plenty of fresh parsley. The second meal is a chorizo-spiced stuffed mushroom. I use my standard chorizo spice mix to flavor the lentil and wild rice blend. The mixture is then stuffed into the mushrooms, baked, and served topped with a generous portion of avocado-lime sauce.

▦ $

▦ DAIRY-FREE OPTION

▦ EGG-FREE OPTION

▦ GLUTEN-FREE

▦ NUT-FREE

"Chorizo" Stuffed Mushrooms

WITH AVOCADO SAUCE

/ RECIPE PAGE 269 /

SUBSTITUTIONS

Make It Dairy-Free:

- **MEAL 1:** Omit the Greek yogurt that is served with the lentils, or use your favorite dairy-free Greek-style yogurt in its place.

Make It Egg-Free:

- **MEAL 2:** Omit the eggs from the stuffed mushrooms.

MEAL 1

CARAMELIZED ONION LENTILS WITH TOMATO SALAD

Serves 4

Active time: 2 HOURS 10 MINUTES

Total time: 2 HOURS 10 MINUTES

For the Tomato Salad

2 tomatoes, cut into ½-inch pieces

1 cucumber, cut into ½-inch pieces

2 tablespoons fresh lemon juice (from 1 lemon)

1 tablespoon extra-virgin olive oil

½ teaspoon fine sea salt

2 tablespoons coarsely chopped fresh dill

1½ cups uncooked wild rice, rinsed

1½ cups dried brown lentils

For the Caramelized Onion Lentils

½ cup extra-virgin olive oil

3 medium yellow onions, cut into slivers

1 teaspoon fine sea salt

1 teaspoon ground cumin

1 teaspoon ground coriander

¼ teaspoon ground cinnamon

½ cup dried tart cherries, plus more for garnish

2 tablespoons fresh lemon juice (from 1 lemon)

1 cup plain Greek yogurt, for serving

¼ cup chopped fresh parsley, for garnish

1 lemon, sliced, for garnish

1. Make the tomato salad: In a large bowl, combine the tomatoes, cucumber, lemon juice, olive oil, salt, and dill. Toss to combine, then set aside until ready to serve.

2. Cook the rice according to the package instructions.

3. Cook the lentils according to the package instructions; do not overcook them, or they'll become mushy.

4. Drain the lentils, then transfer 2 cups to an airtight container with 3 cups of the cooked rice; refrigerate to use for Meal 2 (it will keep for up to 5 days).

5. Make the caramelized onion lentils: In a large skillet, heat the olive oil over medium-low heat. Add the onions and cook, stirring occasionally and adjusting the heat as needed to keep the onions from burning, for 45 minutes to 1 hour 30 minutes, until caramelized to a dark brown. (At this point, the onions and oil can be transferred to an airtight container and refrigerated for up to 2 days. Return the onions and oil to a large skillet when you're ready to finish cooking the dish.)

6. Add the salt, cumin, coriander, cinnamon, and cherries to the skillet with the onions, increase the heat to medium, and toss to combine. Cook until the spices are fragrant and slightly darker in color, about 5 minutes.

7. Add the lentils and rice and toss to combine. Cook, stirring occasionally, for 10 minutes, or until warmed through. Stir in the lemon juice and remove from the heat.

8. Top the dish with the yogurt, garnish with the parsley and lemon slices, and serve with the tomato salad alongside.

TIPS

- The active time for this recipe includes caramelizing the onions, which takes a *long* time, but don't worry—you don't need to be standing at the stove stirring for the full 90 minutes. The onions can also be cooked ahead of time and refrigerated. I recommend doing this a day or two before you plan to serve the dish.

- The tomato salad can also be made up to 2 days in advance.

CALORIES: 642   FAT: 29.6G   CARBS: 77.1G   PROTEIN: 25.5G

MEAL 2

"CHORIZO" STUFFED MUSHROOMS WITH AVOCADO SAUCE

Serves 6

Active time: 25 MINUTES   **Total time:** 50 MINUTES

For the Stuffed Mushrooms

6 portobello mushrooms, stemmed, gills scraped out with the tip of a spoon

1 teaspoon extra-virgin olive oil

2 cups cooked brown lentils (from Meal 1, page 268)

3 cups cooked wild rice (from Meal 1, page 268)

2 tablespoons apple cider vinegar

1 tablespoon fresh lime juice (from 1 lime)

2 teaspoons paprika

1 teaspoon ancho chile powder

½ teaspoon ground cumin

½ teaspoon dried oregano

½ teaspoon garlic powder

½ teaspoon fine sea salt

¼ teaspoon ground black pepper

¼ teaspoon cayenne pepper (optional, for added heat)

6 large eggs

For the Avocado Sauce

1 small avocado, peeled and pitted

½ cup fresh cilantro

2 tablespoons fresh lime juice (from 1 lime)

½ teaspoon fine sea salt

1. Preheat the oven to 350°F.

2. Rub the mushroom caps all over with the olive oil, then place them stem side up on a rimmed baking sheet.

3. Put the lentils and rice in a large bowl and add the vinegar, lime juice, paprika, chile powder, cumin, oregano, garlic powder, salt, pepper, and cayenne, if using. Spoon about ½ cup of the mixture into each mushroom cap.

4. Using the back of the spoon, create a well in the filling in each mushroom. Crack an egg into each well. Bake for 25 minutes for a runny egg yolk, or 30 minutes for a hard egg yolk.

5. Meanwhile, make the avocado sauce: In a blender, combine the avocado, cilantro, lime juice, salt, and 3 tablespoons water and blend until smooth.

6. Serve the avocado sauce drizzled over the stuffed mushrooms.

TIP

- If you want to knock out a little prep the day before this dinner, I recommend preparing the portobello mushrooms and then wrapping them in a clean kitchen towel and placing in the fridge until you're ready to prepare the meal.

CALORIES: 233   FAT: 9.9G   CARBS: 24.4G   PROTEIN: 14.2G

Veggie Buddha Bowl

/ RECIPE PAGE 272 /

ABOUT

While researching how to use butternut squash in one of these dinner series, I can't tell you how excited I was when I finally *nailed* these recipes. I knew I wanted to bring you a veggie-focused Buddha bowl as one of the meals in this series. Buddha bowls are a wonderful opportunity to try new vegetables and incorporate powerful nutrients, like the turmeric in the dressing. The second dinner took some work to create, but it's now perfect. The portobello burgers topped with smoked Gouda are a total showstopper, but it's the butternut squash tots I'm most excited for you to make. They're crunchy on the outside, soft on the inside, and a great use for the rest of that giant butternut squash you cooked for the Buddha bowls.

▌▌▌ **$$**
▌▌▌ **EGG-FREE OPTION**
▌▌▌ **GLUTEN-FREE OPTION**
▌▌▌ **NUT-FREE**

Smoked Gouda Bello Burger

WITH BAKED BUTTERNUT SQUASH TOTS

/ RECIPE PAGE 273 /

SUBSTITUTIONS

Make It Egg-Free:

- **MEAL 1:** Use vegan mayo in the dressing for the Buddha bowls.

- **MEAL 2:** Use vegan mayo on the portobello burgers.

Make It Gluten-Free:

- **MEAL 2:** Use gluten-free panko or other gluten-free bread crumbs for the butternut squash tots and serve the portobello burgers on gluten-free buns.

Tip

- Use frozen cubed butternut squash in either meal instead of roasting squash from scratch. It will save lots of prep and oven time.

MEAL 1

VEGGIE BUDDHA BOWL

Serves 4

Active time: 35 MINUTES **Total time:** 1 HOUR 5 MINUTES

For the Roasted Butternut Squash

1 large (3½-pound) butternut squash, peeled, seeded, and cut into ½-inch cubes

2 tablespoons extra-virgin olive oil

½ teaspoon fine sea salt

For the Dressing

¼ cup fresh lemon juice (from about 2 lemons)

2 tablespoons mayonnaise

1 tablespoon ground turmeric

¼ teaspoon fine sea salt

For the Bowls

1 cup uncooked white quinoa, rinsed

1 mango, cut into ½-inch cubes

¼ head purple cabbage, shredded

1 avocado, cut into large wedges

1 tablespoon black sesame seeds, for garnish

1 lemon, cut into wedges, for serving

1. Roast the squash: Preheat the oven to 375°F.

2. Toss the squash with the olive oil to coat and spread over one or two rimmed baking sheets. Sprinkle with the salt. Roast for 40 minutes, or until easily pierced with a fork.

3. Transfer 3 cups of the squash to an airtight container and refrigerate to use for Meal 2 (it will keep for up to 5 days).

4. Make the dressing: In a small bowl, whisk together the lemon juice, mayonnaise, turmeric, and salt until smooth. (Alternatively, combine the ingredients in a blender and blend until smooth.) Set aside.

5. Make the bowls: Cook the quinoa according to the package instructions.

6. Divide the quinoa, remaining roasted squash, mango, cabbage, and avocado evenly among four bowls, then drizzle with the dressing. Garnish with the sesame seeds and serve, with the lemon wedges alongside for squeezing over the top.

TIP

- If using frozen cubed butternut squash instead of roasting one from scratch, you can actually roast it from its frozen state. Simply reduce the roasting time to 20 to 25 minutes, until the squash is browned.

CALORIES: 424   FAT: 18.6G   CARBS: 60.6G   PROTEIN: 9.9G

MEAL 2

SMOKED GOUDA BELLO BURGER WITH BAKED BUTTERNUT SQUASH TOTS

Serves 4

Active time: 30 MINUTES   **Total time:** 1 HOUR

For the Baked Butternut Squash Tots

3 cups roasted butternut squash (reserved from Meal 1; see page 272)

1 cup grated Parmesan cheese

1½ cups panko bread crumbs

½ teaspoon fine sea salt

1 tablespoon extra-virgin olive oil or olive oil spray

For the Bello Burgers

4 large portobello mushrooms, stemmed, gills scraped out with the tip of a spoon

1 tablespoon extra-virgin olive oil

½ teaspoon fine sea salt

4 slices smoked Gouda cheese

¼ cup mayonnaise

2 tablespoons fresh lime juice (from 1 lime)

1 teaspoon chipotle chile powder

4 hamburger buns, toasted

1 avocado, thinly sliced, for garnish

1. Make the tots: Preheat the oven to 400°F. Line a rimmed baking sheet with parchment paper.

2. In a large bowl, use a potato masher or a fork to mash the squash with the Parmesan until well combined.

3. In a small bowl, combine the panko and salt.

4. Roll about 1 tablespoon of the squash mixture into a ball and form the ball into a roughly cylindrical shape. Roll it in the panko to coat, then place on the prepared baking sheet. Repeat with the remaining squash mixture, spacing the tots at least ½ inch apart on the baking sheet.

5. Brush the tops of the tots with the olive oil and bake for 15 minutes, then flip and bake for 10 minutes more.

6. Meanwhile, make the burgers: Place the mushroom caps on a rimmed baking sheet and brush the tops with the olive oil. Place the pan in the oven (you can bake the burgers at the same time as the tots) and bake for 10 minutes, then sprinkle with ¼ teaspoon of the salt and top each with a slice of the Gouda. Bake for 5 minutes more, or until the cheese has melted.

7. Meanwhile, in a small bowl, whisk together the mayonnaise, lime juice, chile powder, and remaining ¼ teaspoon salt.

8. Top each bun with a mushroom cap. Drizzle with the chipotle mayo, garnish with the avocado, cover with the top buns, and serve with the warm tots alongside.

TIP

- You can grill the portobello burgers instead of baking them if you'd like. Just heat a grill to medium-high. After you flip the tots in step 5, brush the tops of the mushrooms caps with the olive oil. Grill stem side up for about 10 minutes, until the mushrooms have released their liquid and grill marks have formed, then flip, sprinkle with the salt, top with the cheese, and grill for 5 minutes more, until the cheese has melted.

CALORIES: 752   FAT: 39.3G   CARBS: 76.2G   PROTEIN: 21.8G

Green Lentil Curry

WITH QUICK ROTI

/ RECIPE PAGE 276 /

ABOUT

Next to red lentils, green lentils are my favorite. They do tend to take the longest to cook out of all the varieties, but they maintain a lovely texture, even when re-formed and reheated. This clever vegetarian meal series splits one large batch of green lentils and one large batch of brown rice between two fabulous dinners. The first is an Indian curry–inspired dish complete with my favorite meal component of all time: garlic tarka (essentially, a whole bunch of garlic poached in ghee). This green lentil curry is served with a quick homemade flatbread, my take on Indian roti. The rest of the lentils are then transformed into Swedish-inspired meatballs for Meal 2, served over mashed potatoes and topped with the perfect gravy.

▨ DAIRY-FREE OPTION
▨ GLUTEN-FREE OPTION
▨ NUT-FREE

Spiced Lentil Meatballs

WITH MASHED POTATOES AND GRAVY

/ RECIPE PAGE 277 /

SUBSTITUTIONS

Make It Dairy-Free:

- **MEAL 2:** Substitute an equal amount of full-fat coconut milk for the heavy cream in the meatball gravy.

Make It Gluten-Free:

- **MEAL 1:** Use a gluten-free flour to make the roti.

- **MEAL 2:** Use gluten-free bread crumbs or rolled oats for the lentil meatballs, and substitute an equal amount of gluten-free cup-for-cup flour for the all-purpose flour in the meatball gravy.

GREEN LENTIL CURRY WITH QUICK ROTI

Serves 4

Active time: 50 MINUTES

Total time: 1 HOUR, 30 MINUTES

For the Lentils and Rice

2 cups dried green lentils, rinsed

4 cups water or vegetable broth

1½ cups uncooked brown rice, rinsed

For the Roti

2 cups all-purpose flour

2 tablespoons extra-virgin olive oil

1 teaspoon fine sea salt

For the Curry

1 tablespoon ghee or extra-virgin olive oil

2 shallots, minced

3 carrots, thinly sliced

1 tablespoon grated fresh ginger

1 tablespoon curry powder

1 teaspoon garam masala

½ teaspoon ground coriander

½ teaspoon ground turmeric

½ teaspoon fine sea salt

1 tablespoon tomato paste

1 cup vegetable broth

1 bunch lacinato kale, leaves stemmed and thinly sliced

For the Garlic Tarka

⅓ cup ghee or extra-virgin olive oil

12 garlic cloves, peeled and minced

2 tablespoons fresh lime juice (from 1 lime)

½ cup chopped fresh cilantro

1. Cook the lentils and rice: In a medium saucepan, combine the lentils and water. Cook the lentils according to the package instructions (do not overcook them, or they'll become mushy). Meanwhile, cook the rice according to the package instructions.

2. While the lentils and rice cook, make the roti: In a large bowl, stir together the flour, 1½ tablespoons of the olive oil, the salt, and ⅔ cup water until fully combined, then form the dough into eight equal balls. Using a rolling pin, roll each ball into ¼-inch-thick rounds.

3. In a large cast-iron skillet, heat the remaining ½ tablespoon olive oil over medium-high heat. Add one dough round to the pan and cook for 1 minute, or until browned on the bottom, then flip and cook for 1 minute on the second side. Wrap the cooked roti in a clean kitchen towel to keep warm and repeat to cook the remaining dough.

4. When the lentils and rice are finished cooking, drain any excess liquid from the lentils, then transfer 2 cups to an airtight container and refrigerate to use for Meal 2. Set the remainder aside. Transfer ½ cup brown rice to a separate airtight container and refrigerate to use for Meal 2 (both will keep for up to 5 days). Set the remainder aside.

5. Make the curry: In a large skillet, melt the ghee over medium heat. Add the shallots and carrots and cook, stirring occasionally, for 5 minutes, or until softened. Add the ginger, curry powder, garam masala, coriander, and turmeric and stir to combine. Cook for about 1 minute, until fragrant, then stir in the salt, tomato paste, broth, the remaining cooked lentils, and the kale. Bring to a simmer, then reduce the heat to low.

6. Make the garlic tarka: In a small pot or skillet, melt the ghee over medium-low heat. Add the garlic and cook, stirring occasionally, for 4 to 5 minutes, until the garlic is golden brown (do not let it burn). Pour the garlic tarka into the pot with the lentils, add the lime juice and cilantro, and stir to combine.

7. Serve the lentils over the remaining rice, with the roti on the side.

TIP

- If you want to save time, pick up some store-bought roti to go with the lentil curry instead of making your own.

CALORIES: 744   FAT: 28.4G   CARBS: 104.1G   PROTEIN: 22.6G

SPICED LENTIL MEATBALLS WITH MASHED POTATOES AND GRAVY

Serves 4

Active time: 35 MINUTES **Total time:** 45 MINUTES

For the Lentil Meatballs

¼ cup fresh parsley

½ cup bread crumbs or rolled oats

2 cloves garlic, crushed

2 cups cooked green lentils (from Meal 1, page 276)

½ cup cooked brown rice (from Meal 1, page 276)

2 tablespoons extra-virgin olive oil

½ teaspoon onion powder

½ teaspoon fine sea salt

¼ teaspoon ground black pepper

¼ teaspoon cinnamon

⅛ teaspoon allspice

⅛ teaspoon ground cloves

1 large egg

For the Mashed Potatoes

1½ pounds Yukon Gold potatoes, peeled and cut into 1-inch cubes

3 tablespoons extra-virgin olive oil

1 teaspoon garlic powder

½ teaspoon fine sea salt

¼ teaspoon ground black pepper

For the Gravy

2 tablespoons salted butter, ghee, or oil of your choice

2 tablespoons all-purpose flour

2 cups vegetable broth

¼ cup heavy cream

¼ teaspoon fine sea salt

¼ teaspoon ground black pepper

1. Preheat the oven to 400°F and line a rimmed baking sheet with parchment paper.

2. Make the lentil meatballs: In a food processor, combine the parsley, bread crumbs, and garlic and pulse until broken down to a fine, crumblike consistency. Add the lentils, brown rice, olive oil, onion powder, salt, pepper, cinnamon, allspice, cloves, and egg and process for about 1 minute, until the mixture is smooth and fully combined.

3. Form the lentil mixture into tablespoon-size balls, then place them on the lined baking sheet. Bake the meatballs for 15 minutes, or until browned.

4. Meanwhile, make the mashed potatoes: Put the potatoes in a medium saucepan and add water to cover. Cover the pot and bring to a boil over medium-high heat, then reduce the heat to maintain a low boil and cook for 15 to 20 minutes, until the potatoes are easily pierced with a fork. Drain the potatoes and return them to the pot.

5. Add the olive oil, garlic powder, salt, and pepper to the pot with the potatoes. Using a potato masher or a handheld mixer, mash the potatoes until smooth and well combined with the other ingredients. Keep warm until ready to serve.

6. Make the gravy: In a medium saucepan, melt the butter over medium heat. When it begins to sizzle, add the flour and whisk to combine. While whisking continuously, slowly pour in the broth and whisk to combine. Bring the gravy to a simmer, then stir in the cream, salt, and pepper and reduce the heat to low to keep the gravy warm until the meatballs are done.

7. Divide the mashed potatoes among four bowls and top with the meatballs. Pour the gravy over the top and serve.

CALORIES: 521   FAT: 21.1G   CARBS: 68.8G   PROTEIN: 16.8G

dietary restrictions

PAGE	RECIPE	DAIRY-FREE	EGG-FREE	GLUTEN-FREE	GRAIN-FREE	LOW-CARB	NUT-FREE
30	Barbecue Chicken Casserole with Sweet Potato	x*	x	x	x		x
31	Baked Chicken Chimichangas with Beans and Slaw	x*	x	x*	x*		x
34	Chicken Sloppy Joes with Ginger Carrot Slaw	x	x	x*	x*		x
35	White Enchilada Casserole with Tomato Avocado Salad	x	x	x	x*		x
38	Sun-Dried Tomato Bacon Chicken Pasta	x*	x	x*	x*	x*	x
39	Jamaican-Inspired Bowls with Mango Salsa and White Rice	x	x*	x*	x*	x*	x
42	Teriyaki Chicken with Brown Rice	x	x	x	x*		x
43	Bacon Ranch Loaded Potato	x*	x*	x	x		x
46	Green Curry Meatball Bowls with White Rice	x	x	x*	x*	x*	x
47	Chicken Parm Meatball Skillet with Butter-Garlic Pasta	x*	x	x*	x*	x*	x
50	Buffalo Zucchini Boats with Ranch Roasted Potatoes		x*	x	x		x
51	Alfredo Chicken Lasagna with Simple Italian Salad		x	x*			x
54	Herb-Crusted Roasted Chicken with Lemon-Garlic Orzo	x*	x	x*	x*	x*	x
55	Curried Chicken Sheet Pan Dinner	x*	x*	x	x*	x*	x*
58	Lemon-Garlic Roasted Chicken and Veggies	x*	x	x	x		x
59	Sesame Chicken with White Rice		x	x*	x*		x

X* denotes recipe offers substitutions for dietary options.

PAGE	RECIPE	DAIRY-FREE	EGG-FREE	GLUTEN-FREE	GRAIN-FREE	LOW-CARB	NUT-FREE
62	Paprika Spatchcocked Chicken with Green Sauce and Plantains	x	x*	x	x		x
63	Stir-Fried Noodles with Chicken		x*	x*	x		x
66	Roasted Chicken and Potatoes with Fresh Arugula Salad	x*	x	x	x	x*	x
67	Butter Chicken Bowls with White Rice	x*	x	x	x*	x*	x
70	Crispy Roasted Duck with Warm Beet Salad	x*	x	x	x*	x*	x
71	Duck Fried Rice	x	x*	x*	x*	x*	x
74	Roasted Garlic Turkey Breast with Lemon-Dill Quinoa	x*	x	x	x*		x
75	Spiced Turkey Potato Soup	x	x	x	x		x
78	Chipotle-Maple Turkey Bake with Sweet Potatoes	x	x*	x*	x		x
79	Southwestern Turkey Casserole	x*	x*	x	x*		x
82	Asian-Inspired Lettuce Wraps with Rice Noodles	x	x	x*	x*		x
83	Turkey Taco Casserole	x*	x	x	x		x
88	Dry-Rubbed Barbecue Brisket with Zesty Cabbage Slaw	x*	x	x	x*	x*	x
89	Cheesesteak-Stuffed Peppers with Wild Rice	x*	x*	x	x*	x*	x
92	Classic Brisket with Gravy, Mashed Potatoes, and Asparagus	x*	x	x*	x*		x
93	Mongolian Beef Bowls	x*	x	x	x*		x
96	Beef Taco Night	x*	x	x	x*		x
97	Cottage Pie	x*	x	x			x
100	Beef Enchilada Casserole	x*	x	x	x*		x
101	Teriyaki Ground Beef Stir-Fry with White Rice	x	x	x	x*		x
104	Classic Meatball Boats	x*	x	x*			x
105	Wedding Soup with Orzo	x*	x		x*		x

PAGE	RECIPE	DAIRY-FREE	EGG-FREE	GLUTEN-FREE	GRAIN-FREE	LOW-CARB	NUT-FREE
108	Loaded Avocado Bacon Burgers with Wedge Sweet Potato Fries and Chipotle-Lime Mayo	x*	x*	x*	x*	x*	x
109	Crispy Beef Hash with Simple Tzatziki	x*	x	x	x	x*	x
112	Beef Burrito Bowls with Cilantro-Lime Rice, Black Beans, and Corn Salsa	x*	x	x	x*		x
113	Cheeseburger Pie	x*	x	x	x		x
116	Balsamic Beef Roast with Red Wine Mushrooms and Purple Potatoes	x	x	x	x		x
117	Onion and Roast Beef Soup with Lemon-Dill Salad	x*	x	x*	x*		x
120	Chipotle Beef Roast with Yuca	x*	x	x	x		x
121	Barbacoa Tacos with Mexican Pinto Beans	x*	x	x	x*		x
124	Garlic-Peppercorn Beef Roast with Creamy Horseradish Sauce, Roasted Carrots, and Mashed Potatoes	x*	x	x	x	x*	x
125	Shredded Beef Ragu over Pappardelle Pasta	x*	x	x*	x*	x*	x
128	Herb-Crusted Beef Roast with Potatoes and Chopped Veggie Salad	x*	x	x	x	x*	x
129	Beef Stroganoff with Mushrooms over Egg Noodles	x*	x*	x*	x*	x*	x
132	Perfect Stovetop Steaks with Baked Sweet Potatoes and Simple Spinach Salad	x*	x	x	x	x*	x
133	Beef Ramen Noodle Skillet	x	x	x*	x*	x*	x
136	Tender Balsamic-Pepper Grilled Steaks	x*	x	x	x*	x*	x
137	Chipotle Beef Tacos with Jicama-Carrot Slaw	x	x	x	x*	x*	x
140	Hearty Beef and Veggie Stew	x	x	x	x		x
141	Shredded Beef Tostadas	x*	x	x	x		x

PAGE	RECIPE	DAIRY-FREE	EGG-FREE	GLUTEN-FREE	GRAIN-FREE	LOW-CARB	NUT-FREE
144	Beef Chili with Cheddar Corn Muffins	x*	x	x*	x*	x*	x
145	Green Curry Beef Bowls with White Rice	x	x	x	x*	x*	x
150	Chorizo and Potato Taco Bake with Pineapple Salsa	x*	x	x	x		x
151	Thai-Inspired Pork Salad Bowls	x	x	x	x*		x
154	Pork Bolognese Pasta with Italian Salad	x*	x	x*	x*	x*	x
155	Lemony Sausage and Veggie Soup	x	x	x	x	x*	x
158	Madras-Inspired Curry Meatballs	x	x	x	x		x
159	Minestrone Soup	x	x	x*	x*		x
162	Slow Cooker Balsamic Pork Roast with Scalloped Potatoes and Easy Steamed Broccoli	x*	x	x	x	x*	x
163	Pulled Pork Sandwiches with Classic Creamy Slaw	x	x*	x*	x*		x
166	Bacon-Wrapped Pork Roast with Purple Cabbage and Sweet Potatoes	x	x	x*	x	x*	x
167	Crispy Ginger Pork Stir-Fry	x	x	x*	x*	x*	x
170	Butter-Garlic Pork Roast with Goat Cheese Pasta and Swiss Chard Salad		x	x*			x
171	Tacos al Pastor with Charro Beans		x	x			x
174	Perfect Carnitas with Roasted Mexican Street Corn	x*	x*	x	x*		x
175	Sticky Honey-Garlic Pork with White Rice	x*	x	x*	x*		x
178	Bánh Mì-Inspired Bowls	x*	x	x*	x*		x
179	Loaded Nachos	x*	x	x	x*		x
182	Cuban-Inspired Stewed Pork with Black Beans	x	x	x	x		x

PAGE	RECIPE	DAIRY-FREE	EGG-FREE	GLUTEN-FREE	GRAIN-FREE	LOW-CARB	NUT-FREE
183	Pork King Ranch Casserole with Mixed Baby Greens Salad		x	x*	x*		x
186	Pulled Pork Chili Verde		x	x	x		x
187	Barbecue Pork Mac 'n' Cheese Bake		x	x*			x
190	Chili-Rubbed Pork Tenderloin with Cilantro Chimichurri and Tostones	x	x	x	x		x
191	Asian Fusion Bowls	x	x	x	x*		x
194	Honey-Mustard Tenderloin with Roasted Green Beans	x	x	x			x
195	Breaded Pork Medallions with Mashed Potatoes and Gravy	x*	x	x*			x
198	Island-Style Pork Tenderloin with Wild Rice	x	x	x	x*	x*	x
199	Pork Ramen Bowl	x	x*	x*	x*	x*	x
206	Old-Fashioned Crab Bake	x*	x	x	x*	x*	x
207	Seafood Bisque	x*	x	x*	x*	x*	x
210	Lemon-Pepper Halibut with Broccoli Salad and Wild Rice	x	x*	x			x
211	Chile Verde Halibut Melts with Chile-Lime Tartar Sauce	x*	x	x*			x
214	Dill Aioli Salmon Bake with Fingerling Potatoes	x		x	x		x
215	Salmon Cakes with Pan-Seared Green Beans	x		x*			x
218	Teriyaki Salmon Bake with White Rice and Asparagus	x	x	x	x*		x
219	Salmon Burgers with Sweet Potato Fries	x*	x*	x*	x*		x
222	Blackened Shrimp Taco Bowls with White Rice and Zesty Slaw	x	x	x	x*	x*	x
223	Seafood Jambalaya		x	x*	x*	x*	x
226	Chili-Lime Tuna Steak with Tricolor Quinoa	x	x	x			x
227	Tuna-Noodle Casserole	x*	x	x*			x

PAGE	RECIPE	DAIRY-FREE	EGG-FREE	GLUTEN-FREE	GRAIN-FREE	LOW-CARB	NUT-FREE
232	Plantain Black Bean Bowls	x	x*	x	x*		x
233	Barbecue Bean Casserole	x	x	x	x*		x
236	Enchilada-Stuffed Zucchini Boats	x*	x	x	x		x
237	Vegetarian Chili with Vegan Corn Bread	x	x	x*	x*		x
240	Baked Falafel Bowls	x*		x*			x
241	Goat Cheese and Mushroom Quiche	x*		x*			x
244	General Tso's Cauliflower	x	x	x*			x
245	Cauliflower Tinga Tacos	x	x	x			x
248	Vegetarian Taco Casserole	x*	x	x			x
249	Tofu Satay Bowls	x	x	x*			x*
252	Pesto Potato and Mushroom Pizzas		x	x*	x*		x
253	Smashed Potato Bowls with Cauliflower Tabbouleh		x	x	x		x
256	Harvest Stuffed Squash	x*	x	x	x*		x
257	Yellow Curry with Squash and Crispy Spiced Tofu	x	x	x*	x*		x
260	Black Rice Salad	x	x	x			x
261	Rustic Lasagna Soup		x	x*			x
264	Ricotta-Stuffed Eggplant			x	x		x
265	Eggplant Pepper Skillet	x		x	x		x
268	Caramelized Onion Lentils with Tomato Salad	x*	x	x	x		x
269	"Chorizo" Stuffed Mushrooms with Avocado Sauce	x	x*	x			x
272	Veggie Buddha Bowl	x	x*	x			x
273	Smoked Gouda Bello Burger with Baked Butternut Squash Tots		x*	x*			x
276	Green Lentil Curry with Quick Roti	x	x	x*	x		x
277	Spiced Lentil Meatballs with Mashed Potatoes and Gravy	x*		x*			x

Acknowledgments

"If I have seen further it is by standing on the shoulders of Giants." —Isaac Newton

In a perfect storm of blessed, lucky, and privileged, it's my honor to recognize the giants who've been so integral in bringing this bold and daring book to life.

First, to my endlessly patient husband, Austin, who truly deserves recognition: If I happen to make life as a working mom look easy, it's only because you're behind the scenes in full support of this work and my role as both mom and author.

Next, to the Fed + Fit team, including Amber Goulden, Lauren Moore, and Brandi Schilhab: While empowering healthy lifestyles was my first mission (at fedandfit.com), creating great jobs for great people was my second. You are a dream of a team, and our work is better and more fun than ever because of your commitment. Thank you for all you did to help make this book come to life. You washed endless dishes, tested countless meals, and helped me workshop the concept over endless hours, all while pouring belief, joy, and your best work in at every possible step.

To my wise and steadfast agent, Lisa Grubka; clever and inspiring editor, Justin Schwartz; and enormously gifted and joy-filled photographer, Kristen Kilpatrick: I treasure our working together and hope you know how much respect and admiration I have for each of you.

Finally, to the Fed + Fit Community: Serving you with creative, practical, and polished solutions to some of life's most perplexing daily problems (like "what will I make for dinner?") is one of the great honors of my life. Thank you for trusting these recipes and leaning on me as a resource. I hope you feel truly supported and that maybe, just maybe, life feels a little easier and a bit more joyful because of my work.

Index

q

r

PSALM 119:105